SHUT UP

HE

EXPLAINED

Kate Lardner

SHUT UP

HE

EXPLAINED

The Memoir of a Blacklisted Kid

BALLANTINE BOOKS

NEW YORK

A Ballantine Book
Published by The Random House Publishing Group

Copyright © 2004 by Kate Lardner

All rights reserved under International and Pan-American
Copyright Conventions. Published in the United States by
The Random House Publishing Group, a division of
Random House, Inc., New York, and simultaneously
in Canada by Random House of Canada Limited, Toronto.

Ballantine and colophon are registered trademarks of
Random House, Inc.

www.ballantinebooks.com

Library of Congress Cataloging-in-Publication Data is
available from the publisher upon request.

ISBN 0-345-45514-2

Text design by Barbara Sturman

Manufactured in the United States of America

First Edition: May 2004

10 9 8 7 6 5 4 3 2 1

for Carlo, Ellis, and Maude

Are you lost Daddy I arsked tenderly.
Shut up he explained.

—RING LARDNER
The Young Immigrunts

CONTENTS

Acknowledgments

I would like to thank my agent, Liz Darhansoff, for saying Yes and guiding me. Chuck Verril for teaching me about proposals. My editor, Elisabeth Dyssegaard, for her right-on suggestions, perfectly timed check-in calls, and one droll sense of humor.

Pat Trese for showing me how to stay in the game one pitch at a time. Lucy Rosenthal for her expertise and unique delivery. Lou Peterson for first comprehending my intentions. Sally Fisher and company for helping me get them rolling. The denizens of NBW for support and wisdom.

My lifelong friend Nora Heflin Kaplan for feedback and encouragement. And more friends for a multitude of reasons: Leila Gastil, Quincy Long, Mitzi Scott, Will Blythe, Kathy Preminger, Julie Boak, Doxie Forrest, Barbara Suter, Linda Selman, Sally Dorst, Lynn Lobban, Rachel Reichman, Bruce Allan, Caroline Hwang. And the most extraordinary Katherine Wessling: I can't begin to count the ways.

My old friends Victor Brandt and Dick Seymour for helping me remember, and Ben Koenig, Ann Lauterbach, and Jane Vern (who in some cases let me interview them interminably) for bringing the castle on the hill to life then and now.

Russell Hill for sharing with me everything he knew about David.

My cousin Lonnie for her enthusiasm and love. My siblings—Peter, Ann, Joe, Jim—for their assistance in his or her way. And above all: my parents who stood up for their beliefs.

SHUT UP

HE

EXPLAINED

Prologue

My mother said she thought my troubles began when my father went to jail. I think they could have started sooner.

ACTUALLY MY REAL FATHER WASN'T RING. My real father was David Lardner, a war correspondent for *The New Yorker* who was killed, and my mother remarried. She married his brother Ring, who had been married before and had two children—Peter and Ann.

"Where's my daddy?" I asked, or am said to have asked soon after my real father was killed in Aachen, Germany. He was twenty when he began writing for *The New Yorker* in 1939. By 1944 he was eager to see something of the war. He was young and a writer and felt he should be part of it in some way. In mid-July David went to London for the Office of War Information. (He had been rejected by the army because his eyes were bad. "Big brown eyes," my mother said, "but he couldn't see anything out of them.") He said he hoped to return within six months to a year.

A couple of months later David asked to be relieved by the OWI and went to the front to represent *The New Yorker* with the

First Army. The magazine had promised to use his material if he could get press accreditation from the army on his own. "Darling, things are set now so that it looks as if nothing can go wrong," he wrote my mother. "You may not hear from me for a little while, but

it will be only because I'll be moving around and because the mail may be a bit less certain.... I must say that once the Army was persuaded I was a well-meaning fellow it scampered around and got things done nimbly enough. I'm enclosing a spare shot of me in my new role, but I must warn you that it's deceptive, because actually I'm getting as bald as an egg, or at least as I dimly remember an egg to be."

He spent a little more than a day in Paris and then was driven to recently liberated Luxembourg by Walter B. Kerr of the *Herald Tribune,* a corporal and an old family friend. When he arrived, David was chilled to the bone and shivering. The weather was cold and he had no heavy winter clothing with him. It was late but Joe Driscoll, a friend and *Tribune* correspondent, wangled dinner for him and warmed him up with some captured German rum. That night David, Walter Kerr, Joe Driscoll, et al., had a room warming, for Luxembourg had become a piece of old New York.

In a letter to my mother from Luxembourg, in which he addressed her as "Lamb's Lettuce," David wrote: "I guess I won't be through in these parts as soon as I told you I might in earlier letters.... At the time I thought I'd be here for the end of the war in October, do a couple of pieces in Germany afterward, and go home. It took me a little longer to get here than I figured, though, and anyhow it doesn't look as if the war will be over to-morrow or maybe even next week. However, I'll see what can be done."

This was before the last German counterattack and the Battle of the Bulge, when it was still generally felt that the war in Europe was all but finished. David became interested in Luxembourg, where he stayed for about ten days, walking all over the place and interviewing people for a piece about life there called "Letter from Luxembourg." He worked hard on it day and night, rewriting it several times for perfection.

Joe Driscoll had a jeep and a driver and was able to send David's story and messages down to Mackay Radio and Telegraph Company. He drove him out to Arlon across the Belgian border to arrange transportation to the First U.S. Army press camp based in Spa near Aachen, where the first major battle on German soil was still in progress. David, being cold in his light field jacket, wore Driscoll's raincoat over it and a white bath towel around his throat. (He had worn the towel as a robe while working in his room on the piece for *The New Yorker*.) At Arlon they were advised to come back in a day or two. Driscoll made the return trip with him and escorted him onto an airfield where a Piper Cub and Cessna were warming up. It was late afternoon and poor flying weather, but David was impatient to get on to Aachen to do some more pieces. The pilots weren't sure they could haul all his baggage, but promised to bring it up to him piecemeal if necessary. David laughed at his lack of winter clothes and said he would try to get some around Aachen.

A couple of days later he went on assignment to Aachen with *Herald Tribune* correspondent Russell Hill and Richard Tregaskis of the International News Service. It was the big story. The battle was still going on, and the three men were assigned to cover the fighting during the final mop-up. Their first-day plan of action was to enter the city and get as far as Charlemagne's Cathedral. With their soldier driver, they headed toward the western fringe, visiting infantry units along the way. Aachen was a shambles—windows gone, floors and furniture crashed down into cellars, streets covered with twisted wire and rubble, and outside walls of buildings and houses pitted with rifle, machine-gun, and shell fire. There were only a couple of buildings still intact.

They made it to the badly damaged old cathedral, which was the main interest of the city, and passed some time examining it. The cathedral had been taken that day. It was late when they started back, and Hill suggested taking a shorter route than the one by which they had come. Tregaskis decided to stay the night in Aachen, so he didn't return with them.

The shortcut Hill chose was on a surface road several miles shorter than the route the American troops had been using. It led them to a railroad underpass where Allied engineers had cleared a minefield and piled the mines by the side of the street. (The sides of the road were taped, indicating that the shoulders had not been cleared of the mines.) In the darkness, driving with blackout lights, the jeep swerved and hit a pile of mines. Some of them were antipersonnel mines—the jumping mines that go into the air then explode a second time, sending steel balls in all directions.

It all happened very quickly. There was a great flash, Hill recalled, as though he were looking at the sun right down on the road. But it was the jeep burning, and Hill was lying on the road. David was lying on the field. He was wounded in the head. The driver died almost immediately. David and Hill were put in an ambulance and rushed to the evacuation hospital. David was given a blood transfusion and they were getting ready to operate, but he died under the X-ray machine. He was twenty-five.

"Where's my daddy," I asked.

"He's in heaven," replied Grandma Marie, who swore this exchange took place. "Where's my daddy?" she said I asked. "Everyone else has a daddy."

"He's in heaven," she re-peated. "He'll soon come back."

But he didn't come back. And according to my mother who overheard her, it was my cousin Mary Jane, eight months older than me, who set me straight. "She was the one," my mother said, who told me that my daddy was dead. My mother would have preferred to keep it from us.

"See that moth," Mary Jane said when I was two and a half, pointing to a dead one on a dirt road in the country on my paternal grand-

Grandma Marie and Kate

mother's farm in New Milford, Connecticut, the day of my en-lightenment. "It's dead like your daddy."

But nothing else was said, and I only vaguely remember my real father dangling me on his ankle listening to baseball on the radio. So when he died, or was squashed like a moth on a dirt road (which, because I'm literal-minded, is probably what I would have made of cousin Mary Jane's metaphor), I was left with a longing and a dim feeling that never left me that something went wrong.

Santa Monica
Memories

A couple of years after my real father died, we took the train from New York to California to marry his brother. "Going to Canyonfornia to marry Uncle Bill" is how my mother said we kids put it, and this rings a bell. My mother was used to calling her brother-in-law Bill—not Ring, which he preferred—because that's what the family always called him. But my brother Joe, who was two, and I, fifteen months older, weren't used to calling him anything because we hardly knew him. My mother said she hardly knew him, either. He was her husband's brother and she wanted us to have a father in the worst way and it had to be the right kind of father. She said she couldn't marry somebody just for her. It had to be somebody for her and for me and Joe, and she didn't think anybody else was right. She assumed that if he was David's brother and his name was Lardner he had to be okay.

Also there was a letter that had gotten my mother's attention. It was a turning point in a bicoastal correspondence that went on for a year and a half in which Ring said he wanted very much to see her.

Dear Lass, it began. *I want very much to see you even though I am at a loss to know what good could come of it. I suppose the notion in back of our minds is that we might get married someday but when I think about it that concretely it doesn't seem a very likely prospect. I don't think you're in love with me and I'm pretty sure I'm not in love with anyone, and whatever element of sober self-interest there is in my nature would certainly mitigate against falling for any doll with two children. On the other hand, I want to see you which must have some significance. . . . But to get down to one concrete fact, I would like to kiss you.* Signed "Ring."

My mother thought that was pretty nice. In addition, they were both Communists, and I'm told there was a certain rapprochement between them because of it.

Ring had been very impressed by the Soviet Union when he was there in the summer of 1934 and very much antagonized by what he saw in Germany immediately after that. He had stayed in the house of an architect in Munich whose son belonged to Hitler Youth, and just talking to him and seeing the marching in the streets made him feel very worried about what was happening there.

He joined the Party in 1936. With the U.S. recognition of the Soviet Union in 1933, Communist Party membership had jumped dramatically, attracting creative artists, students, and direct-action unionists as well as the disaffected and deprived. In the depths of the Depression (with a quarter of the workforce unemployed) they really had a lot of doubt about whether the system of private industry and capitalism could survive. The Communist Party seemed the most visible force for social change. It was never a question of Communism versus democracy, said Ring. Those who inclined toward Communism or who became members of the Party in Hollywood (as he did) were thinking of trying to institute a new economic system. It seemed as if capitalism had come to an end. It seemed that the whole system had broken down and was not going to be fixed—that it needed a change. Ring assumed that in America, socialism would be achieved by democratic means.

My mother was an actress, and her loose connection with Communism began with her first Broadway job in 1936 in a play called *Marching Song* by John Howard Lawson—a play about a sit-down strike in a factory. The cast included several left-wing actors whom she admired. She didn't actually join the party until sometime in the late thirties, but when the Spanish civil war broke out in July 1936, the actors in the company got involved in working for the Spanish loyalist cause, mostly raising money for medical assistance and ambulances. (The nonintervention policy of the United States didn't permit material aid for either side.)

David had been left of center, though politics just didn't play an important part in his life. But when he died, my mother felt strongly that his death must not be in vain.

Ring and Frances first met in November 1941. Ring had come to New York from California with his wife, Silvia, after the shooting was complete on *Woman of the Year*—the first movie starring Katharine Hepburn and Spencer Tracy. Ring and Michael Kanin had written the script, for which they received a hundred thousand dollars—the highest price paid for an original screenplay at that time. This all happened a couple of months before my mother and David's marriage. The four of them went to the '21' Club to celebrate. My mother and Ring saw each other just a handful of times after that before our move west.

Polly, who came to take care of us three months after David was killed, went on the train to California with us. She was leaving behind, according to my mother, "an unfortunate life" be-

his ornamental lady is Frances Chaney, star of "Grand Central Sta-
n," which recently moved over to WABC, where life among the trai
stles goes on every Wednesday evening from 8 to 8:30 o'cloc

cause she'd been having an affair with her sister's husband (her
sister was my mother's housekeeper). So presumably Polly wel-
comed the move. As for my mother, she didn't give it much
thought. She just said we'll go, and we did.

I remember lots of people turning up at Pennsylvania Station to say good-bye: my maternal grandmother, Marie; good old
friends and actors my mother worked with in radio. (A radio
magazine in the early forties called her one of the country's ten

top radio actresses. And E. J. Kahn Jr. wrote a piece for *The New Yorker* about taking out a girl who looked like a movie star, inspired by one night with my mother as his date when they went to nightclubs and everyone thought she was Constance Bennett. Her hair was long and blond then and hung down over her face.)

They were all well-wishers at the station with wine or champagne or little presents for us kids. And then we took off on the 20th Century Limited and switched to the Superchief in Chicago.

The four of us shared a drawing room. The trip was very pleasant, I had always thought. Then one day, years later, my mom piped up and a mix-up of my memory of it ensued.

I had recently begun interviewing my parents extensively because I wanted to know where the hell they were while I was growing up. I also wanted to know where I was. And I wanted to tell my story of the events I had inherited. A therapist once told me she had the dirty job of ushering me into the real world. And now that I was more or less there, I had decided the time had come.

"It was fine except I got my hand caught in the fan it seems to me," my mother said.

"It's funny, I thought it was I who got my hand caught in the fan," I replied.

"No, I got my hand caught. Not you. It wasn't bad . . ."

"But that's my one memory of the trip."

"Well, I got caught . . ."

"It's interesting I can't remember . . ."

"Yeah, I know, but you make these mistakes from time to time. I don't know that it got caught badly. It was just a small accident. But we were all very excited. It was an exciting thing to be doing."

Our trip took two nights and three days; and, by what can only partially be construed as a coincidence, Ring's ex-wife, his two children (my cousins/soon-to-become-stepsiblings), and their maid (as they were then called) were leaving Los Angeles at roughly the same time. It was estimated that we'd pass one another in the vicinity of Kansas City.

When we reached our destination, my mother, Polly, Joe, and I moved into a stone Basque house on a hillside in Coldwater Canyon, which Ring had been sharing with his best friends Alice and Ian Hunter and a very large housekeeper, Margaret. The Hunters moved out to make way for us, while fat Margaret stayed put. I shared a room with my brother Joe. Then, after a six-day acclimation period, so designated by our elders, Ring and my mother Frances took off for their nuptials in Las Vegas and a honeymoon trip Ring planned to familiarize my mother with the West: from Death Valley (the lowest part of California—282 feet below sea level) to Mount Whitney (the highest—14,494 feet high) and then on to Lake Tahoe, Yosemite, and Carmel.

The trip was geared toward giving Frances a shot at the open road where she could practice her driving. Driving was a recent undertaking for her. Ring was told by his friend Phil Dunne that he had just made one of the most touching gestures of faith ever toward a bride who had only recently undertaken driving instruction. "Jesus it was awful!" my mom exclaimed after a particularly unnerving lesson. *"I've got to learn!* Only I wish people would stop saying 'any dope can drive a car.'" In addition to having his entire car overhauled, the backseats repaired, and a new top provided, Ring had also had the fenders straightened and repainted so that, to all outward appearances, they were virgin territory.

By then the Cold War had started, but almost everyone in and around the U.S. Communist Party was still holding on to a dream of permanent world peace. The cooperation that had once existed between Russia and the United States still looked possible to them. Their optimistic thinking was that the sentiments of peace and harmony might win out. But a month before our move West, a series of editorials ran for eight days in the *Hollywood Reporter* and caused a good deal of talk. "Is Hollywood a Red Beach-Head? Yes—and no" the articles began, in an effort to promote the idea that Communists were seeking to control the Writers Guild and "the thought that goes into American letters, arts and sciences." On the third day, the series had hit home. "Let us take a look at another member of the Guild's executive board—Ring Lardner, Jr. . . . The Reporter has this to ask Ring Lardner, Jr. Are you a member of the Communist Party? Are you at present assigned to the Party's Northwest (propaganda) section? Do you hold Party Book No. 25109?"

People in New York read the story and told my mother about it. "I don't remember the details," she said. "All I know is it made little shivers go through my heart." She said she had no way of knowing that our life was going to take the turn it did. No one really did, my mother said. She never thought about it. And it wouldn't have stopped her from anything if she had known. She knew Ring was a Communist. They had that in common. "That was good." She just thought they were all kind of peculiar in Hollywood with all their money. They should be making little pictures about the working class. Like the Italians: *Open City* and *The Bicycle Thief.*

For the time being, this editorial seemed to do no serious harm, for as Ring reported in a letter before our move, his career as a commercial screenwriter was making phenomenal progress. He signed a contract with Twentieth Century-Fox for two thousand dollars a week, with the number of weeks he worked pretty much up to him. But the Cold War intensified very quickly, and by the tail end of the honeymoon there were rumors in the Hollywood Communist Party that subpoenas were going out from the California State Committee on Un-American Activities. My parents got word that the committee might be investigating Ring, and friends suggested they delay coming home.

Meanwhile, my brother and I were taking in the wonders of our new home in Coldwater Canyon, which included a dumb-waiter in the kitchen that sent food up to the second floor. This predated more puzzling juvenile wonderings about such things as "Reds," "subpoenas," the "left wing," "stool pigeons" . . . (The Mostel family didn't say *stool pigeon*, but used *informer* instead, because of their tender feelings for pigeons.)

What I remember most about Coldwater Canyon is an old wooden gate falling on my head. I don't know how this happened.

Then a year later we moved to a big house in Santa Monica with a tennis court and I lay in the backseat of the car watching the palm trees go by.

Our move came just after a subpoena had been served. The rumors about the California committee had proved false. But an investigation of Communist subversion of the movie business was under way by the House Committee on Un-American Activities in Washington, and a U.S. marshal came to the door with a subpoena for Ring. However, *subpoena* sounded like *penis* to me, and *penis* reminded me of Charlie, an older boy in Santa Monica, masturbating in his doorway, telling us it was good for you. So this thing was served and it was fortunate the interior decorator hadn't cashed the checks my parents had given her because the decorating in the new house had to come to a halt.

Still, the tennis court located behind the house—which was four blocks from the ocean—got a good deal of use, for a while anyway. At a minimum, my stepfather-uncle—whom by then I thought of as my father—had a doubles game every Sunday afternoon and sometimes it was made available in the morning to Greta Garbo, our neighbor. The tennis court had a hard surface, not cement (probably asphalt), with a tall referee's chair. My brother Joe and I climbed the chair and roller-skated and bicycled on the court.

You could label our stretch in Santa Monica a mixed bag. There was Will Wright's peppermint-stick ice cream, the roller coaster at Beverly Park (in West Hollywood) that I rode up front, and the construction sites my brother and I frequented, where slugs popped out of electrical boxes and dropped to the floor. They had no value, but to me they resembled coins and I collected them. And in our household there was the unpopular notion that American Communists were among the most fervent and farsighted supporters of such basic principles as freedom to organize and demonstrate, freedom of speech, and equal rights for minorities and women. I was spanked for using the word *nigger* even though I didn't know what it meant.

And I started taking some of these issues to heart.

The spanking happened on the sidewalk in front of our house by the ocean on Georgina Avenue under the palm trees where I was jumping rope spouting a new rhyme I had heard around the block. "Eenie, meanie, miney Moe, catch a nigger by the toe"—when *nigger* sent my father flying. Intent on repairing my nigger-saying ways, my dad took me in hand and gave the word meaning. I fell to the ground from the swat he administered and a boil on my knee bled and oozed. When I recalled the incident for him many years later, he said, "Fortunately, I don't remember this." It seems in hindsight it made him wince. His behavior and the ooze. "However, I think it had a good effect," he quickly added, offering beneficial evidence and curtailing a wry grin. "Because by the time you were in your teens you were more sensitive to this issue than either of your parents."

The issue he was referring to was the issue of discrimination toward blacks, and he was thinking about where I wound up at the tail end of a day that began with a young man standing at the foot of my bed (when I was nineteen) as I slept naked. Naked under the covers meant I must have been going through a successful dieting phase. I was always dieting.

"Selling magazines," the uninvited guest smiled when I asked what he was doing in my bedroom. "Working my way through college," he further replied. I was a college student, too, attending the Columbia University School of General Studies after two academically challenged years at a college in the Midwest.

But, of course, none of this would have happened if Tommy Kerrigan, the elevator operator, had been on the ball. Living in New York City on a floor with just two apartments, my parents kept their front door unlocked, so when the magazine seller got by Tommy, he was home free.

"Come back later," I said because my parents were still sleeping down a short hall in their bedroom with their ears plugged to muffle noise and black masks over their eyes to block out the sun—even though there couldn't have been any sun because their windows were double-hung with heavy dark shades. Neither my actress mother nor my writer father subscribed to early-morning rising. "Come back later," I intoned helpfully because my parents were the magazine subscribers after all. And the stranger left the premises with no further ado on the heels of an invitation to return when sale opportunities might improve.

Later that morning over breakfast I filled my dad in on my morning so far (my mother hadn't made an appearance yet). My unique morning encounter eliminated my usual need to stumble over potential conversation matter in search of interesting material. My regular quandary had been temporarily stamped out. I had something to say. Something original to talk about had just landed in my lap, and I proceeded to boldly recount the magazine

merchant incident, relieved not to be drifting to a mumble. (If nobody listened I would start wondering if I was stupid or something. Mumble, mumble.) Then together my father and I puzzled
over possible entry routes with suspicious eyes cast toward a
Tommy Kerrigan blunder—and that was pretty much it in the
kitchen in the back of our apartment near the back door, which
we concluded was the college-bound interloper's probable point
of departure. My father wrote screenplays in the little room off the
kitchen, and my brothers and I often had to keep it down back
there because he might be working. But I knew this day had
begun with a story that would capture his attention, and following its telling I left home for the day feeling it had brought us
closer—a connection I was often seeking.

Well, I had no idea that telling my dad about the man at the
foot of the bed would precipitate so much activity. I could have
sworn we were on the same page with the event. We hadn't
chewed the fat over it or anything. That would have been a new
one. But I was certain we were of like mind in a shared silent
recognition of the unique merit of the thing. Jointly basking in
the unexpected charm and humor of an interchange of two
strangers together in an unlikely spot. A white sleeping damsel,
a young black magazine seller gone astray, and a one-of-a-kind
resolution. The fellow and I had an amicable exchange really
and we reached an understanding of sorts. That was the way I
saw it. No big deal. And my father, for his part, remained cus-
tomarily calm when I informed him of the adventure.

It was only way after, when everybody got so carried away, that
I cast a backward glance and zeroed in on some potentially in-
criminating details. Trespassing, for example. And it hadn't even
dawned on me yet that my parents were already up to their eye-
balls in magazines—mostly left-wing crap and not bloody likely
the fellow's periodical company's fare. So old Ring and Frances

probably didn't add up to realistic subscribing prospects after all. But I swear, nobody said anything about danger. My dad wasn't alarmed, but rather taken, I thought, with my morning glory. Although as he pulled most of his lines without altering expression it was hard to tell sometimes what he was thinking. Frankly, my racial infraction in Santa Monica yielded a splashier display.

But my father sure must have gone right on thinking about it after I left because he then got Tommy Kerrigan in on it, and beady-eyed Mr. Levy, the landlord who lived in our building on a much higher floor—and much to my surprise they were all in on it at the end of the day. It certainly wasn't *my* idea to call the cops. My story—my special breakfast tale—was slipping away from me in plain view. It had spread to a cross-examining crew now parked in our living room, and I unfortunately was being relegated to a backseat. Actually, I wound up odd man out—in a clothes closet where I fled posthaste because I was certain the crowd in the living room would want to know if my intruder was black. They'd assume it, in fact. I just knew with them it would be a foregone conclusion.

So I hid in my closet and my father, well, he wound up pacing back and forth trying to persuade me that it was more sensible to come out and give a description if I could. Now, in the best of all possible worlds it probably would have been better if my guy had been white. But he was black all right. Still, he could just as well have been some other color, so don't go making the assumption that he wasn't because that just made you prejudiced and that was the one thing I couldn't stand. And P.S., I wasn't about to exchange unnecessary words with the law. I didn't trust cops, which you could pretty much hang on my dad being an ex-jailbird handcuffed to a U.S. marshal escorted to the Federal Correctional Institution in Danbury, Connecticut.

So I remained hidden in my spur-of-the-moment sanctuary, waiting for the coast to clear, unwilling to cooperate with a committee brought in to ask a question that as far as I was concerned was none of its business. It was dark and I was all alone in there, but hey!—maybe it was hats off to the lesson I learned at my father's knee with the Georgina "one two"; the Santa Monica reprimand. And maybe Emmett Till had something to do with it—the fourteen-year-old black whistling boy from Chicago who couldn't swallow the cold hard facts in Money, Mississippi, that got his neck wired to a seventy-four-pound cotton gin fan and sunk in the Tallahatchie River, one eye gouged out, a bullet hole in his head . . . dead at fourteen. He was only two years older than me when this happened for God's sake. And of course the two white men who dragged him from his bed in the night were set free.

"What else could I do?" one of the men who killed him explained to a magazine writer. "He thought he was as good as any white man." As for Emmett Till wolf-whistling at a white woman: He stuttered or lisped due to a childhood attack of polio, so his mama had told him, "If you get hung up on a word, whistle—and go ahead and just say it."

"Pretty extreme," declared my father from outside my bedroom closet. "You shouldn't carry the feeling about blacks this far." God knows what he was saying to the assembled guests in the living room. But as long as they were on the premises I remained firmly planted, displaying what my father came to call my extreme sensitivity. He would have told them the man was black and played down its relevance, he said, but I was of the opinion that confirming what they thought made me one of them, so I took my stand against the black assumption in the safety of my closet.

. . .

Well, I concluded somewhere down the road, people probably didn't like hearing this story any more than they liked hearing the ones (that occurred almost ten years later) about the
dried-out cat (Curtis) or the cooked feline (Jennifer) and the
broiled chicken. And then, practically right smack in the middle
of contemplating this and pondering possible links between
black-stranger-in-room and dried-and-fried-cats, I had this
dream (maybe it was the clue to the bridge, maybe it was the
bridge itself): There was a small moving lump under the covers
of my made bed. The top layer was puffy white down, and the
puff turned out to be a young black girl. A small robber, hidden
away under my white down cover—much the way the calico cat,
Polly, curls herself—who upon being discovered didn't have
much to say, except to act miserable, because she was uncovered
before getting her hands on something. She thought she was
owed something—like a goddamn door prize. So we searched
my chest of drawers for a *cabecita* among the tiny stone heads
right out of a brick quarry site of an ancient pre-Columbian bur-
ial ground. Actually it was a toss-up for the little darling, who
could have been me, according to what I've heard about dreams,
between two lovely pottery shards. Some of the blacklist crew—
some of the Hollywood refugees seeking shelter in Mexico in the
fifties—collected these archaeological treasures, and my parents
made off with a small haul. None of them really occupied my Korean peasant chest. Only in my dreams. Anyway the little girl's
endeavor was becoming a stiff pain in the neck. An inconvenience. She was losing me even if she was me. The other robber—the real robber, the magazine seller or whatever—didn't
boss me around.

However, small girl lump reminded me of calico moving
bump, which you have to be careful not to sit on and squash. So

I jumped into the little girlie's shoes to see what all the fuss was about and I could see where she was coming from. Then I wound up sympathizing with the slumbering poof and her lousy attitude. Her poaching and plundering could have been the result of neglect on somebody's part, I concluded. Maybe nobody listened to her goddamn stories—like with the gruesome cat stories I couldn't resist telling. And I'd rather sweep it under the rug, but the little thing wasn't alone in the larceny department, either. So chalk it up to an emerging affection for the girl that I mention thieving on my part and, in no particular order, disclose a partial list of past stolen goods: Marie Ziegler's toy cash register, money for the ice cream man on the other side of Ocean Avenue, which I was forbidden to cross, the deluxe box of Crayola crayons with all the goddamn colors to replace the puny starter kit my parents saddled me with, a red plaid Laura Ashley dress, black leather pants from Henri Bendel, Seconal, Valium, Thorazine (even though I didn't know what it was), and comics. (I was afraid I would never stop loving comics. My dad and his three brothers mastered the fundamentals of reading and writing at age four, and by six, reading for them was practically a full-time occupation for God's sake. Whereas at nine I was deeply engrossed in comic books and teen romance novels instead of *The Count of Monte Cristo* or *The Vicomte de Bragelonne*. It was in that context that I worried.)

I didn't know why the cat stories kept popping up or why it was I couldn't resist the urge to relate them in all their gory splendor. I usually laughed when I told them. Ha ha. Even though they were definitely not funny. Sometimes with tears streaming down my face from laughing so hard. Just like my cousin Mary Jane, who practically split a gut at Granny's funeral all those years ago.

There were two of them. Two charming Siamese kittens. Curtis for an elevator man on West End Avenue, and I don't know where the name Jennifer came from. All I know is she must have slipped behind the stove through the broiler opening when its parts were being scoured. Later that night Gwen (the deaf Jamaican housekeeper) turned on the oven and put the chicken in. Frankly, I don't remember if she was broiling or baking. She was especially good at frying and too bad for Jennifer that's not what she was doing that night. Then shortly thereafter, we were alerted by a sound. A desperate cat noise which, of course, flew right past deaf Gwen (although she might have sniffed something was wrong), and we all came running from the front of the apartment. (The big apartment in the Belnord where I was living with my second husband, Tommy Lee Jones, and my two children from a previous marriage. The writer Isaac Bashevis Singer lived across the courtyard and sometimes I'd sit in one of my bedroom windows looking for him down below.) Well, it was Tommy who located the problem. The poor cat squealing for help. The cat calling for release from her stuck position in the hot stove. When he tracked her down he recognized that she was too far gone and, out of everyone's sight, he wrung her neck. In fact, the rest of us never laid eyes on charred Jenny's fur and thank God Tommy was from Texas and knew how to put Jenny out of her misery.

Curtis's demise was another story that took place just a short while after. Another story with nothing cheery going for it. Yet I couldn't leave him out of it. I seemed to have to deliver the whole cat package even when everybody could see where it was headed, including me.

I was doing laundry, and this was where the demise of the old boy came in. It was the night before I was to check into the Hospital for Joint Diseases and get my leg rebroken. Tommy and I had been in a motorcycle accident and after traction, a body cast, and three leg casts, the compound fracture I'd sustained as the result of flying thirty feet into the air and landing on River-side Drive hadn't healed properly. So after all was said and done, my leg wound up crooked and I was doing laundry for the up-coming hospital visit/leg-straightening procedure; the femur rebreaking-resetting course of action. And the dryer was left open after a dry spin. Curtis must have stepped in, settling on the damp but warm clothes that remained within. Unknowingly I shut the door, and the cat went for a spin. Pretty soon, but not soon enough where Curtis was concerned, I noted the dryer walking forward into the room. From some imbalance, I guessed. And upon opening the door and witnessing his stiff dried-out body, I screamed. Yet I couldn't put the lid on it as far as the cat catastrophes were concerned. In fact, I was usually doubled over with laughter by the end.

IN SANTA MONICA I started gaining weight. My mother said I was imitating her. She was pregnant with my brother Jim. I was called "Potato Dumpling" by my dad, in a story he would make up about my brother and me; and Joe—well, he was called "String Bean" in this tale, a name I would have preferred. When I objected, "Tomato" was the name my father held in reserve for me in case of shrinkage. If I dropped a few pounds, got smaller and firmer, I would become "Tomato." Also, Billy Michaels, the Catholic boy next door, said he'd marry me if I lost weight.

But I did find inspiration in *The Churkendoose*, a brother-hood tale in disguise. I identified with the odd bird, listening often to the record. I even sang along with Ray Bolger (the Churkendoose) when he went on about being different. The story I cherished was about a gigantic chicken egg incubated by the chicken that laid it with the collaborative efforts of a turkey, duck, and goose. The result was something unique, but perceived as ugly and peculiar in the collective eye of the barnyard inhabitants, who considered him dangerous. They wanted to kick him on the head, poke him in the eye. Eliminate him. But fortunately there was a freethinker among them who stepped forward and called for a group conscience. Nothing wrong with that. Thank God for the odd bird's advocate. I, for one, experienced similar relief and, in my case, deliverance from third-grade oblivion about a year later, thanks to Polly, the teacher at the progressive school we attended during my father's incarceration, who stepped in and declared me better suited than all-the-rage Janie Gordon to execute some dumb letter the class was sending out. Old Janie had initially won the vote hands down. But I won the revote thanks to Polly's prompting. And what do you know, old Janie's father went on to become a stool pigeon, which I usually pointed out about somebody when it applied. After initially resisting the House Committee on Un-American Activities in 1951, her dad, a director, went on to name names.

Dismissed while the other animals privately convened, the Churkendoose danced sadly out of the henhouse (he didn't walk, he danced) to await his fate and tearfully study his reflection in a rain puddle. While mournfully scrutinizing the situation and singing some pertinent refrain about perspective and perception, screams and confusion emanated from within because a fox had invaded the henhouse. My feathered friend tapped back as fast as he could. The fox was running this way and that, snapping at all the fowl. But when he got a load of you-know-who, he took off.

This made our strange fellow a hero, and the others came to substitute their previous selfishness and meanness toward him with kindness and praise, apologizing and begging him to stay. And everyone wound up helping each other and learning from one another, which frankly was a personal dream of mine at the time.

Kate and Jo Jo

My mother said she tied my troubles to the time my new father went to jail because of a photograph of me taken soon after his departure. In the picture I was standing barefooted, holding the Hunters' collie by the leash and wearing a tight sundress in which she said I looked fat. I was skinny when we arrived in Los Angeles, so this photo caught her attention. In the portrait she called lumpish I actually have a smile on my face, united as I was for the moment with a dog called Jo Jo.

"You probably began to experience difficulties then," my mother said. "Probably" meant that it was possible I never experienced any difficulties—but if I did, this was when they began. "I think it was from not having your second father around," she said. "Now, there might have been problems also about my behavior, God knows. First of all, I had terrible sexual problems. I mean I was a frozen fish. It was during that time that I became involved with Joe." The director Joseph Losey was around our house a lot while Ring was in jail.

But I think my troubles began sooner because, frankly, everything that occurred before my dad's incarceration—my real father's death, moving west, the six designated days, my mother marrying my uncle, the "subpoena" thing, and Billy Michaels's provisional marriage proposal, coupled with the disgrace of being likened to a potato—felt like trouble to me.

FOUR MONTHS BEFORE my sixth birthday my mother gave birth to my brother Jim, and just before the actual festivities my father left Los Angeles for Washington, DC, so he could get a passport quickly in order to fly away to Zurich. It was still possible then for him to get one. A Swiss producer named Lazar Wechsler had borrowed Cornel Wilde from Twentieth Century-Fox to star in a film, and Ring was accompanying Wechsler to write the screenplay. Twentieth Century-Fox would no longer allow my father to pass through the gate, but the studio, wanting the picture to be good enough for their star, was reassured when Wechsler told them he was hiring Ring. That's what persuaded them to lend Wilde in the first place. They weren't the ones releasing the picture, so they figured they weren't breaking the blacklist.

My father waited for the passport outside Mrs. Ruth Shipley's office at the passport bureau in Washington. She was in charge and noted for being anti-Red. Ring knew that Adrian Scott and Eddie Dmytryk had received passports to work in

England stamped GOOD FOR ENGLAND, FRANCE AND ITALY ONLY. So when he received his, he anticipated these constraints. "I want to see what restrictions there are," he said, opening the document while expressing his concern, and the young man who'd handed it to him said, "What?" Then he took the thing back. In a few minutes he reappeared, stating there were no restrictions at this time. But this was the last passport my father was given until 1958. After Harry Truman was elected in 1948, and up until 1958, it was not considered in the best interests of the United States for Ring to travel abroad.

A couple of months after Ring left, my mother joined him in Europe. It never crossed her mind for one minute to stay with us kids, for that would not have reflected life as she saw it.

"The way you have children, if you're an actress," she said, "you have somebody take care of your children. And then you can be an actress. The work comes first. Like a fire horse you go. When the work comes that's what you're supposed to do. It never would have occurred to me to stay home." My mother coached the two French actresses in Mr. Wechsler's picture and served as dialogue coach. She had a small part, but it was cut out.

We were left with Polly, the only person for whom I felt affection, and a baby nurse named Miss Peterson for my brother Jim. She fed him orange juice, egg yolk, cow's milk, and prunes because he was constipated and held him on her lap, and together they watched the men on the tennis court. My new father's friends still came to play. I announced to a car pool of kids, "You all think I'm going to be an actress because my mother is. Well, I'm not." Then on one of Polly's days off, I stood on our tennis court in Santa Monica and asked God how things were going to turn out. I was beginning to wonder if anybody was ever coming back. My parents told me I could be any religion I wanted and I went to Sunday school once to investigate, but I knew what they believed. Everything, they said, including evolution, was determined by chance and necessity, and Ring said he considered the existence of God highly improbable, even if he couldn't prove it. But I was desperate.

I attended Sunday school with somebody on the block, Marie Ziegler, I think. She was my friend, although my mother begged to differ. She told me once that Marie was a crazy little girl. We made fun of her, she said, and all the kids pulled down her pants and my mother claimed she was sort of a local victim. I never knew this about her and was distressed to hear it. I knew Marie could be bamboozled and cheated as she had been by me in the deal concerning her toy cash register—I got caught by her parents traversing their living room with it. But she was my friend and I remember nothing about pants. Actually, it's my underpants that I remember something about. But that's another story.

My Sunday school trial run with Marie went badly. I got called on and was asked a question I couldn't answer. So I figured I didn't belong and I never returned. The only spiritual comfort I had was Polly singing "Swing Low, Swing Chariot" to herself, often enough so I learned it from her. *Swing low, sweet chariot, comin' for to carry me home. Swing low, sweet chariot, comin' for to carry me home. I looked over Jordan and what did I see, comin' for to carry me home? A band of angels comin' after me, comin' for to carry me home.* But when my mom was in Europe, that wasn't enough. I missed her. So with my limited experience in spiritual endeavors, I turned to God on the tennis court.

Sometime in April, while my parents were still away, I wrote "Dear Mommy and Daddy" in my big block printing with a pen Polly had given me. "We are so happy that you are coming home earlier than you thought. We miss you very much. Joe had a good party." There was more in my letter about the pen and money from Granny (our paternal grandmother, Ellis), Easter bunnies from Grandma Marie, and an Easter egg hunt at the Rossens'. So it must have been before the director-screenwriter Robert Rossen became a stool pigeon that I wrote this because we wouldn't have been caught dead at the Rossens' after that. At his second appearance before the committee, May 7, 1953, Rossen became an informer, naming fifty names.

I signed my letter to my parents "Katharine," because that's how I was known then.

Soon after my parents came home, the situation got worse. The next thing I knew, my father was telling me he might have to go to jail because some men in Washington had asked him things they had no right to ask and he'd told them so. He was shaving in the bathroom in front of a mirror when he said it—his back to me, addressing the task at hand. He said "might" and I clung to that word.

"Mr. Lardner, are you a member of the Screen Writers Guild? . . . a Congressional Committee is asking you: Are you a member of the Screen Writers Guild? Now you answer it yes or no." But my father refused to submit to a yes-or-no limitation and wanted in the course of his answer to challenge the committee at the very foundation of its existence. It was a dumb question anyway. They could have found their answer by reading the guild stationery or magazine because in both places Ring was listed as a member of the executive board. However, they kept on asking until Chairman J. Parnell Thomas, perched on a District of Columbia telephone directory and a red silk pillow to appear taller for the cameras, moved them on to the next question. "The sixty-four-dollar question," he called it.

"Mr. Lardner, the charge has been made before the Committee that the Screen Writers Guild which according to the record, you are a member of, whether you admit it or not, has a number of individuals in it who are members of the Communist Party. This Committee is seeking to determine the extent of the Communist infiltration of the Screen Writers Guild and of other guilds within the motion-picture industry.

". . . And certainly the question of whether or not you are a member of the Communist Party is very pertinent. Now, are you a member or have you ever been a member of the Communist Party?"

Well, my father told the House Committee on Un-American Activities he could answer their question but if he did he'd hate himself in the morning. He stuttered when he said it, holding a cigarette in his right hand. The stuttering was a throwback to his youth. But, like most of his responses before the committee, this one was delivered in pieces. He started to say, "I could answer the question exactly the way you want, Mr. Chairman," when Thomas broke in from his pillow perch with thoughts that had just occurred to him on the subject of "real Americanism." My dad waited until he drew a breath—determined to get one complete parsable sentence into the record to justify the efforts of his childhood English teachers. This time he picked up the thought with "I could answer it"—the words "exactly the way you want" being incorporated by implication. What he meant was that he would subsequently reproach himself if he ever yielded to the committee's terms entirely. He said he has always associated the words "I'll hate myself in the morning" with a situation in which a previously chaste woman was succumbing to the indecent blandishments of a scoundrel and very likely launching herself on the road to prostitution. This was the analogy he wanted to suggest.

Then my father was forcibly removed from the witness chair by the sergeant at arms and cited for contempt along with nine other men who came to be known as the Hollywood Ten. He left murmuring, "I think I am being made to leave by force."

Stuttering was something my father did as a kid. The fact that he was made to write with his right hand instead of his left is what he thought accounted for it. In an attempt to overcome it he signed up for public speaking and discovered he didn't stutter so much if he was debating or making a speech. However, by the time he more or less stopped stuttering, he didn't talk as much as he had. He talked a lot more as a kid—more than anyone in his family. In fact, he was considered veritably gabby and voted second windiest in his class at Andover. But from the age of nineteen or twenty he became comparatively taciturn— imitating the family feeling that people who expressed their emotions or talked about them were on a slightly lower level.

And here, in no particular order, are some of the things we never talked about: my mother marrying my uncle (Ring). My new father's imprisonment. My college board scores. Ring crashing drunk into my room in the middle of the night, breaking a special plate of mine (he was headed for my brothers' room was all he said). My real father's death and my mother not saying anything to us when he was killed. "Darling, you were . . ." I was twenty-one months old, for God's sake, and Joe was six months. "Of course I didn't say anything," she said. "Don't be silly. Nothing. Nothing. There was nothing to say and nothing to do."

My mom didn't stay home with her babies and mourn the loss of her husband. She couldn't. She could no more do that than jump out the window. So what she did was fly around town like a chicken with its head chopped off. She went back to work right away. She found out about David on a Saturday and Monday she was back at work and she had "such pride about this thing," she said that she would walk down the hall of the third floor of NBC and nobody dared come up to her to say, "I'm so sorry, Frances."

"It was so private. It was so personal. It was so painful. We were so unique. We were so exceptional. David was so exceptional that I mustn't be human about this."

All I know is this reminded me of a rabbit we once had. We were living in North Hollywood and this bunny we had died. And we were encouraged to consider him missing. Well, I didn't remember much about the actual rabbit, except I had a feeling it wasn't white. And I only dimly remembered feeding it and thinking a little bit about what food to give it—vegetables or something. But what I recalled vividly was searching for it up and down the hill and all along the brook behind our house on Holly Drive until it got dark, before the truth was revealed. Now, I know a bunny's not the same thing, but it had a familiar ring.

I was also pretty good at secrets.

Like in Santa Monica when the bubble gum boys, as I alone referred to them, would come on their bikes and I'd be waiting and off we'd go to the vacant lot across from my house to lie, in exchange for bubble gum, in the overgrowth and among the hillocks with my underpants down, which I didn't mention to anyone.

My mother said stories like that were all the rage. Like when I finally told her about my stepbrother taking me into the back room onto the single bed after pulling down the shades. My mother wanted to know what he did there. I don't remember what he did there. "Did he put his penis in you or rub up against you?" she asked. He did say, "Is this what your boyfriends do?" But I didn't tell her that. I was only eleven when this happened and overweight, flattered he even thought I had boyfriends. My mother laughed when I told her he said not to tell. That it was our secret.

"Of course," she said, and then volunteered one about her cousin Bernie. "Back then," she said, "it wasn't this big thing. You just knew it was something you didn't want to tell anybody."

My mother said incest was all the rage. "The thing that all the girls were talking about. A lot of it is bullshit," she said. "I know goddamn well that I crawled into bed with my father. The three of us had one bedroom, and my mother was away working at night. When I'd wake up and my father would be lying there in the morning I'd come and poke his eye open and crawl into bed with him and I know goddamn well that his penis hung out of his pajama bottoms. But I don't believe he ever did anything molestatious. I'm sure he didn't. I think if I wanted to interpret that penis sticking out of his pants, I could say he should have been careful and not allowed anything like that to happen. But he didn't rub it up against me and if I thought he did I'd be making it up because I don't believe he did. He loved me so much that he would have to protect me from that."

Eric Johnston, president of the Motion Picture Producers Association, told the Ten's attorneys in a private meeting, "I will never be party to such a thing as a blacklist." That was in October 1947. By November about fifty of Hollywood's chief executives and producers had met in one of the public rooms at the Waldorf-Astoria hotel in New York. "We will forthwith discharge or suspend without compensation those in our employ, and we will not reemploy any of the Ten until such time as he is acquitted or has purged himself of contempt and declares under oath that he is not a Communist," said the document that came to be known as the Waldorf Statement. Darryl Zanuck at Twentieth Century-Fox told Ring that he would respect his contract until commanded otherwise by his board of directors. His board promptly met in New York and so commanded. My father was reached at a meeting with Otto Preminger in Preminger's office and requested to leave the premises.

MY DAD HAD to go to jail for almost a year, which he explained would seem a long time but really wasn't. "It won't be a long time over your life or mine," he said. "Just a passing thing."

The Penal Interlude

Augilst 30.
       Frances: *Katie has been pretty "big blonde" lately.*

Well before I knew what it meant I didn't like the sound of
it. (I was seven.) Nice reference, Mom. Dorothy Parker's Hazel
Morse—a peroxide doll in a boozy world where everybody wanted
her to cheer up and be a flabby pretender when really everything
looked lousy to her. I mean "[m]isery crushed her as if she were
between great smooth stones." So after about "a couple [a million]
evenings of being a good sport among her male acquaintances"
she tried to kill herself with a hypnotic called Veronal, a sodium-
barbital-type sedative you could readily lay your hands on in Jersey. Only thanks but no thanks to the young sleazebag doctor
living on the ground floor—who was lasciviously occupied and
"none too pleased at interruption"—the old gal got her stomach
pumped, thus returning her to yucky status quo. Thanks, Mom.

*I think it's just the natural restlessness of a fairly inactive
summer,* she explained about <u>my</u> "misty melancholies" to my
dad, who was in jail, which was why she was writing this little tid-
bit in the first place. *Both children will be much happier once
school starts,* she said. *Joe has a great deal of activity around
Holly Drive but once again there is a girl shortage.*

The New York Times, **Thursday, June 30, 1950.**

Eight Hollywood figures who refused to tell the House Committee on Un-American Activities whether they were Communists were convicted of contempt of Congress...and six were immediately taken to jail.

Convicted were Albert Maltz, Samuel Ornitz, Alvah Bessie, Ring Lardner, Jr. and Lester Cole, writers; Adrian Scott, writer-producer; Herbert Biberman, writer-director, and Edward Dmytryk, director....

(Two others of the so-called Hollywood Ten who defied the committee, Dalton Trumbo and John Howard Lawson, were fined a thousand dollars each and began serving one-year jail terms on June 9.)

...Still protesting their innocence, the prisoners took the verdicts calmly and made brief statements. Lardner said there was only a minor difference between forcing a man to say what his opinions are, and dictating what those opinions should be.

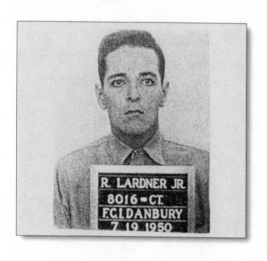

"Whenever men have been compelled to open their minds to government authority, men's minds have ceased to be free," concluded my father.

My mother was doing a radio show when my father was sentenced. "A pretty horrible day!" she proclaimed. "There was the tension of doing a show and sorting out what the hell was going to happen." She said once my father was sentenced she had to take hold of herself and she did. "And the truth is that I took hold of myself before that. It was I who decided that you kids were not going to be going to a public school in Hollywood and you were going to be safe and protected. Safe and protected. That's when I went to the Westland School and got you guys scholarships. I wasn't going to have you going to the local public school and not be surrounded by love."

When my father went to prison we had to move.

OWNER GOING TO JAIL

One of the Taciturn Ten offers 10-room house for immediate sacrifice sale. Tennis court—Nr. Beach in Santa Monica. $26,000 in direct sale by owner; $11,000 cash required. Call **S.M.** 5-7272

My parents had to sell our big house in Santa Monica. We needed money to live on while Ring was away. So toward this end he placed an ad in the *Hollywood Reporter* and before dawn a Beverly Hills doctor who was in Las Vegas doing research in emotional stress at the gaming tables climbed into his Cadillac and by midday wrapped up a deal that left my family with a net loss of nine thousand dollars.

All federal prisoners who were tried in the city of Washington went directly to the District of Columbia Department of Corrections, a maximum-security prison, along with everybody else who was arrested in Washington for municipal offenses. My father was put in a cell. *A combined bedroom, living room and bathroom for two*, he wrote my mother—*with almost the precise linear dimensions of the bed you are now filling so inadequately.* And the door locked behind him. His first six hours in custody were pleasant enough. *I don't anticipate any hardships beyond possible boredom*, he said.

Ring: *If we only stay here nine days, I may not be able to exceed the weekly quota of three letters.... So you may not hear from me till I have reached my permanent home-from-home.*

My father's new roommate, an amusing fellow with four counts of armed robbery against him, told my father about having machine-gunned nine Japanese prisoners during the war.

Actually, right after starting in Washington my father had a bad night. He said it was just a feeling of it all having come to a head. There had been a certain amount of suspense about how it was all going to turn out right up until the Supreme Court decided not to hear the cases of Trumbo and Lawson. (The Ten had thought they had a pretty good chance of winning in the courts. And if they had—if the Supreme Court had said they had a perfect right to do what they did—then the movie producers would have had to rescind their blacklist.) It was just an accumulation of bad news. And then the Korean War broke out. My father was very unhappy and didn't know if he would be able to get through it comfortably. He felt sad and cried. He didn't know exactly what it was going to be like in prison or how he was going to react to it. But when he found he wasn't too depressed, he felt he could handle it all right. He said it was just a question of waiting it out.

We didn't know where my dad was going next. Some federal institution. They weren't sending any more than two of them to the same place. One of my father's lawyers (Robert Kenny) put in a plug for the Federal Correctional Institution in Danbury, Connecticut. If anybody was headed that way, let it be Lester Cole and Ring, he told the head of the Bureau of Prisons. (Kenny, having been attorney general of California, was well acquainted in Washington.) They both had mothers in Connecticut and were going to be far from their families in California, he explained.

Thursday, June 29.

Ring: *Dear Pals* [this was directed to Joe and me], *I am in jail at last and it isn't really so bad at all. I hope you are finding the new house is as much fun as it looked like it would be. It will probably be a couple of weeks before you can write to me, which you can do most easily by adding little notes of your own to Mommy's. . . . Have a lot of fun.*

When my father began paying his debt to society, my mother, my brothers, and I relocated to a rental on Holly Drive with a small wooden front porch, a big picture window, and an oak door with beveled glass. We were to pass the penal interlude in a Hollywood-style bungalow on a shady site near what is now the Hollywood Freeway. The new house had a creek out back full of aquatic treasures, excellent for capturing and transferring to old jam jars. And along with the rest of the neighborhood youth, we jumped off our garage roof with umbrellas onto mattresses— wondering how long we could stay suspended in air. We rode our bikes around the Hollywood dam and Johnny Black, a chipped-tooth fellow, possessed the first TV—a tiny RCA, an eight-inch thing. His father, a bricklayer, offered up his biceps for our chinning purposes. And there was Spencer, a boy in the neighborhood somewhat on the bad side of Johnny Black. While Johnny Black was only borderline—the kind who never did anything clearly wrong—Spencer ran afoul of most people, talked back, and pulled pranks. My brother Joe remembered him being accused of cursing a woman once and when she got hold of him all he said was "too-too-too." Not too likely, but that's what old Spencer claimed he said. And Roy Rogers lived up the hill on Ivarene, for God's sake. Too bad he was a mean bastard throwing rocks at Victor (Vicky) Brandt's dog Pedro, who gobbled up chickens and snatched fish out of Roy's pond. But hey! His stone throwing broke poor Vicky Brandt's heart. For Roy Rogers was a cowboy hero. Vicky Brandt was our friend (his father was never formally blacklisted, but suspicions that he was a Communist cut his career midstream). He turned up every Saturday morning at eight, parked his bike in the driveway, climbed through the window to sit with Joe and me listening to *Big John and Sparky*.

Polly moved with us and took care of us, and my mother kept trying to work.

Frances: *Our next door neighbors have a nine year old who's away a great deal of the time, or has been because of an ailing grandfather who has recently passed on. Only now the family came into a little money—which has enabled them to take a short vacation so Katharine's only girl companion on our street anyway—Diane White, is off again.*

This was my mother tying up her interpretive thread. But not included—the girl inhabiting an iron lung (attracting a hell of a lot of attention) with the dreaded disease of the fifties for which there was no cure. No vaccine. Infantile paralysis.

I wanted polio.

The New York Times, Thursday, June 30, 1950.

...Maltz, Cole, Lardner and Bessie were sentenced to serve one year and pay $1,000 fines [like Trumbo and Lawson]. Dmytryk and Biberman were sentenced to six-month terms and must pay $1,000 fines.

So the main concern on everybody's mind was, What gives with the switch by the third judge? Why only six months per culprit when all their offenses were identical in every significant detail?

It is a good sign, wrote my father of Dmytryk's and Biberman's good fortune, especially as it might affect parole. But there might be a tendency for people to get overly optimistic, he warned.

Ring: *The fact that you or I or anybody else thinks it's incon-sistent for there to be a difference in the sentences doesn't mean that judges or parole boards will see it that way or that there's anything legally wrong with it under a code which leaves sen-tences to the discretion of judges.*

Parole was one of the many subjects to which my father said the lawyers contributed sustained obfuscation.

He had heard it before in unconfirmed fashion. But never definitively until his lawyer Marty Popper showed up and stated as absolute fact: No such thing as parole on a one-year sentence for a misdemeanor. Which left the only chance for the eight achieving equalization (a six-month sentence for one and all) resting on the slender chance of a petition for executive clemency in the form of a pardon or commutation of sentence. *But if there is still any con-fusion in legal minds* [for Christ's sake] *I suggest it be clarified forthwith,* said my father.

Ring: *Baby darling . . . I may have implied in my first letter that there wasn't much point in your writing me here. If I did, it was a grievous error because there would be nothing more reviv-ing than to hear from you in the next few days. . . .*

My father was beginning to get more or less adjusted to the new life but with little danger, he said, of coming to prefer it to *connubial existence on, as we prison types say in our quaint jar-gon, "the outside."* And he was putting on weight. A process he would try to counter with exercises learned from a weight-lifting, "directorial" character.

Actually there are photographs of all four of the Lardner boys looking plump. But Ring, by his own estimation, was definitely the fat one. And he suffered occasional blows as the result of it. I'm thinking of what happened after he made a remark to charm a girl with whom he was smitten. "Hello, little Buttercup," he sweetly addressed her. (For that was her role in the school production of *H.M.S. Pinafore.*) "Hello, little Butterball," she shot back. Nailing my twelve-year-old dad with her cheeky reply.

And Uncle John wrote a song: "I have three young brothers Dave and Bill [Ring] and Jim. Bill is like all mothers. The rest of them are slim."

But in 1950 my father was "tall, slender, bespectacled," as *Time* magazine described him in a National Affairs piece titled "Ring & the Proletariat" that also featured a photo of him handcuffed to Albert Maltz.

Unfortunately, in the same *Time* magazine story my mother was referred to as a bit player.

"Like an extra almost!" she exclaimed, summing up the whole affair.

> His first wife had divorced him; he married his brother David's widow. In the three years since the hearings, Ring has been fired by his studio, and has had only one job.... His wife earned money as a radio actress and by playing bit parts in the movies.

"I wanted to kill myself," my mother declared. "I just couldn't tie in blacklist," she said, giving the subject a cold shoulder. "I mean, to me it didn't matter. I didn't care, blacklist, no blacklist. Miss Chaney a bit player—what are they, crazy?"

"Acting was my higher power, baby," she cried out on another occasion. "That's the only place that I knew about God."

Sunday, July 9.

Ring: *I have converted to nylon and look forward to the time when we can do our bathroom laundry together. I am also very glad I decided to wear my new suit because flannel would be very tough in this climate.*

You may receive two separate parcels of my clothing....

My paternal grandmother, Ellis (Granny), was sending us my

dad's briefcase and its contents. But my father didn't know what they were going to do with the clothes he'd worn in. And there was more confusion on the parole issue. It seemed now he would be eligible for same after four months.

Ring: *It is incredible and annoying that we are still left in doubt on this point. . . .*

[But] you shouldn't get the impression that I am undergoing any grievous punishment or that these months will sear an indelible imprint on my tender soul. This kind of confinement is not in itself a problem to anyone as inured to inertia as I am. I read, smoke, talk, eat and sleep a little more than I am used to, and try to work. My greatest problem is the familiar one that it is so much easier to read than write, especially when I know that I won't be allowed to keep the notes I am now making when I am shipped from here to my more permanent location.

The main drawbacks to the whole situation, outside of not being with you and the children, are the psychological factors that it is involuntary and senseless. Senseless, I mean from any point of view, including that which holds we were justly convicted of a misdemeanor against legislative authority. What conceivable benefit to whom, now that they have won their judicial victory, is served by our being locked up these six or ten or twelve months?

Moving day hadn't arrived yet, but my father thought it would momentarily and with it the prospect of a less confining routine.

Sunday, July 16.

Ring: *If you hear where I am before I am able to let you know, pass the word to my mother as I have an idea she will want to visit me. Incidentally there is no such danger to fear from your mother because she can't qualify as a close enough relative. . . .*

Do you feel as I do that the prospects for world peace are looking up? No matter how many other explanations are thought up for the Korean disaster, the only question of the hour is why do North Koreans fight better than South Koreans? No one can escape the implications and its logic leads to finding, however reluctantly, a formula for co-existence.

Tickle Katharine's feet and throw Joe into bed for me and give Jimmy a taste of something sweet in my name. You are loved, madam, by

RING LARDNER, JR. D.C.D.C.85577 CB1-113

Another day and still no word about departure for those of them who remained.

Letters of commendation didn't seem as important as they would be in the usual case, said my father, where the problem was to establish the applicant as having some sort of respectable past and record as a sober, law-abiding citizen; but they wouldn't do any harm, he concluded. *Otto Preminger is a good idea*, he wrote. *And of course* [Darryl] *Zanuck would be great.... I'd rather Hepburn wasn't asked.* Due to his letter-writing limitations, my mother was the one responsible for rounding up proof from people that my father was a good candidate for parole.

Monday, July 17.

Ring: *Tell Polly, Katie, Joe and Jimmy that I love them, am having a reasonable time and don't wish they were here....*

My father's final letter from the Washington jail was held up twenty-four hours because he inadvertently violated the local standards for polite correspondence with a phrase roughly equivalent to "to the nether regions with it." It was sent back to him for use of profanity. He changed it to "forget about it."

Mail Form No. 4
Rev. June, 1946

UNITED STATES DEPARTMENT OF JUSTICE

PENAL AND CORRECTIONAL INSTITUTIONS

Instructions to Correspondents

You have been listed as one of the persons with whom the inmate, whose name appears in the box, may correspond. All mail addressed to inmates must be opened for review. May we have your cooperation in making it possible for your friend's or relative's mail to be handled promptly by following these instructions:

1. Address the envelope as shown here:

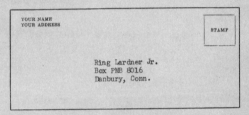

YOUR NAME
YOUR ADDRESS

STAMP

Ring Lardner Jr.
Box PMB 8016
Danbury, Conn.

2. Be sure to sign your name in full at the end of every letter and write in your correct address.

3. Please limit your letter to two sheets of paper and use only one side of each page.

4. All letters must be written in English. Special permission must be received before any correspondence can be carried on in a foreign language.

5. Do not send postage stamps or stationery. The institution furnishes writing material and the Government pays the postage on the number of letters your correspondent may send out. Money in small amounts is acceptable for deposit to your correspondent's account unless you have been notified to the contrary. For your own protection DO NOT SEND CASH. Use postal or express money orders.

6. Do not send packages of any kind unless you have received special permission to do so. Inmates are permitted to purchase books and magazine or newspaper subscriptions through the institution commissary. If special permission is received from the Warden, correspondents may furnish printed material to the inmate provided this comes direct from the publisher.

7. Please limit your correspondence to one letter each week unless you are advised that special arrangements have been made for you to write more frequently. These arrangements can only be made when letters from other correspondents are eliminated or restricted.

Your observation of these instructions will insure prompt delivery of all mail and will help us handle the very large volume of mail received.

FPI—LK—10-31-47—25M—5158-

. . .

LEAVING WASHINGTON things got better, said my father—starting with traveling (with Lester Cole) in the custody of a couple of marshals along with a guy who was being sent up for having broadcast for the Nazis during the war. "Just the fact that the marshals didn't know how to change trains in South Norwalk and I had to tell them by directing them under the tracks." After a pleasant trip they arrived in Danbury. And old J. Parnell Thomas (no longer committee chairman) was there when they pulled in. Having received a two-year prison sentence for putting nonworkers on the government payroll and appropriating their salaries for himself, he was now custodian of the chicken yard at the Federal Correctional Institution, Danbury, Connecticut. "The blue prison fatigues hung loosely on the weary perspiring man," my father remarked. (Thomas had dropped about fifty pounds.) "Still pushing the chicken shit around," Cole greeted him. This always got a big laugh in our circle of friends.

Thursday Night.

Frances: *My dearest honey, I heard of your transfer yesterday, but this is the first chance I've had to write. Yesterday started with a 9:30 appointment with the La Jolla Summer Theatre in Beverly Hills and then a meeting with Jonnie [Cole] about general matters, & specifically about coordinating the legal eagles, then a ladies luncheon at which I spoke and read Trumbo's poem....*

The wives had a lot of things to do. (There was a sense of community, my mother said. A sense that you weren't totally alone.) They solicited letters for parole. There were parties to raise money. My mother found speaking at various gatherings on my father's behalf helpful for her personal morale. She was the one delegated to read Dalton Trumbo's letters. It was a good way of raising money. (Trumbo wrote very moving letters, but his wife, Cleo, wouldn't read them aloud.) "On the other hand," she said, "you began to feel like a pariah because a lot of people dropped off. I mean a large mass of them dropped away."

Frances: [T]*hen* [there was] *a rehearsal for an evening eulogyzing (I don't know whether that should be y or i) Maltz which lasted till seven, for which I was the narrator—home for a bath and to kiss Joe and Jimmy. And back to the New Globe Theatre at eight—for the performance. Then dinner at 12 and bed by 1:30. Today was Thursday and you know what that means.*

Thursday meant Polly's day off.

Frances: *So having explained I'll go on.*

Today we finally got the word (official) on the parole question. I was so joyful I couldn't stand it. I've made myself calm down a bit because applying for it in four months doesn't mean an automatic release, but it's the best news we've had yet and I think we'd all be silly not to rejoice a little. . . .

I was in Balboa, California, a subdivision of Newport Beach, practically the birthplace of the John Birch Society, with my stepsister Ann and her mother, Silvia. I'm not sure how this happened. (My stepbrother Peter was visiting Granny in Connecticut.) I got off to a bad start with old Ann. (But she did have one hell of an imagination.) I was prey to her wit on several occasions. In one case it was all Ann. Another, a collaborative effort, when both Peter and Ann were staying with us in Santa Monica while Silvia was putting the Balboa house in order (they returned to southern California in the summer of 1948 because Silvia found fault with her relatives in New York and Ann kept getting sick there). "You can get a big prize for a couple of dust particles," Ann told me one day—referring to grit bits caught up in a ray of sun shining through my bedroom window. A guy would give me diamonds if I nabbed one or two, she promised. And I believed her. Then Peter and Ann both nabbed me on the

Back row, left to right: Kate, Ann
Front row, left to right: Jim, Peter, and Joe

next one. "What kind of water do you like, hot or cold?" they asked in unison after I was tucked in bed. "Cold," I swooned willingly. And cold is what they dumped on my head.

We were in the middle of a heat wave in Balboa, I remember. I got a lousy sunburn and it was put on display everywhere we went. Ann accused me of snoring (I was left to sleep alone) and a debate over my recent tonsillectomy ensued. But there was a beach at the end of every street and I got to swim in the bay. A very nice bay. In fact, I swam quite well by the end of the visit.

Meanwhile, Joe got to go in a Hollywood friend's pool diving headfirst with a lifesaver. He could swim and dead man's float. Pool crazy, my mother called him. He finally fell asleep at ten

o'clock with her sitting, singing to him "Yankee Doodle Dandy."
And, she said, Jimmy must have gotten wind of the parole news
because he asked "Where's Daddy?" about thirty times in one
day. He wasn't saying "Daddy's gone bye-bye in a car" anymore.
I guess the car ride seemed too long.

*Tell Katie when she comes home that I envy her her daily
shower and hope she appreciates it properly,* wrote my father.
*And pass the word to Joe that typewriters are out but he shouldn't
worry about it too much because I can and will work with pencil
and pen. . . .*

My father wished he could write us separate letters, but he
was saving up a fund of bedtime stories instead.

July 20, 1950.

Ring: *The contest between this hostel and our previous one is
all to the good. . . .*

More restricted during a two-week quarantine and orientation period than he would be later, my father felt less confined in
a larger space all to himself with relatively free access to common rooms, a large yard, and the library. This was immeasurably
better than the DCDC, as it was known. Eventually he would be
allowed two visiting hours a month, either all at once or in two
sessions—immediate family only and no more than three people
at a time.

In his last letter (held up a day because he named someone
in the place and had to take it out) he forgot to mention that he
hadn't been able to listen last Monday to *Broadway Is My Beat.*
But, he said, in Danbury he could probably catch any network
show my mother did, with advance word.

At the end of this period my father would be classified into
some sort of a job. His inclination was toward an outdoor, physical one (a healthier ten months, he concluded), most of which

were outside the prison walls. They had some animals, raised vegetables, and most of the food served came from the inmate-tended farm. My father had no idea what he'd end up with. (Later he found out he was classified medium security, and medium-security people couldn't have jobs outside the walls. Lester Cole had been classified minimum security. My dad never knew why there was this distinction between the two.)

July 23, 1950.

Ring: *Tell Katie and Joe I won't mind if they get thinner and fatter respectively but it doesn't matter too much because they looked lovely the way I last saw them.*

Give Jimmy constant messages from me in terms adapted to his gathering comprehension so he will remember the form if not the content of a male parent.

[To Mom.] *I trust you and Polly are raising an occasional glass together to my health. Give her my love (but only if she re-membered to deliver your birthday present today).*

It was my mother's birthday and we gave her a funny card. It said:

> Another Birthday Comin' up—
> Well, you needn't worry, you needn't fret—
> There's plenty of wiggle in your Fanny yet!
> Many Happy Returns—

Signed—"Jimmy, Polly, Katharine—Joe L."

Then my mother was presented with the bottle of Femme perfume my father had entrusted with Polly before taking off. Well, she never thought he'd remember that far ahead. She said she was a lucky girl. Jail or no jail.

Still not completely satisfied with the parole information, my father wanted to raise the following questions. He kept a copy of them to facilitate my mother's reply.

July 27, 1950.

Ring: *(1) Is it an established fact that a revision of the D.C. code would apply to a case coming under the general Federal code? (2) Several fellows I ran across in D.C. were given sentences of less than a year and a day, but the judges had specifically stated them as "3 to 9 months" or "4 to 12"—just the way they do with 1 to 3 or 3 to 9 years. Why did our judges say simply "12 months" or "one year"? (3) Are there any precedents for the application of parole to our situation or are we making a test case? (Bob [Kenny] used the word "unique".) (4) If this applies as Bob says to all terms over 180 days, why not to Biberman and Dmytryk, whose sentences are for 183 days?*

P.S. We weren't to expect my father's clothes because they were going to be kept there.

P.P.S. The Connecticut summer was cooler than any he remembered—it had been consistently comfortable so far.

My mother was full of questions herself. And facts. For example, did my father know, on release, if not picked up by close family member there was the possibility of getting shipped home by slow freight with visits at every way station en route? And in case of parole . . . *A man must have a job to go to.*

She wasn't positive about this one.

Frances: . . . *I think it's the respectability of having a job, rather than the actual income that matters. Anyway don't worry . . . it can be arranged from my end. . . . After all you can type. We'll get you a job as a secretary to any number of guys. . . .*

My father in the meantime had come to recognize the strangely familiar feeling he'd had since arriving in Danbury. It was almost like going away to boarding school for the first time, he said.

Ring: [T]*he uneasy but curious appraisal of your new surroundings; the initial shy exchanges with one's classmates; the absorption of rules and routine both from official sources and from the often more enlightening standpoint of the other boys; the final sense of separation from family and home that only becomes a complete reality at your ultimate destination; the wide gulf to be bridged between the new boys and the sophisticated upper classmen; the good and bad features of an exclusively male environment; the constant knowledge that you are under the scrutiny of pedagogues determined to strengthen your character and generally convert you into a fit citizen. The analogy is virtually complete, but the reaction is hardly as stimulating at thirty-five as it was at thirteen....*

Greater love hath no man,

RING

My father attended Phillips Academy, known as Andover—from the Massachusetts town—from 1929 through 1932.

In the quarantine and orientation section acquiring great facility with mop and broom (but with many months in which to forget these talents before anyone exploited them on Holly Drive floors), my father launched into the preliminary stages of a play. He was going to try to complete it during his prison stay. His attitude, subject to change, was that it was provocative and difficult material worth writing even if it turned out to be nothing more than an exercise in the form.

July 30, 1950.

Ring: *... Please tell the Hunters that my correspondence with Ian ... must still wait on some sort of a check on his suitability, which I understand is merely intended to cover possible past criminal connections.*

Tuesday—August 1st.

Frances: *Darling honey—I can't report any work unfortunately ... hope something pops soon ... I miss you enormously as you know and . . . terribly envious of all the ladies who have been able to visit. . . .*

Sue Lawson had already seen her spouse; Cleo, Mitzi, and Chris were on their way to visit Trumbo; and Margaret Maltz and Jean Dmytryk were planning a trip to West Virginia.

I can hold out awhile, allowed my mother, who was also toying with the idea of subletting our house furnished and appealing to Granny's hospitality in Connecticut.

Frances: *[B]ut . . . after you are settled and more certain of procedure it might be . . . good . . . to look into . . . extra visiting time privilege in the case of a visitor (wife type) who travels a long, long distance. . . .*

New Milford (where Granny lived) seemed pleasant to her but work seemed less likely. But, my mother said, things could change.

Frances: *The children are getting along well—our back yard is once again full of kids—and they've generally gotten settled. . . . I'll get them to write occasionally, but it's more satisfying to just tell you about their goings on. . . . I'll send snaps as soon as I can. . . .*

Thursday—Aug 3.

Frances: *Polly and I cheer you at every opportunity. She sends her love. She is a great girl to have around. The children are great too. Katharine is playing with Kathy Endfield and I'm taking Joe and Jimmy to Beverly Park after Jimmy's nap. I'll report on his reaction to Merry-go-Round stuff next time. . . .*

August 3, 1950.

Ring: *Today was matriculation day. I made my appearance before the classification committee and was assigned the job of clerk in the parole department. . . .*

This was a fate my father received with mixed but predominantly favorable emotions. He said his occasional yearning for physical culture hardly amounted to a consistent compulsion. And although he didn't know the nature of his duties yet, he figured they would probably be as suited to his temperament as any other. Also he'd be able to follow all the proper procedures in relation to his own application—toward which he maintained his steady pessimism. He was more convinced, however, that he was at least technically eligible. As for supplementary letters, my dad did want Burgess Meredith and Katharine Hepburn to be included.

Ring: *Dear Katie—I still haven't heard what you think of Holly Drive, etc.*

Dear Joe—I guess you're a really good swimmer. . . . You'd better not forget how . . . because next summer I'm going to race you. I'm going to see Granny and Pete tomorrow—they're coming over from New Milford. I wish I could see you but it's too far away.

Dear Jimmy—Hello. Remember Daddy? What do you know that's new? I'll be home again sometime.

Monday Morning.

Frances: *I have a job tomorrow on "Stars Over Hollywood." I am so pleased because there's just been nothing at all and now I'm hopeful again.*

MY FATHER'S ENTRANCE into the "population" meant a switch from a house with individual cells to a dormitory housing nearly fifty men in one large room. Because of the greater freedom of movement involved, this was supposed to be a great step forward, but he didn't see it that way. Nor did he subscribe to the theory that having a job made time pass more quickly. He supposed it made some sense for men who couldn't exploit their skills locked up, but his prison work just meant he didn't have the time or energy to do some for himself. And he found it hard to sleep because of the light and noise. My father had this sensitivity to light. And a light was always left on in the big room. When they came around and counted at night they flashed one right on you. So as not to be awakened, my dad wrapped a nylon undershirt around his eyes. But the first time he did it, the shirt slipped off and down around his neck and the guard set off the alarm. It was his opinion my father was strangling himself.

But my dad said there were things to report on the positive side. The secretarial employment my mother mentioned, for example, was something he should be well qualified for by the end of the whole ordeal. The first two days consisted entirely of transcribing from Dictaphone records, and the material he typed was interesting and valuable as research in human character. He was transcribing the correspondence of the Office of Classification and Parole. The parole officers would interview each inmate as he arrived and then dictate a report on the basis of the interview and the papers they received from the court, the probation officer, or another institution. What they were dictating from all this was basically the history and record of each prisoner and recommendations to the parole board. So my father would get substantial facts about each case. He said then guys would talk in the yard about what they were in for. They'd talk about their cases and the nature of their trials, and so forth. And, having seen their records, he knew which guys were telling the truth and which were making things up. This would help him know, he said, which people you could count on and which people you could believe generally when they talked about their past experience.

Ring: *I . . . think* [New Milford] *would be pretty tough on the kids in the winter and I incline much more toward a quick trip by you alone after the parole illusion has been dispelled.*

Give my love to the wee and well-cherished, and be good to your sainted mother, even sending her some dough if you can squeeze it out.

Incidentally, I realize you are probably resolved to protect me from all worldly worries but . . . would really like to hear how plans are working out and what the inevitable unforeseen problems which beset any budget specifically are.

```
                                    'ednesday afternoon,

  Dearest Honey,

          I can|t figure out how to set the margin, but
  since I don|t know anything else about this infernal
  machine, you'll just have to put up with me. There's
  no reason that I can think of which doesn't permit my
  taking up any suggestions you may have for Katharine.
          First let me answer all immediate queries
  parole and/or clemency letters. At this instant it seems
  to me and, as far as I can make out, the eagles as well
  adress all such documents to The U.S. Board of Parole,
  Gentlemen:- and etc., send them to me. I in turn will
  pass them on to the lawyers, who will attach same to
  proper parole application after it has been sent in by
  you- the application I mean. Let me also at this point try to
```

Drop a few lines on Mommy's next letter, beseeched my father. He said Silvia had written him I was a good girl, but did I have fun? And include something about Holly Drive. *Maybe on the typewriter. So it won't take up too much room.*

And hardly taking up any at all, I offered the following:

Katharine claims she's going to do a bit of writing so I'll leave room. I love you, love you, love you. I wrote to Ellen - mostly repetitions of the first part of this letter

Dear Daddy
Ihhad a good time in Balboa.
How are you. I like theenew house.
                                    LOVE KATH ARIN E

Jimmy says Daddy's gone byebye in the car.
Jimmy can say Danbury too.
            We all love Daddy - Polly & Katie & Joey
And Jimmy and   Frances Lardner
                              2048 Holly Dr.
                              Hollewood 28 Calif.

If you pick up any office skills in your new job, concluded my mother, *maybe we can be a joint secretary to someone.*

August 11, 1950.

Ring: *We are all—you, I and the lawyers, wasting too much time and too many words on the parole theme, and, though I have a few more points to make on the subject, the most important of them is that I am better acquainted with the procedure than any of you on the outside can be ... you shouldn't worry about any phase of it. There is a regular routine here for checking on employers and parole advisers. . . . If you have Lastvogel set as adviser by the time you get this, that's fine. If not, Michael Abel at 20th Century-Fox. He used to be parole officer here at Danbury. . . . The only other things you have to do ... send me the name and address of my next employer; send whatever letters you get to the Federal Parole Board ...; and ... if it seems worthwhile to you ... one of the most influential letter-writers is the applicant's wife, especially if one makes a convincing case for the need for her man at home, not only economic but in terms of his relation to the children.*

Marty Popper (the attorney) showed up for a visit without identification, and for that and/or other reasons was only permitted to talk to my father and Lester Cole in the presence of their boss.

And speaking of visits, it looked like my mother could probably get approximately the same treatment as Cleo Trumbo. Even under the strictest interpretation, by being around on the last day of one calendar month and the first day of the next, my parents would have four hours out of forty-eight, provided my dad knew enough in advance to bar other visitors during the preceding month. But my father still thought the expense and trouble might outweigh the benefit.

The Royal Typewriter Co., wrote my father, is very proud of its "magic margin" lever on the left side of the carriage which you simply bring forward while you establish the margin anywhere you want, but your report indicates it wasn't as foolproof as they thought. Which reminds me . . . don't quite understand your function in the secretarial team you suggest—typing is what I do. As a matter of fact I do it interminably these days, but not in the familiar company of my muse.

Frances: *Yesterday Katie, Joe, Jimmy, and I drove out to Salka's for dinner.* Salka Viertel lived in Santa Monica Canyon. She was known for gathering the literary set on Sunday afternoons. Thomas Mann, Bertolt Brecht, and Kurt Weill were frequent guests. It was the place to be in an intellectual sense. A sense of community and friendliness. And Salka wrote movies. The most famous, *Queen Christina*, starred her good friend Greta Garbo.

Jim was an angel, crowed my mom, because he'd remained lively as usual, even on the ride home. And it was a miracle, she said, because he had just caught on to the fact that he could break out of his crib, which he did all during nap time before our departure. And speaking of the ride home, there was somebody honking at us on the way back. Scared she was being tailed, my mother's heart started racing. She thought somebody wanted to arrest her or something. "The panic was so great," she said one day, remembering. "The fear of what might happen to all us Reds and former Reds because of the Korean War. The terror in Hollywood as a result of the hearings, the Cold War situation, and the Korean War was awful."

Frances: *Darling, there are many things I wish I could talk to you about. I* think *you're probably right about my waiting until after we hear about parole—but I'm not certain. Anyway if you should change your mind—I could do it the first week in September.... You're also to remember that I have great faith in your careful and considered judgment ... and will act accordingly. I seem to say this in every letter!*

P.S., my mother concluded New Milford in the winter might be lovely.

My mom was so busy she practically didn't have time to job-hunt, she said. Saturday night she read Trumbo's verses. Friday night—spoke along with Adrian as a sort of good-bye to him. (Adrian Scott entered jail later than the rest.) Then verses again—along with a movie showing. (Just before they took off for their various places of incarceration, the Ten hurriedly produced a twenty-minute film, *The Hollywood Ten*, about the case, which they intended to use as a means for carrying on the fight and raising funds to pay their huge legal costs.) The rest of the time—checking on stuff with lawyers, wives, and so on ...

Frances: [A]*nd I suppose it's a good thing because then I don't have as much time to worry about the fact that I don't have many jobs.*

*Honey, don't worry about finances. They'll hold—I don't have
any budget. I just don't spend money on anything that it doesn't
absolutely have to be spent on. Of course it's true there are vary-
ing definitions of <u>absolute</u>. Beverly Park might not be considered
absolute necessity by some people—but Katie and Joe look on it
as such and I figure their views are to be respected.*

(We were instructed to read menus from right to left. Which
meant concentrate on the cheap stuff and don't splurge.)

My father reported a very refreshing triple visit—Granny,
Uncle John, and my stepbrother Peter (Sunday, Peter would be
returning to Balboa)—at which, Granny stated my father looked
better than he had before. He claimed the only difference was
that he took the time to wash his face and apply a comb to his
hair. He was fine, he said, and actually the place was full of interesting people. And if you were selective, the level of political
discussion was profound.

In Danbury, there was always something going on you could
get interested in. There was a daily conclave to analyze the day's
news, exchange profane and obscene anecdotes, and criticize
authority in general. As for engaging fellows—there were two
brothers, for example, who used to run a steel company that
provided a lot of it for the government, only they bribed the congressman (who was head of the House Military Affairs Committee) to steer contracts their way. (The congressman was doing
time, along with Trumbo and Lawson, at the federal penal facility at Ashland.) One of them was an excellent bridge player and
my father spent time playing bridge, something he hadn't done
since college and shortly thereafter.

Granny had sent two books. You couldn't send or bring just any
book. It had to arrive directly from a reputable bookstore or publisher. Otherwise the prison censor would have the burdensome
task of having to check every page for words marked in some way

(underlined or something) with a code message about how to execute a prison break or something. If sent by a well-known publisher or store it would be new and devoid of concealed information.

August 15, 1950.

Ring: *Thank Katie for her nice letter and tell Joe to keep his right hand up and lead with his left. What are you and Polly doing socially. I crave vicarious participation in gay life.*

The Department of Justice gave its "full blessing" to the Ten's parole eligibility and instructed all the institutions to put them on their parole dockets. My father had the pleasure of making copies of the ruling for various files.

Ring: *Dearest love—I cannot give the slightest support to any notion (yours of 8/14) of a trip east in September, unless . . . primarily motivated by a valid and sound career consideration such as a genuinely promising opportunity in a play. Outside of such relevant but secondary factors as the growing need for thrift, my thinking on the subject is based on one main fact. That . . . despite the long odds against parole, the determination of that question will be the critical point in this whole experience. If it should go through, then the affair will be a fairly minor event in our lives and certainly not to be regarded as a serious ordeal. But the difference between four months and ten months is even greater than an arithmetical computation would indicate. When, probably in the first part of October, we learn that we're facing the full siege, accompanied by the malice that denial would reveal in a case where all the conventional bases for parole exist, I think we'll both undergo a qualitative change of attitude and there will be a real need for communion between us which would just be a pleasant event at this stage. I'd say make it about mid-November or early December, but naturally other considerations affecting your time should finally determine that. I'll be available any time.*

Wednesday—August 16.

Frances: *Honey darling, This may come a day early because I want you to get it in time. I love you more than ever now that you are practically 35—because now I can again be younger than you. . . .*

My mother had already turned thirty-five.

My father's birthday (August 19) turned out to be his most exhilarating day on the inside so far. So much so that he said he didn't get around to rereading my mother's "wonderful" letter (in which she said she wasn't going to deal with anything but how she felt about him) until bedtime. He said he spent the morning in overtime devotion to his secretarial chores and then returned to the dormitory to an assortment of wrapped gifts on his bed and a small chorus of Happy Birthday singers. The presents were necessarily limited to items like candy bars and cookies—all purchasable at the local commissary—plus cherished toilet articles from inmates departing in a few days. There were sentimental inscriptions from income tax evaders and grand larcenists alike, and my father was quite taken aback. In the afternoon he played handball for the first time. And, having such a good time, kept at it through a pouring rain.

Frances: *. . . I'll go right back to routine business matters in the next one, but not in this one. You're not even to think of anything at all, but how wonderful it'll be and is to be together. I'm using is advisedly. . . . I'm sorry to sound like some character out of Barrie, but just for a few minutes I want to forget that you aren't here. I've got your picture across from my bed. . . . Oh darling—this is just not good for us—but the simple truth is that I love you on your birthday as I did in May—that K. J. & J. love you as much as any Poppa anywhere was ever loved or missed. . . .*

My mother said she knew exactly what my father needed for his birthday. Three new white shirts, ties, a pair of moccasins, a noiseless typewriter, a nice new tennis racket, and tennis shorts. And T-shirts and a bathing suit. She celebrated the occasion with friends at the Pasadena Playhouse seeing Lillian Hellman's adaptation of Emmanuel Robles's play *Montserrat*. Afterward my father was toasted from afar. It was a pleasant evening, she said, although she was disappointed in the play. *Too much talk. I suspect it makes very good reading.*

Sunday Morning.
    . . . Did you know that Alan Campbell and Dorothy [Parker] *were remarried last week?* queried Frances after attending the reception along with what she called a very mixed-type group. A real Hollywood affair. My mother found the whole business pretty depressing except *Dottie* [in a taffeta cocktail dress] *was very sweet and Dottieish!* At this point my mother had communicated with all the people from whom she received letters regarding clemency asking for new ones for parole. At the party, the Hacketts (the screenwriting couple Frances Goodrich and Albert Hackett) asked best man producer-screenwriter Charles Brackett *(The Lost Weekend* and *Sunset Boulevard)* for one. *You can imagine his answer.*
    Meanwhile Joe and I were at her daily to jump in the car and go see my dad—we missed him—swearing to be good and not carry on about the length of the trip, etc. It would make us a little late for school, but who cared? And my mother perused the options. (1) Leaving Polly with Jimmy and getting someone to drive with us. Or (2) we could all go together, with Polly and my mother taking turns at the wheel and spending a week in New Milford—something my mother was sure Granny would go for. On the other hand (3) we could bag the car trip altogether and (4) my mother would wait and go later on her own, but she couldn't leave Polly alone with us for too long. There was also

the possibility of (5) getting a friend to stay with us while she was gone.

Well, their letters must have crossed paths. Because the one in which my father expressed his views re visiting hadn't reached my mother by the time she wrote on the twentieth. He said what he expressed there was only fortified by her *fantasies about driving east with offspring.*

Ring: *Baby, I have a high respect for both Katie and Joe but I still don't think their statement that they wouldn't mind eight days in the car is very relevant, nor is it fair to them to take it seriously.*

August 22, 1950.

Ring: *[And] [t]he Kings' subsidiary enterprises I wish no part of.*

The independent film producers (the King Brothers) had promised a job for my father (in case of parole) in any number of enterprises in which they or any of their relatives had holdings, such as haberdashery and so on.

Ring: *If they got the message I gave you through Mother and that is all they can muster, then bid them farewell with my blessing, and I will take up free-lance editorial writing for religious journals.*

Ha ha.

August 23.

. . . Oh before I forget—have I ever told you that I don't like California climate, wrote my mother. *I think it would be much better to be in the east when you get out. In fact if you were agreeable I'd be happy to settle us all in New Milford, while waiting for you. Oh yes—of course I've told you and you've said no! By golly, I gotta do what you say. . . .*

Frances: . . . *Five letters are in for you. . . . Incidentally I saw
Gene the dancer yesterday who wants to send one on his own. I
said he could. Is that all right?*

*Darling my social life is great, but like I keep saying it would
be greater in N. Milford. Paul & Sylvia [Jarrico] just got back from
a three week vacation in New Mexico and stopped over last night,
as did Solly & Fra and Irwin Lieberman. (All send their love.)
Tonight I'm going out with Huebsches & Hugo. (Jean's at the
ranch.) We're going to see "Death of a Salesman" (second time for
me, as you know). Sunday night I had dinner at Hunters with the
Reises. So as you can see I'm fluttering around much too much.
Poor butterfly would like to be a nice quiet moth in the cool country air in Connecticut and all those little moths. What of them?*

My father didn't know what the future would be like or
where we'd spend it but was still in favor of starting it from Holly
Drive, whither he'd be sent at government expense. He said
much depended on what he accomplished in jail.

August 25, 1950.

Ring: *Give my love to Ian, Alice, Sylvia, Paul, Bob and
Kathy P., Hugo, Jean, Cleo, Fra, Solly, Budd, Hacketts, Camp-
bells, who never looked prettier than in their wedding picture,
Kate, Ingo, etc. Spread the word among the children that I love
them, kiss Polly for me, and concentrate on keeping as pretty as
you were. The climate in Connecticut is dismal.*

A letter from Gene Kelly was a fine idea, said my father—if
he remembered to write it. He encouraged my mother to call
him expressing his deep and sincere appreciation as a reminder.

Sunday—Aug 27.

Frances: *Dearest Honey, You haven't heard from me in the
last couple of days because I've been working! . . . I planned to*

write to you on the set . . . but even though it was only a two line bit as a nurse—I couldn't manage it. Had a radio rehearsal that night for a show on Saturday and today I'm doing "The Amazing Mr. Malone." Unfortunately I didn't get calls for the two radio things in enough time to let you know. . . .

By now it seems to me that the one thought we can both be certain about is that it's rough to be apart and it seems idiotic for you to be in jail! If parole is granted—oh I've got to stop counting on it—but it does seem more tolerable to think of you possibly being out in about two months. I'll readjust if I have to but it's not going to be easy. Baby doll—don't think I'm having too rough a time of it. It's just that we miss you so and it's so hard to think of you being so far away.

Here is a list of the people who had written testifying to my father's goodness so far: Garson and Mike Kanin, H. Herbert, Philip Dunne, Frances Goodrich and Albert Hackett, Donald Ogden Stewart, Ira Wolfert, Ingo Preminger, Bob Parrish, and D. Parker Campbell . . .

August 28, 1950.

Today brings us to the end of the second month, and I must say I don't find them going very fast, wrote my father, who for various reasons was switching his immediate attention from a play to a book he'd had in mind for some time.

MONDAY—AUGUST 28.

Frances: *I've got another job on Saturday. Maybe you can hear it. The program is called* Line Up *and is on CBS sometime Saturday afternoon. If it's about what I think it is it's kind of fitting . . .*

. . . All right my love. I get it about visiting. . . .

August 30.

Frances: ... *Katie has been pretty "big blonde" lately.*

Well, you heard that one already. I guess I wasn't exactly a barrel of monkeys. Just a flabby pretender due to a girl shortage.

... *Most of the other accessible girls are at camp so it hasn't been too much fun for her lately,* further clarified my mother.

Frances: *However all three children are going to Mark Norvo's birthday party on Saturday and Katie & Joe have Michael Craven's party on Friday as well which will sort of make the week....*

Red Norvo, one of jazz's early vibraphonists and a gifted bandleader, and family lived close by, and his xylophone playing (in his living room) was a regular occurrence when Joe and I visited his son Mark.

Frances: *I just talked to Jean D. who has just returned from seeing Eddie* [Dmytryk]. *She reports that both he and Albert are in fine spirits—Eddie especially. It seems that at their place* [the prison at Mill Point, West Virginia] *they not only have five days off for good behavior a month, but can also <u>work</u> off an additional three a month—which means ... Jean is going to pick Eddie up at the very latest November 15th....*

August 31, 1950.

Your work reports sound very good—compared to Jean Muir's anyway ..., wrote my father in reference to the actress who (though denying Communist connections) was dropped like a hot potato from the cast of *The Aldrich Family.* The General Foods Corporation (the program's sponsor) said she was a "controversial personality" who might offend prospective customers. The inclusion of her name in "Red Channels" (a list of 151 people in show business and statements of the Communist front activities of each) was the basis on which anti-Communist groups had protested her television appearance.

My father also said he followed President Truman's speech with rapt attention—his "Report to the Nation" (September 1, 1950) about why we were in Korea and our objectives there.

Ring: [E]*specially the part in which he defined our free way of life as the right to express our opinions (which I hardly dared dream I possessed), the right to choose our own jobs (which I have missed the last three years), the right to raise our children in our own way (which I am only permitted to exercise in indirect fashion), the right to plan our own future (which I regard as pretty illusory, both for Mr. Truman and myself) and the right to live without fear (which is easy once you overcome a morbid phobia toward prisons).*

Granny sent my mother two hundred dollars to cover transportation. My mom was thinking about not waiting until the end of October to visit after all.

Sunday—Sept. 3.

Frances: ... [P]*arole or no parole ... However ... I won't come that soon __unless__ there's a change of feeling on your part. You know the circumstances __almost__ as well as I do and I'll accept your decision because you're just naturally smarter—although of course I'm more instinctive and everything in me says I should make the visit by Sept 30. ...*

As for the extra good time at Mill Point mentioned above—my father wrote that that was one of the imponderables they couldn't have figured in advance.

September 4, 1950.

Ring: *It is also available here but confined ... to those who work in the glove factory ... our basic industry. And even if I had sought to be assigned there, my performance on the mechanical aptitude tests wouldn't have qualified me, the way my firm grasp*

of orthography and I.Q. rating did for my present employment.
The proletarian bias is so strong that the industrial contingent
also receive money for their labor. But what are these considera-
tions compared to the deep sense of responsibility which sustains
the morale of the front-office worker? The trust and regard with
which I am honored has now reached a point where mine is the
penultimate decision between the use of a semi-colon or a comma
in official business.

As for rumors concerning release procedures—my mother
shouldn't bother her *lovely, medium-sized head* about them, is
how my father put it. It was a highly premature topic.

My father managed to rearrange his day to see *Ticket to Tom-*
ahawk (a comedy-western that included Marilyn Monroe as a
showgirl—her only line "hmmm") in the afternoon in order to
listen to *The Line-Up* in the evening, only then he couldn't determine whether my mother was the "finger-girl" with the Brooklyn
accent or the astrologer. Actually she was both.

Then gazing at his photographs, he concluded that she and
I were very pretty and that he and Joe and Jim were *three of the*
finest examples of young American manhood he'd ever seen.

Katharine Hepburn sent a letter—passed as a "special" because it concerned parole business—in which she informed my
father that she'd written directly to the parole board in Washington. But "if you find that the appeal should be made direct to the
President," she added "and if Mrs. L. could inform me, then I
shall do that." Hepburn was going to be on tour in *As You Like It*
until February, but her mail would eventually catch up to her.

My brother Joe and I were going to start school in four days.

Saturday—Sept, 1950.
...Katie's about to have her first gentleman tutor and is
quite concerned about his looks, explained my mother. *She said*

RECEIVED

UNITED STATES BOARD OF PAROLE

September 1, 1950

Dr. O. O. Killinger, Chairman
U. S. Board of Parole
Washington, D. C.

Dear Dr. Killinger:

Ring Lardner, Jr. is serving a Federal sentence in
Danbury, Connecticut, for contempt of Congress because he
refused to answer questions regarding his political affilia-
tions. I understand he will soon be eligible for parole.

I have known Ring Lardner, Jr. since 1941. To the
best of my knowledge he is a respectable, law-abiding citizen
and I think his present conflict with the law is entirely
conscientious and, however mistaken, should be viewed with
charity.

In view of the fact that his wife and five minor
children depend on him for support, I trust that the Parole
Board will give sympathetic consideration to his case, for
I do not believe that he will use his release from custody
in any way harmful to his country now that the courts have
decided he was wrong.

This letter is written in behalf of an old friend
of whose political views I know nothing, but whatever they
are I believe they are sincere, although they may differ
radically from my own.

Very respectfully yours,

Katharine Hepburn
179 Allyn Street
Hartford, Connecticut

"He better be handsome." Incidentally, you'll be pleased to know that she considers you handsome and me pretty....

My mother said I showed extremely good judgment in that department. She only hoped that I'd be as stable in other fields.

We still had our cat—definitely male and not a prowler type—who was barred from the house except when Polly was away.

My father wanted to hear something about what Joe and I were up to, but we were off the hook until after school started because he was anxious to know what that was like.

I love you both very much, he wrote, *and Jimmy too. You can tell him so if you can find a way to make him understand it.*

Ring: *Dear Frances—I was read a report from Jonnie* [Lester Cole's wife] *about the last wives' session which represents everyone else as showing the strain and you "looking lovelier than ever." Even though I specifically prescribed a more casual and carefree life, I can't resist a minor twinge at this.... I'll listen to Night Beat Monday and see if I can do better than last time.*

EDDIE'S MANIFESTO WAS A BLOW ... wrote my father.

The New York Times, **Monday, September 11, 1950.**
JAILED FILM AIDE PLEDGES LOYALTY
Dmytryk, One of 'Hollywood Ten' Asserts He Is Not
In Communist Party

This statement was taken in the form of an affidavit witnessed by the warden at the federal prison in Pocahontas County at Mill Point, West Virginia. Eddie Dmytryk said he wasn't a Communist or a Communist sympathizer and hadn't even been one at the time of the congressional hearings. He said his original position (as an unfriendly witness) had been taken because of a duty he felt he owed to all Americans to preserve what he believed was a constitutional privilege of substance.

"I have not forgone that principle and do not do so now. . . ."

But in view of "the troubled state of current world affairs," he went on, he was in the presence of an "even greater duty," which was to make it perfectly clear where he stood toward his country.

Eddie Dmytryk wanted off the blacklist—to be free of the Hollywood Ten—and he hoped this would do it.

Once Dmytryk's decision was made, the details had been ironed out in a single visit with his wife, Jean. Through their letters they had concluded one visit from her was all they could afford. At first Jean Dmytryk considered traveling by bus, but when Margaret Maltz agreed to visit at the same time, she somehow found the means to fly. And together they flew from Charleston, West Virginia, shared a motel room, and drove the next morning to Mill Point in a rented car. It was hot as hell that day, and the Dmytryks spent the afternoon on a little outdoor prison patio, right across from the Maltzes, pretending sweet nothings while plotting rebellion. It was Jean who was going to set the wheels in motion. Well, my mother thought there was something fishy about the fact that old Jean hadn't made much effort on Eddie's behalf, but everybody just assumed he was taking care of things himself and he sure was, she said. No one really knew anything. Only what they read in the newspapers. Except possibly for his lawyer Bartley Crum, everyone was equally surprised.

Eddie's manifesto was a blow, wrote my father, *which will serve to fortify my cynicism for the future. . . . I can only figure that he must be swinging a material bargain for the paltry two months left to him.*

Remember, Eddie pulled six months.

Ring: *Otherwise, how much more dramatic to wait till the*

prison door clanged behind him and then ... make his declara-
tion of faith. But this is so craven—and so injurious to those who,
with much more time at stake, won't go along with his surrender.

The preposterous reasoning of the statement itself is, of
course, one more proof that there is no compromise in this kind of
thing. He was defending the Constitution in taking the stand he
did. He still believes in the Constitution. But the troubled state of
world affairs makes it necessary for him to express his patriotic
devotion—to what? Obviously not the Constitution anymore. To
maintain that what was right in 1947 is wrong in 1950 is worse
in a sense than to have taken his present position in the first
place. For that you could at least present a case, in logic, in law,
in principle. But this way, blathering about "an even greater
duty," is to justify the whole cumulative process of oppression—
to say it is right to use Korea as a weapon against civil liberties.
May all his pictures be smash hits and may Jean and the baby
dwell in everlasting luxury. ...

Sadly, my father wasn't able to catch *Night Beat* (my mom's
show) because it began at lights-out—an event that occurred
from one to three hours before his sleeping began. His big problem remained—finding time and discipline to write, especially
after so much typing and lots to read. (My father was reading
John Hersey's *The Wall* and finding it very rewarding.) And the
concentrating conditions being what they were. Addressing the
latter, he got himself placed on a waiting list for a transfer to a
dormitory broken up into little cubicles. Of course, he would
have preferred cellular housing, but this was largely reserved for
quarantines and night workers.

September 11, 1950.
Ring: *Best love to Poll and little ones. And especially to you*
[Mom]—*from one of the Nine Little Indians*

. . .

MONDAY—SEPT. 11TH.

Frances: *My dearest darling . . .*

I air mailed your notebook—registered—this afternoon and . . . hope you . . . get it soon—and . . . find it useful. . . . I was very pleased that in some reference you made to a wife reading a piece of work which her husband had just written and making a fantastically foolish comment—you weren't refering to me! (Darling I wish you'd tell me the rule about doubling consonants in verbs—I'm never sure about it and am too lazy to look it up.)

All right—I'll <u>wait</u> for another six weeks or so, but it's hard to do. However I think you're probably right, although I don't promise not to change my mind—which has always been my prerogative. Let's . . . plan . . . sometime between the middle and the end of October—I'm leaving it flexible now because I feel better about it—and because of the possibility of hearing about parole sometime towards the end of <u>this</u> month. I agree . . . about the horrors of being together for such a brief period and not being able to think of anything except the undecided question. . . . Oh I'm changing—I'm not the impulsive, natural type you used to know. I dare say I'll have an outline all prepared on how our visit's to go. I want it . . . in two parts . . . or more if that can be done. And you've just got to get special dispensation about time—after all 3,000 miles is 3,000 miles and I'm sure your authorities there are very understanding folks. . . .

I don't look all that lovely at all. Jonnie is a nice girl, and . . . prejudiced in my behalf. I'm a little thinner than I've been which is always good and my hair is longer and of course you're right about that. . . . Darling I suddenly remembered about insomniac waking. Starting Wednesday—I must get up at 8 every morning to drive the children to school by 8:30. . . .

School started and my mother had to get up and transport us, which brought on a pretty wild headache that she attributed to her prejudice against early rising and a deep-rooted feeling she had that she was being abused when she did. She also had dental problems (a broken cap) and the emotional strain of Joe's fears (she had to stay with him all morning) and the reward of Beverly Park, two kids visiting until six, and the unexpected desire on Polly's part to see her foot doctor at supper time.

Frances: [T]*hen the final facing of the bills . . . all almost too much.*

On top of it, Joe was going in for high comedy, imitating Victor Brandt. Burlesque was Vicky's department, and Joe and that type of comedy didn't mix. And everyone agreed the result was strange.

It was soon going to be my brother Jim's birthday, so we took him to the Broadway Hollywood Toy Department to (as my mother said) sniff around—before investing in fifteen dollars' worth of loot: a nest of blocks, a stuffed Pluto pull dog, green truck, etc. and a big soft "sleep doll." The kind that had a zipper and a place for pajamas. My mother explained that every kid of hers got one of those things by the time he or she was two. "And Daddy in jail or not can't make the difference." Then she carried on about Jim in a letter. *Oh Ring he's so pretty and big and sweet and fine.* But it was Joe, she proclaimed, who felt my father's absence most of all.

Frances: *Oh, he* [Joe] *had his first dry bed in ages—the first night after the first day of school, and came in to wake me this morning saying "Well thank goodness—I was dry last night."*

Oh he needs you, wrote my mother.

Frances: *Poll and I just can't cope with him physically. He wants the pummelling (please—where's the rule about doubling consonants?) and wrestling and general high physical play that you and you alone can provide. We've told him he's just got to be patient and he understands perfectly, but his energy just doesn't get used up. Oh Lord and does he have it!*

Sept. 14, 1950.

    Ring: Yours of Sept. 11th has been duly noted . . . and is hereby acknowledged. . . . [Y]our misgiving about the spelling "refering" is well founded. One you exclude (a) words formed by adding a suffix beginning with a consonant (commitment, madness, woodenly); (b) words in which the final consonant before a suffix beginning with a vowel is preceded by a diphthong or two consecutive vowels (treating, defeated, sweeter, shooting); (c) words which drop a mute "e" in adding a suffix (hating, unabated, inscriber); (d) words in which two consecutive consonants precede the suffix (insulted, retractable, askance) and (e) words ending, before the suffix is added, in certain soft consonants which it would be unthinkable to double (enjoyable, allowance, boxing)—under none of which circumstances may the consonant be doubled—and confine your consideration to words ending in a single consonant preceded by a single vowel, to which is added a suffix beginning with a vowel, the infallible rule is that the question of doubling the consonant or not is determined by pronunciation. If the syllable before the suffix is accented (which, of course, is invariably true when the original word is a monosyllable), the consonant is doubled; if an earlier syllable is accented, the consonant is not doubled. Thus: referring, excelled, madder, remittance, fitting; but: reckoned, paneled, uttering, editing. The only partial exception to the above of which I can think at the moment is the frequently accepted variant: "traveller" or "travelling," but even here "traveler" and "traveling" are preferable (not preferrable).

Sept. 18, 1950.

Ring: *Dear Katie and Joe—What Mommy writes me about the Westland School sounds fine and I hope you keep on liking it. I'll bet it's still pretty hot in your part of the country. Here it is colder than any September I remember.... I'm having a pretty good time and am surprised every day to find how many nice people there are in jail, but I wish ... I could be back home with all of you. Don't get too big or I won't recognize you. I love you both and Jimmy, too.*

DADDY

MY MOTHER ATTENDED the first parents' meeting at the Westland School rather than an AFTRA (American Federation of Television and Radio Artists) thing scheduled for the same time. She said the director, Lorre, explained a lot of stuff about their way of working that my mother found terribly exciting. She said kids learn when there is an incentive. When they want to and are willing. There was a store at the school, and the older kids had the job of running it—bought supplies, kept accounts, etc. They didn't *learn* arithmetic. Just practiced it! Last year those guys couldn't spell worth a damn, but since they had to write the day of the week on each sales slip, they worked hard (on their own initiative) to learn to spell *Monday, Tuesday,* etc. When they got to Saturday and Sunday they quit—after all, why bother? There wasn't any school on those days and therefore no sales slips.

Incidentally Katie complained <u>last week</u> about there not being school, wrote my mother—*so as you can see—it's a success. Joe is more reluctant but his teacher is already pretty taken with him and said he is opening up.*

Joe was building a boat at Westland. They better not abandon the boat project or he'd resign, he proclaimed. We were in a liberal artistic community. Weaving, spinning, and shop were included.

My mother picked up her autumn activities—a dance class, job hunting, etc.

Frances: *I'm not letting myself think about the fact that as I write . . . the decision about parole may already be a known quantity. . . .*

It was Thursday and you know what that meant. Polly had to be out early. And it turned out we didn't have school. My mother hemmed a smock for me, cooked borscht, gave us all shampoos, and put my hair up in pins. Then she'd had it. And, she said, it wasn't likely Polly was going to return in time for her to get her letter to the P.O. for the 1:30 A.M. postmark.

My mother was now thinking Grandma Marie's birthday (October 28) would be a good day to depart for the visit. She'd spend the night in New York with her mother and leave in the morning for either Danbury or New Milford in order to see my father Sunday afternoon. She said either place because she had no idea how near the Danbury station he was situated.

Thursday Night—late—Sept. 21.

Frances: *I want at least two visits with you—or every day— or whatever is possible. If you're freer (there's no such word, I know) week ends and it would be better for me to leave L.A. on Friday the 27th . . . Please get some dispensation of time. . . .*

At this point she was tempted to take Jimmy. He probably could travel free. But then Joe and I might have a fit. On the other hand, without Jimmy around, Polly would have more time for us.

My mother said everyone was very nice to her at the William Morris office. She just hoped it resulted in work.

A member of the parole board informed my father that the board would now consider his case.

September 21, 1950.

Ring: *And in a sense I suppose they will.* [But] *since they tend to announce the more or less open-and-shut cases first, it may be weeks, even a month or more, before we hear—unless, of course, ours are considered open-and-shut (with emphasis on the latter). . . .*

Granny visited, taking the routine of successive locked gates and purse checking in her usual dignified stride. And, my dad said, they had a nice chat covering such topics as the technique of double-crostics, World Series prospects, and Connecticut weather. My grandmother was a Brooklyn Dodgers fan. Albert Mayer, her German man-of-all-work, drove her. She'd had an accident when Uncle John was a baby in which John was thrown right out of the car. After that my grandfather felt more secure when he did the driving and insisted she give it up. (My grandfather died in 1933.) Now Albert drove her to the prison and waited outside.

Sunday Night—Sept. 24.

Frances: *Today was going somewhere please, Mommy, day—as was yesterday too, but today Jimmy got in the act.* We drove out to the beach with the Premingers. At the ocean I said, "Don't you wish Daddy were here?"

[I]*t was just that the water and playing and having a good time made her think of you,* wrote my mother, *which is as it should be—remembering you during good times. . . .*

Monday.

Frances: *Polly is coming home later and later.*

"How was I to know Polly was an alcoholic," said my mother years later on the subject.

Frances: *Poor girl really needs help . . . what she needs is a psychiatrist and I'm not qualified. Wouldn't it be wonderful if warmth and friendship and understanding could resolve things for people. . . . I just feel . . . badly . . . I can't provide the personal happiness . . . [she] needs which could make her a more stable person. . . . Oh Lord the misery in the world is heartbreaking.*

I've just gotten some fine news! shrieked my mom about a television film with cellist Gregor Piatigorsky for the director Irving Reis. It would earn her a nice little hunk of change. [I]*t's just wonderful (here we go again). . . .*

And although my mother didn't have a lot of lines, she was the only girl in the thing. And she said it was sort of a cute way to bring the classics to the populace. Piatigorsky was a very famous cellist, and Alice Hunter said he used to be quite a ladykiller.

Frances: *. . . Hm! I'm playing a girl reporter again who flirts all through rehearsals etc. . . . trying to get an interview for a television magazine—and Mr. Piatigorsky's desire is to avoid such an event at all costs. Well if I'm destined to be a junior Roz Russell— I can stand it!*

The conversation at the prison (with Granny) re doublecrostics, etc. sounded great to my mom. It was one of the reasons she thought of New Milford longingly. But she'd remain in Hollywood and be a big moving-picture actress instead—at least until late October. She hadn't done anything about reservations, but she was coming without fail.

September 25, 1950.

My dear love, began Ring. *It's a fine and beautiful thing to be able to keep in close touch with you as your fine and beautiful letters make possible though it's not a satisfactory substitute for being with you. Neither, I'm afraid, will visiting be, but I guess we have to take a relative view of pleasures these days and I can't help being excited by the prospect.*

But, my father said, he could make a better pitch on the question of visiting time after the parole game was played to its conclusion. And if there was any problem about reservations, my mother might as well proceed on them before the point was definitely resolved.

As for the notion about bringing Jim, it sounded very attractive on first contemplation, but my father thought the deciding factor should be the balance of convenience and inconvenience to my mother and Polly, rather than any *highfalutin theories about effects of any consequence on us two psychologically sound males.* It would be nice to see him but he didn't think he could do much to resolve Jim's Oedipus complex one way or the other in the fifteen minutes or so he might tolerate the visiting room.

Ring: *In other words, I toss the issue figuratively and, if you decide to bring him, literally back in your lap. . . .*

Darling, this should reach you, as should a nosegay, on our anniversary. . . .

Thursday Night—Sept. 27.

Frances: *This is going to be very short . . . it is now 10:30 and I still have to study three pages of stuff. . . . Today was the usual hectic one that seems to be the pattern for me, in relation to movie jobs. I went to rehearsal only to find myself sitting around while Mr. Piatigorsky, the world's most famous cellist, discussed <u>my</u> part* *with Mr. Reis . . . actually what he was worrying about was the fact that he doesn't get to play the cello till page 5. . . .*

Then quite late in the day everyone started to worry about my clothes—*as usual I didn't have the proper ones, tore over to Macy's with the wardrobe character at 4:30. Finally found three things before the store closed at 5:30—Had them fitted—back to the studio for . . . approval. . . . They . . . got around to looking at me at 6:45. Tentatively approved one—got back to the original theme— Couldn't I borrow something? Went to Louise Losey's house—tore through everything she owned. Found three more numbers—ate— listened to the Louis-Charles fight. . . .*

My mother listened to the Louis—Charles fifteen-rounder as a great champion went into the discard at Yankee Stadium. Then she went through all her clothes again. Finally in bed, she was frantic, worried, and calm all at the same time. *To the nether regions with it!* she said.

Frances: *Happy Happy—our ANNIVERSARY—TOMORROW & YESTERDAY & ALWAYS.*

By special dispensation, my father also listened to the fight. He said it was the first time in twenty-five years he'd been allowed to stay up after bedtime to listen to one.

I'm reminded here of a story about Louis that I heard Ring tell. Well, not just about him but about my real dad's lousy eyesight. His inherited nearsightedness, registering 20/800 in the last vision test he took, and the proportions of my uncle John. Leaving a fight at Madison Square Garden one night, David approached the Brown Bomber and tapped him on the back under the impression he was his oldest brother, John.

Meanwhile, Joe Louis—the fightingest world heavyweight champion boxing ever knew (the *New York Times* said)—came out of retirement to get pounded by Ezzard Charles into a bleeding helpless hulk. Charles had his reward in a victory that was so one-sided there was almost no competition, and Joe was not a pretty sight. His left eye being tightly closed and puffed out in a discolored lump of awesome size, his lips swollen, and his body showing angry red welts.

Well, September 28 was my parents' fourth wedding anniversary. And also the end of my father's third month in captivity. And my father made substantial strides in his struggle for peace and privacy by being switched from Vermont to Connecticut House. This was a dormitory divided into thirty-three cubicles, each about six by eight and a half feet, with partitions four and a half feet high. It was better for writing and sleeping.

SEPT 29, 1950.

Frances: *Yesterday—my first day of actual shooting—was even more unbalanced than anything I could possibly have expected—Reis for whatever neurotic reasons, was a real monster . . . somehow I'm here to tell the tale. . . .*

But my darling, I came <u>home</u> last night—having been away from 6:30 A.M. to get both your wonderful letter and your flowers. I can't describe to you how I felt. . . .

My father was glad the florist fulfilled his assignment. The final selection had been left open after some discussion about the September product before his exit, and he could only hope for the best.

So far the parole board had left the sixty-five or so current Danbury applicants in a nervous state—but, my father said, being free of illusions on that score, he remained relatively calm.

October 2, 1950.

Ring: *Tell Joe that I challenge him to a push-up and chinning contest the week I get home and that he had better do some prac-*

ticing because I am. But I don't intend to get sucked in to any of his specialties like pole-climbing.

As for Miss Katharine, it seems a shame that after she learned to write so well at Roosevelt [I hated the Roosevelt School], *she had to go to Westland, where I understand, they unteach it. Unless I am mistaken about this and I'd have to see some real proof before I'd admit I am, she's probably forgotten every word she ever knew by now and would have trouble spelling her own name.*

Connecticut slightly redeemed itself in my dad's favor with a spell of warmth and sunshine. He played handball over the weekend and Saturday was further improved, he said, by a better-than-average movie—*Broken Arrow.*

Ring: *If you run into anyone who runs into* [writer] *Michael Blankfort or* [producer] *Julian Blaustein, advise them that it was very warmly received here, being particularly commended by the Negro one-third of the population.*

Monday Night.

Frances: *Once again a short letter. I couldn't write yesterday— gave Polly the day off because she'd really had a busy few days with me being a movie actress—and came down with a stiff neck and three kids. . . . I came down with a stiff neck, not Poll. I knew that Reis would blow his top if I arrived today with three scenes to shoot—in different costumes—and physically disabled—I parked the children at the Jarricos' while I got an osteopathic treatment by a doctor recommended by Jack Schwab—said doc also shot me intravenously full of calcium vitamins B&C & I don't know what else. . . . I certainly need every bit of experience I can get and maybe someday I'll end up being a good picture actress. . . . Maybe I'd do better under gentler treatment.*

Tomorrow . . . back to more normal living . . . still undecided about Jimmy. I'd love for you to see him, no matter how briefly, but having him would create problems re my mother, yours, job hunting etc. Oh dear. I'll probably end up coming alone!

    I'm glad you've got your cubicle . . . I wish I could share it.

Thursday—October 5.

    Frances: . . . *a typical Thursday . . . children to school . . . cashed a check at the bank for Polly—then Jimmy and I took her part of the way downtown . . . errands . . . marketing . . . lunch— he got put down for a nap—I prepared fixings for a borscht. . . .*

Borscht was one of the few things my mother could make at the time. It was one of the only things her Russian mother had taught her. Grandma Marie was against my mother learning to cook. Her daughter was an actress and that was it. And if you didn't know how, you wouldn't wind up having to perform the tasks. Plus my mother had no inclination in that regard. But Grandma taught her how to make a Russian meat borscht once when she was laid up in bed and it was done under my grandmother's instruction, when my mother was nine.

    Frances: *I've reserved a seat for the 27th a Friday. . . . The plane leaves at 9:30 A.M. . . . This way* [the children] *can drop me at the Hollywood Roosevelt on their way to school and I can go out to the airport by bus. . . . I'm hoping that it will be possible to have some* <u>extra time</u>, *but . . . whatever time we have . . . will be worth it. I can be gone about two weeks . . . I think . . . Jimmy is out. . . . He's . . . gotten too old to travel for free. . . .*

There was an interruption here in the letter-writing process because Jimmy woke up crying and needed *a little pampering. . . .*

    Frances: . . . *then Katie & Joe arrived with rabbit who had been visiting in school* [Polly let us purchase the bunny for a buck] . . . *only rabbit looked a little weak and he needed pampering—then the borscht needed pampering—then Ingo* [Preminger] *called up and invited me to see "Woman of the*

Year" on Sunday at the Academy—oh in between there were thousands of ants around the kitchen which had emerged from I don't know where. . . .

Tonight I'm going to see <u>M</u>—directed by Joe Losey—a preview. . . .

Joe and I also saw *Broken Arrow*. We loved it.

"Is it not possible that your people and mine can someday live together like brothers?" asked a cavalry scout played by James Stewart, sucking up to the great leader of the Chiricahua Apaches, Cochise (Jeff Chandler). And in the name of peace, harmony, and brotherhood, Stewart inspired Cochise to break his arrow. He even married Sonseeahray (Morning Star), the Apache maiden played by Debra Paget. Too bad she got shot down in an ambush orchestrated by a big-time hater of the Apaches (Will Geer—he wound up blacklisted in real life). "We'll have peace when every Apache is hung from a tree," harangued Geer. But it was Sonseeahray's death—Stewart's great loss—that brought his people together in the will to peace. And without that will, peace treaties weren't worth a damn. James Stewart's heart was broken. However, as time passed, he came to know that Sonseeahray/Morning Star's death put a seal on the peace he struggled so hard to bring about.

Peace just didn't come easily.

Oct. 5, 1950.

Ring: *Darling—The parole results started to come . . . —only a handful and . . . no possible way to predict on the basis of past performance. . . . There could be a considerable delay.*

Your closing report on the Piatigorsky session arrived today. The neck trouble sounds grim. Was there any physical origin to it . . . or was it just a manifestation of nervous strain?

The dearth of things to write about is too challenging for me tonight what with a state of fatigue brought on by a slight cold. . . .

October 9, 1950.

Ring: *Your Thursday letter came Saturday and was as always an aid to morale. The idea of seeing you gets more exciting as it grows closer, though I still have a reservation in some deep logical recess of my mind which reminds me that it isn't a very satisfactory kind of visiting and hardly worth all the effort involved. . . .*

Only one-fourth of the results of the parole hearings were in, and all but one were affirmative. Since 25 percent of a total group of applicants was a fairly high percentage, my father concluded there probably wouldn't be many more granted. He said there was a chance of quite a long delay. Perhaps until after the elections. But he thought there was a greater chance of a routine denial sooner.

My father had a full weekend, including handball, bridge, watching the last baseball contest of the season between FCI Danbury's varsity and an outside team, and two sessions of work on the book. He called it one of the slowest literary projects since the A–B Volume of the Oxford Dictionary (it was proceeding more satisfactorily in a qualitative than a quantitative sense). And because the clerk who'd broken him in at the Office of Classification and Parole left on parole, my father had assumed senior responsibility over a new man.

Ring: *Please apprise Polly and the juvenile brood of my unceasing love. . . .*

Sunday we went to Beverly Park. Joe was furious because there were too many people. Jimmy rode around in a little car. My mother wrote to my father. Then Joe and I went on the whip and everything was great until Jim climbed under the fence and started out toward the street. After his retrieval, we each had six pony rides. The fastest, of course, for Joe and me. Jim, however, had advanced to the trotting stage. The whole place had a nice cheerful quality, and all of us were lulled by the music of the merry-go-round.

My mother called it quits after devoting a week to budgeting her time, with disastrous results. She had the feeling that everything was moving too fast, the borscht wasn't seasoned properly, etc. So it was back to her *own lazy, wasting time pace.*

Sunday she saw *Woman of the Year* and said it was one of the best pictures ever. She loved my father for being such a sensitive writer and, remembering the first time she saw it, realized something she'd forgotten. That was how she had first gotten to know him. The attitudes and understanding he'd written for Spencer Tracy she took to be his. She said it was how he'd won her. When my father's name flashed on the screen, Hugo Butler started the applause, which was picked up quite heartily in the other parts of the house.

Monday—Oct. 9th.
. . . [C]hange of underwear three times a week is fine, declared my mother. *Katie & Joe only get baths every other day now, so we're all changing our habits.*

The neck ailment was a fatigue thing.

October 13, 1950.
Ring: *I waited 24 hours beyond my usual writing time in case some parole word came in today but it didn't. An avalanche of denials arrived Wednesday spreading gloom. . . .*

I have just had a haircut which in turn brought on a shower and a shampooing before settling down to write you. Like most things in old F.C.I., haircuts are systematized to a point where in-

dividual responsibility is non-existent. Everyone gets one every three weeks to the day but it isn't up to him to remember. . . .

Have you heard yet where Adrian is doing his stint?

I read in the course of the American Legion Convention story (and I'm happy to note that those boys are still on the qui vive in these troubled times) that you had the hottest Columbus Day in record history yesterday. The same trend is not evident here. I find it necessary, especially going to breakfast in the close vicinity of dawn, to wear my Navy P-Jacket, which looks as if it had been through the Battle of the Coral Sea but still serves its warming function.

Getting a script into the jail for my father to work on, which he had thought might be feasible, wasn't.

Friday was the hottest day of the year. Jonnie Cole (Lester's wife) said it was earthquake weather and anything could happen. My mother was in bed with the flu and grateful for the opportunity to lie around without feeling guilty when everyone else was tearing around in the 103-degree horror. It was all anyone talked about.

Friday Night.

> *Dear Daddy,*
> *I miss you. My teacher's name is Polly. We want arithmetic only Polly won't let us. They don't unteach writing at Westland. I don't know if <u>they</u> allow me to write a whole letter and I don't like to write.* [I was referring to prison rules, not to my school.]
> *We have a store at our school, but they don't have ice cream. They only have juices. They have paper and pencils and chalk and lots of other things too. I've bought colored paper and plain paper.*
> *Kathy Endfield goes to my school. Janie Gordon used to go to Progressive School too, when I went to kindergarden. We*

play with paints and clay and we study farms. We saw some bulls when we went to the dairy. JIMMY IS STILL FUNNY.

LOVE KATHARINE

They don't unteach it, but they sure come close, wrote my mother, her reservations about private school education mounting. Not because the school and what they were trying to accomplish wasn't good, she claimed. But because of the number of problem children. And because, she said, her brood would probably have been better off in public school. I remember a boy with a fuzzy patch on his face. (His entire cheek resembled a calf.) And a handsome blond kid flying around the yard in a cape. My friend Jan audibly sucked her thumb during naps, and her hair significantly tangled and became one with the comb when I coiffed her locks. And there were some celebrity offspring. The school wasn't a factory. It was sensitive to the emotional landscape. We were taught to embrace all of mankind.

Frances: *Oh dear. I'm always admitting my mistakes when its too late. The children are happy though—and maybe there will be worthwhile results.*

> *Dear Daddy,*
> *. . . I challenge you to a throwing darts at Balloons contest, and if you get more darts popped at the balloons than I can do chin-ups, then I'll give you a dime. We're going to Balboa Sunday if Mommy feels better. I would rather be going to see you.*

LOVE JOE

My father said one benefit he was deriving from his enforced absence was a more objective attitude toward Hollywood and American culture in general. An Esther Williams picture played at the prison over the weekend, and he said it was with great difficulty and reluctance that he was beginning to admit his judgment could have been corrupted by material considerations or distorted by close-range viewing. In the past he would have been merely appalled at the movie as an individual item of stupidity and bad taste.

October 16, 1950.

Ring: *But here and now it is more than that; it symbolizes a degeneracy so hopelessly far advanced that hanging* [producer] *Joe Pasternak or Dore Schary* [soon to be head of MGM] *or* [writer] *Jerry Davis or Esther Williams would be, while an act of simple justice, a pathetic gesture as well. There would be some consolation in the fact that the whole fabric is doomed if it weren't that it were being swallowed by a monster even more horrible than itself.*

A little checking around with local residents who had had visits on the weekend revealed that they were generally regarded as less satisfactory than under the quieter and less crowded conditions of weekday afternoons.

Ring: . . . *Dear Joe—Okay, I'll take you up on the dart-throwing at balloons deal. I hope Mommy was well enough for you to make the trip to Balboa. I miss you very much and next time I make a trip it will be home.*

Dear Katharine—It's very nice to hear from you and I like to know things you do at school. I want you to talk to that Jimmy character about me and show him my picture once in awhile so he won't sock me in the nose when I come home. . . .

Well, the flu germ really got into my mother, and the Jarricos wound up taking Joe and me to Balboa. It was nothing but a great big nuisance, my mom declared about the bug. It was Monday and she was still in bed, but she said she better get cured quickly because she'd gotten a call to do a radio show and couldn't indulge it beyond Wednesday. She said there hadn't been a bug yet that couldn't be chased by a job or the prospect of one. Paul Jarrico treated all the kids (his son Billy along with Peter, Ann, Joe, and me) to a boat trip.

IT WAS PAUL JARRICO who wound up checking out our library on Holly Drive. Rumors were spreading about break-ins to examine books in homes, so he came over and eliminated the troublesome ones. We were loaded with political volumes, and my mother didn't know what to do, so Paul went through our bookcases and hid the potential offenders down in the basement.

"I don't know what good it was supposed to do," said my mother. "But the fear was so great. It really was. You began to feel the way people felt in Germany—on a much lesser scale, because nobody was wearing Stars of David. But there were stories going around Hollywood that anybody who ever belonged to anything was going to be incarcerated. They were going to be in concentration camps." My mother said people remembered when the Japanese were interned. And if the Hollywood Ten could go to jail, anything could happen.

Her ailment was finally diagnosed as infectious mononucleosis, which was quite common in southern California that season, but she did her show anyway and had gotten up to do one on Tuesday. A last-minute thing.

Her reservation was set. Don't worry about the weekend thing, she told my father, because she'd be around for at least a week and a half and they could have subsequent visits on weekdays.

Frances: *I know how terribly inadequate it will be, but I think it'll be good anyway. I miss you so and. . . . it will be fine just to sit and talk. . . .*

My father said the parole board had been uncommunicative for nine days. He would have thought it was a special tactical

delay in respect to the Hollywood cases, except there were seven
other Danburyites still "in suspension."

He hoped to hear soon that my mother had recovered from
the flu. He suspected low resistance due to undereating as a con-
tributing factor, and if she looked too thin, she would have some
explaining to do.

Saturday—Oct. 21.

I wish I were leaving <u>now</u>—this minute! wrote my mother.

Frances: [D]*on't worry about the fact that there hasn't been
word on parole . . . and may not be before our visit . . . it will be
very good for both of us to see each other, no matter what the circumstances. . . . We can't deny from each other, at least, that this
confinement for you is a grueling and interminable ordeal and
that the separation for both of us is exceedingly difficult, to put it
mildly. But I think that we're . . . managing . . . as well as possible. . . . [S]omehow we've both been made so that we can with-
stand whatever has to be withstood—I don't know what makes
me so <u>certain</u> of our strength or why I think we can be tested in
this way—but certain I am and know you are too. . . .*

*. . . I told you I would give you my most recent reactions to the
whole question of Hollywood. I feel somewhat differently than I
did as recently as just a couple of months ago. . . . I'll never think
of this place as a perfect choice for a permanent home—but if you
still are for it—I at least know how I could swing it and be happier doing it. I still think all the same things I've always thought
about the whole business of making movies, and all the unbeliev-
able compromises and the intrigue and nonsense that is all part
of it, but probably because I've had these few little jobs and have
tasted the pleasure of work I believe that it would be all right—if
you wanted it for us (I mean Hollywood) in the future again. Also
there is the fact that I've had to make friends on my own and*

function alone that makes me feel more as if I belonged a little.... Have I made myself at all clear? The one constant factor outside of my feeling for you and the children is the terrible attachment I have for acting. I'm afraid I'll never lose it.... And I never want to, but I think I'll get a chance to do it—even in pictures—even looking as I do—anyway I'm not afraid anymore.

Jim had taken to saying "Let's go see Daddy," which meant the picture of him.

Frances: *Ringly—so many people send their love.... Everyone hopes you'll be home soon and for once I'll allow myself the joy of thinking it might really happen.*

My father reported going through a contemporaneous infectious period in the form of a boil or abscess on the base of his left nostril. But, he said, it was well under control after five penicillin shots. He thought he should mention it because there might be some vestigial scar when my mother visited, which might otherwise startle her. He was granted the privilege of an extra two-hour visit. Assigned, because it had to be assigned to one month or the other, to November. He suggested that my mother go to New Milford Sunday night or Monday, and to Danbury for the first time Monday afternoon, October 30. Weekday visiting time was afternoon only, starting at 1:00 P.M., and he said the closer to that hour she could make it, the better.

I love you ... and ardently await seeing you ..., he wrote.

The Visit

My mother stayed with Granny, and Albert drove her to the prison. It was strange, she said. They drove up in the car, and my mother was asked her name and that of the person she was visiting. Then a loudspeaker boomed out both her name and

Ring's. There she was being driven by a chauffeur (Albert) going to see Pop in jail, and she'd decided she was going to look great. My mom wore her mink. And she was shown around as if she were a visiting celebrity. "Mrs. Lardner, here we have our football field," her host said. "Here we have our baseball diamond." So, there was that, she said, and then ultimately going into this place through a gate, and then another gate.

"Whatever," said my mother. "And then sitting down and there was Dad across from me. Pale. And somebody staying at the end of the room from us. It was terrible. You couldn't . . . You couldn't anything."

They looked at each other and they talked. And, she said, they had a good time, for the days and hours allotted them until my father walked out of the room and she couldn't see him anymore.

Even so my mother said it was worth going. "It was very important to have some kind of contact with each other besides those goddamn letters." She was determined on getting there. "Poor little bastards. What a terrible thing to go through."

Then my mother returned home and it was all as it had been before. She drove us to school and Joe proudly wore his Daniel Boone hat—his coming-home present from her. But she had been right, after all, in her more positive feeling that visiting then was a necessary part of maintaining contact, acquiesced my dad.

He said it had begun to be something of a strain for him— going along on circumstantial evidence of my mother's existence. Now the links were forged a little more solidly with her and, through her, the rest of the world. There remained, however, the cumulatively debilitating strain of the parole business, which he earnestly hoped wouldn't go on much longer.

November 10, 1950.

Ring: . . . *Please tell Miss Katharine Gigglepuss Lardner that if she draws or paints a picture on a piece of paper small enough to go in the envelope along with one of your letters . . . I have some wall space that needs decorating. The same for Joe Stevie Scott Lardner, whom you had also better tell to start practicing up on his getaways because I have thought up some new tricks for playing Giant that will make it dangerous for him to come within six feet of me.*

Please give my love to Polly and thank her for letting you visit me.

Sunday—Nov. 12.

. . . I know we'll all calm down a bit after we know what gives, but at the moment everyone including the lawyers, is very high—either with hope or despair, wrote Frances.

One of them assured my mother that the feeling locally was all for equalization.

Jimmy was getting wilder and needed constant supervision because he could now climb over both back and front fences.

My father had no way of knowing whether the news was given out to the newspapers or communicated to the lawyers as quickly as to them—him and Lester Cole.

November 13, 1950.

Ring: [S]*o this may be your first word that parole has been denied. . . .*

MY FATHER ASSUMED the same decision was made in the other Ten cases as with the pair of them. They made it a little tougher to take by dragging out the suspense for so long. But there was at least an element of relief in knowing for sure what they were up against.

It's unpleasant, unjust, indecent but not unbearable, he wrote.

Ring: *The only possible explanation I can think of for the delay is that one or two members of the Board must have had a small spark of integrity or conscience that took a certain amount of effort to extinguish.*

The mail arrived with the letter containing the grim detail just as my mother was leaving to join Hugo, Joe Losey, and director Bob Aldrich for lunch. She carried the unopened missive with her to Lucy's El Adobe, a Mexican restaurant on Melrose Avenue, planning to read it while the men hashed out their various deals. She said its contents were rough and completely unexpected that day, but she was glad it was revealed to her in that way—at Lucy's. My mother proceeded to order a couple of drinks. She ate no lunch and was fairly drained of everything.

Frances: *Even though we hadn't hoped and said we wouldn't, I guess we had.*

November 20, 1950.

Ring: *Baby darling—I'm glad you operated as you did with the particular letter containing my news from Washington—taking it along to lunch, I mean, and reading it with a bar handy.*

My dad said it was precisely the convenience he missed. And let the clemency petitions go in, and photostats of the parole letters, etc. (if character references were needed). But don't let anyone take the gesture seriously, was his thought.

And now that Thanksgiving was heralding the approach of the festive season, my father appointed Granny official designated family member to send him the single Christmas package permitted. He said the restrictions were rigid, and it was easier to discuss them in relation to his tastes during her next visit rather than by

mail. Books (as long as they were mailed under the aegis of a reputable bookstore), however, were still an option for anyone else
wishing to make a seasonal gesture. My father's preference was
still for nonfiction (though not overwhelmingly so), and in about a
week he could arrive at a definite suggestion. In recognition of the
fact that it was more blessed to give than to receive, he was feeling
some remorse over not having taken advantage of the prison craft
shop's leatherwork facilities. (Engaging in craft work would have
been a first for my dad.) Because then he could have sent gifts to
the whole horde, as he called his immediate family. But he was
sticking to the idea that the prose he wrote instead might eventually have more value and was, as he said, probably better wrought.

Ring: *Please tell Potato Dumpling and Stringbean that their
crayon work is beautiful. I guess P.D.'s Indians make their wig-
wams out of asbestos—if they don't the open log fire would be a
little dangerous. Anyway, it's pretty and that's more important.
How did Stringbean ever get to be so neat with his colors?*

JOE WANTED TO KNOW if there was any chance of Dad making it
home for Christmas, even though he was told this wasn't going
to happen until soon after he turned seven in April. So he started
spreading the word that he was practically there.

Cleo Trumbo was in town with her gang, and all Hunter,
Butler, Trumbo, and Lardner offspring (except Jim and Emily
Butler) were at the Progressive School Fair. Along with a few
hundred other small characters, as my mother called them. Afterward, some of us took in the planetarium, where she and Joe
were equally bored by the lecturer.

Thanksgiving in jail went about as well as could be expected,
reported my dad. Tables were covered with white sheets mas-
querading as tablecloths and everyone received half an institu-

tional chicken. It even snowed. The weather was turning cold for a southwestern type like him and he was grateful he didn't have to be outside more than a few minutes at a time. But on Thanksgiving he got trapped into what he referred to as a Bob Hope fiasco—*Fancy Pants*—so he abstained the next day from *Where the Sidewalk Ends* on the grounds that it was too much concentrated pleasure. The holiday weekend was going to give him a chance for some work, and he hoped to be well into the third chapter by Monday.

My father was eager for reports concerning the return of Eddie and Herbert to what was known in parole office parlance as "the normal community."

And he told us about a letter he had received in six different Lardner handwritings executed on Thanksgiving afternoon in New Milford, full of warm sentiments: "I hope you'll be out soon. I wish I could get you out, love John N. Lardner." Cousin Johnny was seven. (The same age as me.) Cousins Mary Jane, eight, and Susan, ten, and the level of their penmanship, remarked my father, was notably superior to the standards in Balboa and Hollywood.

We went to Hope and Jeff Corey's for Thanksgiving. They had a couple of kids and seemed to think we ought to spend it with other children. The Christmas parade ran the night before and Joe and I stayed up until nine-thirty viewing it on Vicky Brandt's TV.

There had been no radio work for my mother since her return, so she was going crazy waiting for two movie things to be resolved. Then, after an on-again, off-again routine, she was offered two scenes in Mike Kanin's picture *When I Grow Up*. Nobody thought she was right for the part because she didn't resemble a girl from the other side of the tracks. But it was decided she had better qualities for it than anyone else, so they took a chance.

Disposing my mother in favor of Granny as Christmas donor was okay by her, as was lack of leatherwork. My father was going to be with us no matter where he was, she swooned.

Saturday.

Frances: *Potato Dumpling & Stringbean have constant colorings for you. Some a little large to include in my letters, but there are these for the present.*

My father said jail was the place to spend a hurricane because of how detached you could be when you simply didn't care what happened to the neighboring countryside. Or for that matter your own living quarters. And everyone was well protected from the elements (even when the wind blew up to eighty-five miles an hour) by the surrounding solid walls. He said he was only buffeted about a little—when crossing the quadrangle for meals, for instance. The only inconvenience really was the loss of electric power. The prison operated through the weekend on an emergency generator, which didn't furnish enough power for more than a few lights in each dormitory, so reading and writing were out but my father spent Sunday playing bridge.

November 27, 1950.

Ring: . . . *Your letter mailed on Thanksgiving arrived Saturday and the one you mailed Saturday night came today. The latter . . . with the latest art work . . . probably all . . . the traffic will bear. . . . But thank the artists for me. . . . [B]oth are unsigned and both look like Katie's work, but if . . . animal in . . . circus wagon is not hers but Joe's, then I am genuinely impressed because it represents a big step beyond the drawing he was doing last spring.*

Thursday Noon.

Frances: *I guess the mail call around here is just as important as around your house.... [D]idn't write yesterday because your letter hadn't come ... but today nothing either. I only hope ... it's a delay because of the Thanksgiving holiday. Our mailman knows the days that matter ... and assured me today that the storm in the east may have caused the delay....*

La Guardia's field was under water for about thirty-six hours. They probably sent the airmail by train.

Frances: *No definite call for my part—but it's due on the cast list for Wednesday and Thursday.... You can imagine the state I'm in—about whether I'll be any good or not—whether I'll freeze— whether I'll be honest and natural—whether the characterization will get in the way and keep me from being simple. Oh nuts!*

Hair and costumes were approved and my mother looked a fright, which pleased her no end. She wasn't going to use makeup. Just whatever was necessary to make her look drunken and glazed.

Here are some books she thought would spark my father's interest: *Pageant of the Popes*, with portraits of fourteen of them, and *Beyond Humanism*. (Research material for the book he was writing that was going to deal in a light vein with the contradictions of Roman Catholicism in America.)

Hugo Butler was up for more jobs, reported my mother, and was rewriting on the set of the Roberts picture—just ahead of the camera.

The doorbell rang one of the times he was visiting our home on Holly Drive. I went to answer it but was shoved aside by this friend and told children don't answer the door. I didn't know it then, but Hugo was probably in hiding and afraid I couldn't handle a U.S. marshal with a subpoena.

My father said he wanted *Neuroses and Sacraments* and *Beyond Humanism*. Perhaps my mother could recruit someone to finance one of them, and in case she ran across any characters who wanted to send books, he also wanted Bishop Sheen's *Lift Up Your Heart*.

Joe and I meanwhile envied the Biberman kids. Their father (Herbert) was back home. His wife Gale Sondergaard ("the Spider Woman") invited wives and lawyers to get together with him—just twenty-four hours after he arrived. Herbert was feeling so bad (at liberty) about the rest of them still incarcerated he'd composed a letter to the parole board on his way home. He insisted they should make another appeal. My mother said it wasn't that my father didn't want everything being done that could be—he just didn't want anyone to get their hopes up again.

Eddie Dmytryk was also back but he hadn't been seen yet.

November 30, 1950.

These were stirring days in the newspapers and in life too, wrote my father. *One of the very few advantages to being in the East . . . is . . . you can read complete texts of speeches and statements in the Times, the news columns of which aren't any less one-sided than the ordinary papers. But you can ignore these and read what Senator Austin and General Wu actually said and judge how the sense is apportioned between them. Of course it's frightening, terribly so, to realize that there is real danger of somebody pushing or blundering the world into war every day, and yet it seems to me the odds are strongly that there won't be any war. There isn't a country outside of this one which would fight under the leadership of MacArthur in any broadening of the present operation, and I don't think either America or China wants a war just between themselves.*

My father said he was beginning to put on weight as a result of exercising and having quit smoking. The latter, he thought, would be a permanent thing if his reaction continued as favorable. So far it had cut his coughing considerably and eliminated the postnasal drip that used to result in violent coughing and gagging in the morning. And the unseen benefits to the internal organs *ravaged by the vile drug* were incalculable. The only possible drawback was that it would be physically/morally impossible for him to live with anyone (my mom) who was herself *a slave to the repulsive poison.*

Ring: *Please kiss Joe for me and tell him to kiss Katharine for me and tell her to kiss Jimmy for me and tell him (Jimmy) to kiss Polly for me and tell Polly to kiss Joe (second time around for him) for me and tell him to kiss you for me. . . .*

Frances: *Did I tell you that our cat is still with us—that he looks like a pair of kittens we had in Santa Monica and that I suspect we'll have him always. I know <u>you'll</u> like him. He's pretty & friendly and very well mannered.*

Yesterday was my mother's first day on the picture and she looked really broken down—without lipstick, with red around her eyes for bleariness. Her hair greased, no pancake, and stuff on her teeth to take down the cleanness.

Thursday Morning.

Frances: *Potato Dumpling & String Bean were a little put out at not getting a message. . . .*

MY FATHER SAID if stubborn souls were inclined, there were two ways to get a parole decision reviewed: sponsorship by the confining institution and outside pressure. The first was out at Danbury. But the second method could be started with a visit to

Washington by Margaret Maltz and Sue Lawson to make simple inquiries. Why were their husbands denied? In what branch of the usual requirements for parole were they deficient? What could they do in the next month or two to improve their chances?

Also the prisoner could address the board directly. My father had already done this, feeling that no one could state the arguments on his behalf in *quite such deft and exhilarating prose.* However, about 99.97 percent of the prisoners denied parole felt their cases should be reconsidered, so that process was a spectacularly ineffectual one, he cautioned.

December 4, 1950.

Ring: . . . *Above all, remember that none of this . . . is to be taken seriously enough for agitation one way or another. What does matter, as of the way things looked from Monday morning's newspapers . . . is that there's world truce—a breathing spell at least—in the making.*

Love to what-do-you-call-her and what's-his-name.

Sunday.

Oh—before I forget—I don't think I did as well on the final stuff in the picture, said my mother, *but I have some fine theatrical stills which I can't send . . . because . . .* [t]*hey look like a poor broken down French guess what?* [H]*ardly the sort of thing to send to one's husband . . . maybe I'm wrong. . . .*

Frances: *I was told by Cleo today that Herbert & Eddie had written a joint letter. Please God it'll help. . . . They both feel that it is absolutely unjust that the rest of you are still in prison— Everyone feels that way. Surely the Parole Board will have to reconsider. . . . What will they say to Margaret & Sue. What would they say to me. . . .*

The meritorious good-time regulation was changed at the

prison so it could start three months after beginning of sentence instead of six, and my father (the first beneficiary of the new system) was awarded two days per month retroactive to October 1. So unless the award was withdrawn because of something construed as a lapse of diligence on his part, he said he was going to get thirteen days off and be released on April 16 instead of April 29.

December 7.

Ring: *Please tell Joe that I'll make it home <u>very soon</u> after his birthday.*

It was very touching, he added tongue in his cheek, to know that Herbert and Eddie had written letters.

Ring: *It is probably conceded pretty generally that we ourselves are in favor of getting out but certainly the second least startling revelation is that our codefendants support us. After that in order of nonsurprise would come the open and unqualified endorsement of our wives and children.*

Dear Katie—I loved getting your letter. . . . written in what I think is just about the most beautiful printing I've ever seen. I never saw an envelope made from wallpaper before but I think it's a very smart idea. . . .

Wednesday.

Frances: *There is great feeling among many people about the unfairness of your still being imprisoned and they are expressing themselves to the Parole Board asking for reconsideration.*

My mother sent my father two books through Martindale's— *Lift Up Your Heart* and *Come Back, Little Sheba*. She wasn't sure if she was delighted or furious with him about stopping smoking because it placed a terrible burden on her. She didn't know what effect it would have on her course of action.

Frances: *Dumpling & String Bean . . . out this afternoon visiting friends so Polly and I will probably be alone for dinner—although that's hardly fair to Jimmy. . . . [H]e . . . joins us some days now. We remove his tray and his high chair fits very well under the kitchen table and he's as pleased as can be.*

My brother Joe lost another tooth and all three of us went to see the clown who appeared in my mom's movie do tricks on the set at a publicity-type party.

Sunday.

Frances: *Dearest love—This letter isn't going to be about anything much. . . . It's warm out—very—and I feel queer and nostalgic and it's a great indulgence on my part. The Nostalgia. Possibly it's because there are so few shopping days left till Christmas—or maybe it's because we're finally into the second lap of this infernally long separation—or again and most likely—I have no immediate acting job in sight to get stirred up about—whatever the reason or reasons I'm suspended in day dreams. . . .*

DECEMBER 13, 1950.

The Supreme Court decision in the Blau case seems like the first important step in the history of our fate since the sentencing of Eddie and Herbert, wrote Ring referring to *Blau v. United States.*

The Court had decided for the first time that unwillingness to admit Communist Party membership was adequate grounds for invoking the Fifth. On the question of Communist Party membership—a witness could therefore avoid being in contempt of court or Congress.

Ring: *Although we invoked Bill of Rights in toto we put emphasis on First rather than 5th Amendment. The practical difference between the two is the difference between saying, "You have*

no right to ask me that question" and *"I don't have to answer
it . . ." Justice Dept. spokesman quoted in newspapers take for
granted new decision will apply to Congressional as well as
grand jury investigations and that questions we failed to answer
will no longer be permissible. Thus principle for which we stand
is now vindicated while we remain in jail. . . .*

My mother was in a car wreck. Having just emerged from a
stop-sign street (creeping along), she was hit broadside by a fast-
traveling lady. (The other driver had the right-of-way.) She deliberated and deliberated and then changed her mind about
telling my dad.

Thursday.

Frances: *[B]ut . . . silly not to, because it's not serious and I'm
fine. . . . It was pretty spectacular because my silly head got cut
open and had to have some stitches in it. Will leave a small scar
very near my hair line on the right side of my forehead. . . . The
car will of course be completely repaired as will I, thanks to the
insurance. . . .*

She was probably going to write the parole board and tell
them she wanted my father home for Christmas.

Saturday.

*. . . I personally feel that your expression of the situation is as
clear . . . as can be,* she said, *and the Parole Board should act fa-
vorably, but we'll see. People are writing letters to the Board—
and our lawyers here . . . [are] hopeful. . . .*

Ingo Preminger sent my father *The Information Please Almanac* along with *The Lady's Not for Burning*, the Christopher
Fry play my mother saw opening night in New York after visiting
my father in jail. [It] *seemed to be about something,* she wrote,
but the resolution was terribly pat . . . not all in keeping with its

early promise. . . . I was most impressed by the brilliant acting of Pamela Brown . . . the most exciting woman I've ever seen perform. She . . . knows best of all how to make everything she says absolutely comprehensible. I wish that some day someone might say this of me. . . .

Ring—you do understand . . . I'm hoping harder than anyone, but I'm afraid to talk about it or really think about it, or anything.

Katie Becker (a friend) picked up our laundry from the Laundromat during this no-car period.

Dec. 19, 1950.

Ring: *. . . I know how upsetting and generally horrible the accident must have been at the time . . . the fact that you were still without a car eight days later means it has been a pretty grim inconvenience.*

We have been having a persuasive foretaste of winter in the area before it is officially upon us.

My father said some eight or nine inches of snow fell in one storm, and it had stayed cold enough to keep a good part of it on the ground. He expected eventually to be inundated with books (from the number my mother reported en route). But delivery was fantastically far behind dispatch. The delay, he said, was caused by grave deliberations in Washington as to their acceptability.

Ring: *Please tell Stringbean and Potato Dumpling to have a very merry Christmas, likewise to James and Polly. . . .*

Tuesday.

Frances: *There's the usual last minute preparation for the children's day—somewhat complicated by . . . car . . . still in repairs, but I'm managing to get rides. . . .*

It's going to be a queer Christmas without you. . . .

. . .

IT SNOWED STEADILY in Danbury on top of what was already a pretty substantial residue, and my father was gripped by a strong nostalgia for a green Christmas. Anti-eastern sentiments were mounting and, he said, he longed to be in a pleasant place with a sensible climate: LA. But writing plans (even with sinister influences conspiring to delay execution) were still intact. So the two upcoming long weekends were crucial. If he could just get a substantial chunk accomplished he might come reasonably near his schedule by the end of January. At which point he would be eligible for the "pre-release house" that offered the great advantage of a private room.

Dec. 22, 1950.

Ring: *This will probably reach you the day after . . . and should find you in a pretty exhausted state. The idea of a vacation period without the car is appalling, even though it's better on Holly Drive than it would have been in Santa Monica. . . . If the florist down on Cahuenga is still carrying out the terms of our accord, you should have received another bundle of posies on Christmas morning. . . .*

Please ask Miss Pretty-puss and the young man of the house to let me know how they felt about their Christmas. . . .

Thursday.

Frances: *. . . I was going to write yesterday but yesterday came and went and today has, almost—and nothing from you. I'm sure that it's the holiday delay. . . . [I]n the meantime . . . I'll pray that this reaches you Saturday. . . .*

I got Jimmy a musical rocking chair and a sort of desk thing with a black board along with a number of small stuffed creatures and Katie a doll (because it's probably her last year for one) and a bracelet and a dress and a basketball to share with Joe who is also getting a gun that shoots ping pong balls, and a car that is worked by remote control—of course there are other things like a wonderful belt (western type) and a small walking bear and I think Christmas will be all right for them. . . . Today we bought the tree . . . a fine type of tree. . . . Our curtains have all been washed and . . . hung again—clean and starchy—and I've remembered the mailman and the milkman. . . .

By January 1st—it'll be three and a half months unless some unexpected loveliness happens—and then it'll be less than that—and then even less—and then Joe's birthday and then you'll be home! If they give you turkey on Christmas as they did on Thanksgiving [they served chicken]*—and if your main meal is in the evening (which it probably isn't) we'll be eating at about the same time . . . at about 2:30 or 3. . . . I'll think of you very hard at special moments of the day—first when the children wake me—then when we finally start opening packages—then we'll drink to you (with champagne . . .) then when we eat, then when the guests have gone, then when I've said good night to the children. . . .*

Darling—please get this in time. . . .

DEC. 25, 1950.

Ring: *Baby, there is a wonderful chance for a big publicity break if it is handled right. . . .*

A story appeared in the *Herald Tribune*—page twelve (movie news)—about the Motion Picture Academy bidding five hundred dollars at a public auction to prevent an Oscar from falling into alien hands. And my father was proposing another trade paper ad: "$498—OSCAR—$498—Sacrifice Sale—Genuine Academy Award—Winner in straitened circumstances far from home." If the five-hundred-dollar price hadn't been publicized locally, he'd change the beginning to "OSCAR FOR SALE—Sacrifice—No reasonable offer refused." He figured my mother would get calls not only from the Academy, but from city desks and wire services as well. He said the ostensible purpose of the ad should be carried through and for all the money the traffic would bear.

Ring: *I'm afraid I may have disturbed and misled you by my inconsequential complaints about the East in my last letter.*

My father said he jettisoned all former reasons for continuing in California and could operate equally well (or badly), in the East or the West. The way he judged the situation was that there would be no more employment in Hollywood—white, black, or gray market—for ostracized characters like him and though the opportunity for anonymous story sales would probably still exist, that was almost as easily conducted from New York as California. So my mother's career should determine the place of our future home.

Ring: *How do you look this Christmas, my darling? How long is your hair and are you still too thin?*

Tuesday.

Frances: *Christmas was fine for the children. As usual I managed to get them to stay in their room till 8. Then they got their stockings and opened presents and had breakfast before the official unveilings. Years from now some analyst will think I was some sort of monster for keeping my children from their packages until 9 A.M. Jimmy was delighted with all the proceedings—carried all his stuffed creatures around—rocked in his new chair—pulled candy canes off the tree and had a splendid time generally. Joe as usual couldn't believe when the final present was unwrapped that there wasn't any more. Joe got a ukelele which of course Katharine wanted and so on. But all things considered (which really means one) it was a fine day. . . . Hugo, Polly, Jean* *and I drank you a toast at about 11:30 A.M.—Champagne, honey—at 2 P.M. your plant and message arrived.... How you were able to concern yourself with X'mas, anniversaries, birthdays etc last May or June.... Anyway <u>everyone</u>—Salka, Beckers, Mosses, Brandts, Trumbos, Sam Spiegel, a guy named Jack Solomon, Premingers, Dick Wilsons, Parrishes—everybody (I've left out hundreds) wanted to be remembered to you....*

December 28 marked the end of my father's first six months in confinement, and winter struck the area with full force, dropping to five below. When it wasn't snowing it was extraordinarily clear and the sky radiantly blue. Physically he was holding up about even.

Ring: *I probably look pretty pallid, but in general I feel fine.*

I don't know how closely you are following events on Broadway. Apparently King Lear is in pretty solid on Broadway despite mild dissent from [Clive] Barnes....

In the field of the cinema, my father said it was Judy Holliday all the way.

...I don't know why I mention these things at all. Happy New Year to Katie, Joe, Polly, James and Frances—Ring

MY MOM DELAYED giving her final judgment about the Oscar (the newspaper story had appeared locally but didn't get much play) until after consulting with a variety of friends. She then decided not to do anything about it. The consensus was that any good accomplished (in terms of publicity) might be negated by some irritation due to the seemingly smart-aleck attitude toward the award in general. Moreover, some people thought my father would work in the community again—at least partially—so no point in promoting antagonism among certain characters who at the moment were only neutral.

Saturday.

Frances: *Darling angel lamb—I'm not quite as thin. I weigh 112½ lbs—my hair is longer. I know, still no picture but sometime someone'll break down and take one of me. . . .*

I meanwhile (having been put on a diet) had just knocked off two pounds, and my mom concluded I was terribly interested in the whole process.

Frances: *My God—do you think you'll be able to stand having two of us going on about diets when you come home? String bean and Jimsy and Miss Turnip send their greatest hugs and kisses.*

Also, we were introduced to a new sitter. An old French lady named Delavau who lived around the corner on Primrose. Polly had taken off for the whole night. My mother was visiting the Jarricos for an evening's amusement. And old Delavau read *Heidi* to us.

Jan. 1, 1951.

New Years, always a pretty pathetic holiday, was even more so here . . . , wrote Ring, whose predictions regarding the international scene weren't materializing with the rapidity he would have liked. But, he said, the general shape of events was as he anticipated.

Ring: *Only the blindness of a few characters to even their short-range self-interest is delaying the process, and I still think the odds favor a quite prolonged period of peace (or maybe absence of large military conflict is a better phrase for it).*

Now that a little time had gone by, my father said, he wanted to hear more about the hairline scar my mother dismissed so casually right along with her casual dismissal of the whole accident. And while she was at it, how did she look generally, disfigurements and all.

Ring: . . . *Give my regards right back to all those people who sent theirs and tickle the young ones for me, except Joe, that is, who hasn't got any ticklish places since he is all skin and bones and muscle. I've been wondering what a girl who was kind of giggly and rough-house when she was seven gets to be like when she comes close to being eight, and if you have any information on this subject, please let me know.*

My father didn't see how his Oscar proposal could be regarded as irreverent or even a joke. He had just hoped to realize a little cash and useful publicity. He said actually the idea of doing it publicly came second when it dawned on him that the public relations value might be the major of the two elements involved.

Jan. 4.

Ring: *Can there be anyone in or out of Hollywood to whom our kind of issue could conceivably appeal to whom censorship by blacklist isn't of more moment than the formal dignity of the Academy?*

My dad said if he weren't in bad circumstances, then someone might possibly say it was a smart-aleck gesture, but how could Jean Hersholt himself question the reasonableness of the standards behind his offer?

We got our car back and although the other driver might have been at fault after all, my mother didn't think it mattered. Our Ford was in good shape, she kind of liked her scar (with its slant)—and it would fade in time. All her other bruises were pretty well gone. She said she had gotten a bad shaking, but not too bad all in all. Just scared about what might have been. *I look great,* she wrote, *or as great as I can without you.*

Frances: *Oh my love I wake every morning now with the joyous realization that each day (no matter how long it takes to pass) brings your homecoming closer. What I would really like to do—is not* wake—*but sleep till you're back. But I can't, can I? . . . [A]fter Katie's birthday—it'll be sooner and so on and so on and so on. . . .*

Joe is really straining for you, dearest.

He wanted to be shown on the calendar just how long, and a little over three months seemed too long. Jim was recovering from a bad siege of runny nose, etc. But my mother said it probably wasn't going to take long for him to make the connection between "Daddy's picksha" and Daddy.

I had now dropped five pounds, and my mother said I only had one stomach. It was slightly large, she said, but there was just one of them.

After the snow on the ground in Danbury finally disappeared, it started snowing again. The ground was covered once more and my father was brooding about his prison habits. Wondering if they would carry over to domestic life on the outside. Probably not the reflexive bed making, he concluded, or sweeping upon rising, but his change in eating routine might linger. For more than six months he hadn't missed a meal on a three-a-day basis. And, it shamed him to reveal it, but he was packing away plenty of candy in between. Other eating-habit changes included an addiction to the prison brand of coffee merged with milk and sugar. And in the name of a balanced diet: an enforced conversion to coleslaw. It was practically the only form of salad available. This was the longest my father had ever gone without drinking. Several people who worked with tractors in the garage on the outside got hold of antifreeze and strained it through some kind of cotton thing, but he heard this was also done at Lewisburg where a few inmates had expired. And there was something used in the mimeograph machine containing alcohol. My father used the mimeograph machine all the time—but, he said, he wasn't tempted.

He promised that his next letter would be along less narcissistic lines.

Granny visited and declared that it marked the end of two-thirds of the sentence. But being a fundamentally conservative type, she hadn't adjusted yet to the meritorious good-time reduction so her calculation was based on the April 29 date.

The Lady's Not for Burning and *Best Plays of 1949–1950* had been released to my father.

JAN 10.

> DEAR KATHARINE—
>
> I almost said "Dear Potato Dumpling" but then I thought maybe that wouldn't be a good pet name for you any more because from what I hear you have been losing a lot of pounds. How many is it now? Of course really you don't have to lose more pounds at all. What you should do is just not gain any. . . .
>
> I was thinking about what to send you for a birthday present and I finally decided the best thing would be just love. But when I tried to put my love for you into the envelope along with this letter, it wouldn't fit and I had to make a separate package of it which I wrapped up in some invisible wrapping paper and addressed with invisible ink and have sent so it will arrive in the same mail as this letter. If you haven't noticed it yet, look around and when you open it please give some to Joe and Jimmy.
>
> DADDY

Thursday—Jan 11.

Frances: *Please don't worry about your profile because I'm not as tight as I might be . . . not as cadaverous as I was. . . . Honey dear I'm also glad to hear that your smoking is contingent on mine . . . maybe I'll cut down then—although I don't really anticipate that. Actually I don't imagine it'll be long before all our old patterns are reestablished—which won't be such a bad thing at that. . . .*

I had lost six pounds and my mother said I looked a lot better. (This was getting to be a goddamn theme.) And we celebrated my birthday with a party. A fried chicken lunch for eleven girls and Joe. And instead of the usual baskets full of candy and what my mother called junk, we each got a roll of assorted Life Savers and a package of gum. Cupcakes and Popsicles. The favors were pins with suggestive messages: STOP, ICY, CAUTION, etc. Then we went to see Bing Crosby in *Mr. Music.* My father's birthday letter arrived and I said, "Oh, I know—a hug." And then the whole thing was over even though I didn't turn eight until 2:30 A.M. (January 14).

My mother hadn't had a single radio show since her return. She said maybe there would be a movie job, although at the moment she wasn't sure she had an agent.

Ninety-one days to go and my father was looking forward to the added grants and privileges to come with the passing of the seven-month mark: eligibility for the pre-release house, which featured individual rooms with doors, curfew advanced to eleven-thirty, and, instead of army-type cots, something approximating a bed with a relatively soft mattress, wide enough so you could turn over and still remain within the borders.

Regarding cooked cabbage and sauerkraut, frequent items on the prison menu, he said, his resistance was still formidable, fortified by exposure to the forceful smell of it in huge quantities.

He received an unsatisfactory communication from the parole board. It contained the words *No change in the order of denial is indicated at this time,* which my father was inclined to interpret as the final word.

I attended the First Presbyterian Church of Hollywood with

Diane White's family—and intended to become a permanent fixture there but spent a good part of the afternoon alternating between the Bible and the Whites' TV. My stepbrother Peter assured my mother that my church attendance was a passing thing.

The William Morris office assured my mother of their faith, interest, etc., and said they were doing their damndest to get her work.

Jan 18 (88).

Ring: *... The only reason I didn't answer your letter ... before today ... is that I had to devote myself last night to the care of a boil (now past the crisis) and the preparation of a debate for the local debating society, before which another Californian and I made our debuts tonight.*

The subject, my father explained, was "Resolved: that jails serve a useful social function." The other Californian and teammate upheld this proposition with *the crafty argument* that jails promoted crime and crime held society together. Since my father and his teammate (on the negative side) maintained that nothing could be achieved by force and that anybody who said it could was upholding the un-American and un-Christian doctrine that the ends justified the means, all speakers were in substantial agreement in their opposition to the prison system, and the judges declared the affair a draw. My father said a splendid time was had by all. It was a busy social week. Sunday night he was entered in a bridge tournament for the institutional championship.

Jan 19.

Ring: *New England has just played a malicious trick on me. Inured as I am to the idea that come the signs of spring it will be time to return to you, I awoke this morning to a display of thun-*

der, lightning and April-type showers, and walked out as the clouds dispersed into a warm, vernal atmosphere. Now a series of meteorological anti-climaxes lie ahead.

Thursday Night.

Frances: *Every day is just a lovely day because it's another one gone by.*

Jimmy can practically read—he's making such progress—Did I tell you I'm reading "Heidi" to the children and that I wish I loved it as much as they do. We did get a fine laugh ... though— I said that when I got mean and shrill I was like Fräulein Rottenmeier and they laughed in recognition—so you see I haven't changed a bit. ...

Jan 21 (85).

Ring: *We got through the first round of the bridge tournament today but even that excitement in the same week as a debate isn't quite enough to relieve the monotony. It would be better if I were functioning on the book but I've hardly advanced during the very month in which I counted on doing the most. ...*

Sunday.

Frances: *Darling, I know it sounds prejudiced, but I'm sure you'll agree with me when you see him. Jimmy Lardner is the most wonderful almost 2½ year old there is.*

My mother said he was reminiscent of Jimmy Savo, some vaudeville character with gleaming eyes and bulging cheeks.

A RECENT DEVELOPMENT opened up a subject that previously stumped my father. His ex-wife, Silvia, acquired a 1951 Pontiac to replace her 1941 Chevrolet. (Her employers paid for it outright.) It was two-tone job. Gray on the bottom and baby blue on top. As the signs of a long shortage increased, my father worried about our car situation and Silvia's but didn't see how to meet both needs (or either for that matter) and couldn't really make much of our hardships with a '47 item in face of hers with a '41. He didn't know quite what the situation was— but if waiting lists were necessary, maybe my mother should jump on one. Even if deposit money had to be borrowed from Granny.

Johnny Black, Vicky Brandt, Joe, and I (among others) unearthed lots of cowboys, Indians, buffaloes, and pioneers in the empty lot near our place. About ten thousand in all. Little play ones about two inches tall. They were made of plastic and we didn't know how they got there. But they were perceived as buried treasure. They were probably molded rejects before they came to be great loot.

Jan. 24.

Ring: *You have succeeded eminently in whetting my parental appetite in regard to young James (Savo) Lardner. I hope next April will find him in some need of being tossed in the air . . . the only beneficial use to which my arm and shoulder exercises can be put is in flinging him about—after, of course, whatever readjustment period it takes before he accepts me as something more than an intruder in the maternal bed and general domestic routine. I'm also developing a good deal of curiosity concerning the other four creatures and look forward to resuming my paternal function. For that matter I'm anxious to resume my husbandly function too.*

. . . Late bulletin on the astounding relation of smoking to weight: In eight days since resuming I have lost four and a half of the nine pounds I gained.

Frances: *Oh Ring it's too long—much too long—but getting shorter. . . . NO More BOILS!!*

JAN 26 (80).

Ring: *I want you to convey an earnest message to Herbert [Biberman], who I hear is still keeping office hours and organizing . . . in behalf of a nonexistent cause. . . . Now that the parole issue no longer exists and neither . . . do the Hollywood Ten, there is no constructive direction activity can take. Mind you, I am not so naive as to say there is no possibility of activity . . . but . . . am resolutely and irrevocably against agitation for agitation's sake. Take publicity, for example. It is the one thing we have all had a serious overdose of and the thing most devoutly to be avoided from here on. . . .*

Thursday.

Frances: *The last two days . . . heavenly—somehow the smog's been temporarily blown away and the air . . . delicious . . . quite hot, but very clear . . . with just enough of a breeze. I long for . . . small Plymouth . . . the convertible part. . . . Do you think— someday. . . .*

Cleo was planning to meet Trumbo when he was released and take about a week or two getting home. When Joe and I got wind of this we said no way and were assured our parents weren't planning any such thing. But there was talk of a small trip without us sometime after my father returned.

Polly was about to take off on a vacation. My mother said her depressions had increased and she hoped a week would help.

Frances: *[T]here's no question of the fact that she richly deserves [it]. On the other hand there is the strong possibility that it may prove to be just a "lost weekend. . . ."*

Saturday—79 days to go.

Frances: *Yesterday I finally went on a job interview that looks promising—an independent feature called "Skid Row."... The part I'm being considered for (an alcoholic) is being rewritten, of course....*

Poll departs tonight ... and I'm ... praying ... all three children stay well while she's gone....

Frances: *The weather's gloomy ... cloudy and cold—which doesn't help my disposition.... I stopped by the Roberts office yesterday during my job hunting.... They're always so sweet and friendly and I'm always so grateful to get that kind of reception that my cheerfulness should have carried over till today.... I've gotten more and more short tempered and you know how hideous I am during these flare ups. Terribly penitent afterwards, but that doesn't do much good.... If only I could curb myself—if only counting to ten helped or something....*

Jan. 29.

Ring: *You may have noted ... a seeming contradiction between my advertising proposal* [to sell Oscar] *and my attitude toward publicity in my admonition to Herbert. But actually the difference is simply a dramatic expression of what I feel is a drastically changed situation. Though pessimistic, I favored a measure of effort prior to the original parole hearing; was against it ... once the major opportunity was lost; called for an outburst of energy when the Blau decision restored a possibility of effective action; and now make an earnest plea for general acceptance of the need for demobilization and the craving for obscurity which I for one propose to indulge.*

DEAR KATIE,

Thank you for your very nice letter. I don't know where you got the pretty writing paper but I'll make a guess that it was a birthday present. I wonder if an eight year old girl looks enough like a seven year old girl so I'll be able to tell whether Mommy kept the same old Potato Dumpling or traded her in on a new one. . . .

LOTS OF LOVE DADDY

After asking around, my mother concluded that there wasn't a car shortage after all and the prices were frozen. So a new one could wait until my father came home, unless he felt strongly about doing something sooner.

Thursday—74 days.

Frances: *Darling, for no special reason that I can think of, it occurs to me . . . I may as well confess right now that although I read over several times in fact, the letter about doubling conso- nants, I never . . . studied it or memorized the rules. . . . [S]ome- time before you return I'll have the thing learned—unless of course I discover that my not knowing . . . is one of my fatal charms—in which case I may just save that letter for our children when they get to whatever grade it is one has to get to to learn such things. I myself skipped that one as you know.*

My mother read Trumbo's poem Saturday night at a party and never did so well.

Frances: *No new news on my job thing—still being rewrit- ten. . . .*

Honey dear—how about a convertible—Wouldn't it be nice and . . . much more sensible . . . in this part of the country . . . , pro- posed my mother. *Some people . . . think . . . we should do some- thing about getting a car now. . . . If you want to empower me to undertake this transaction—I want to know how much power I've got. I also want to know how <u>we</u> feel about cars—what make etc. Because like the citizens of Bali, about whom I recently saw some* *film, I believe in arbitration and discussion and an arrival at a completely unanimous opinion.*

My parents agreed in their desire for and expectation of congenial unanimous determination of the car question. But they were miles apart (my father said) on at least one aspect of it. Because the main reason for even considering buying one at this time (of all times) was the long-range economy involved, which was in his present opinion: a standard, hardtop, two-door job for us.

My father's move to the pre-release house got postponed pending an institutional policy decision but would probably take place the following week.

Saturday.

Frances: *This one has to be short . . . for many reasons— Among them Jimmy who wants attention. . . . Ring—he's delicious, enchanting, sensitive, good, well-adjusted (horrible word), beautiful, strong, manly, kind. He burst into tears the other day worrying about a small cat that wouldn't come down out of a tree. Jimmy was afraid it couldn't get down. Actually the silly thing didn't want to get down. Anyway I think it was a surprising display of concern for another creature's welfare.—Oh, wait till you see.*

Katharine said I was to tell you that the writing paper was not a birthday present—just a piece of indulgence on her mother's part—for no reason—

She read the letter very well—protesting all the time that she couldn't.

A NEW ANGLE on the car thing hit my father in the night. The main reason for buying one at all was long-range economy. But now he wasn't sure this was sound doctrine. He said it might be franker to regard it as an extravagance and go ahead and do it anyway. His new notion derived from two facts. The kind of transportation he'd get out of Danbury would be a seventy-dollar non-negotiable tax-less coach ticket, which would take another hundred dollars to convert to a Pullman fast train with berth. And he was striving (with some promise of success) to get fifty dollars in cash instead—with the idea of putting it toward a plane ticket. The second fact was that cars cost about three hundred dollars less in Detroit than in LA.

Feb. 5 (70).

Ring: *This makes it an attractive idea for you to follow the frequent practice of turning a car in in L.A. (getting the higher-price on the turn-in) and accepting delivery in Detroit. . . .*

Of course, the cheapest procedure would be for my father to go to Detroit, pick up a car, and drive it home. But a more pleasant one, he concluded, would be for my mother to meet him there and the two of them make the trip home together. He said the savings on the car would roughly cover her fare, the driving expense, and room and board (for five or six days) en route. They would also be having their vacation trip. It would be a nice time of year, etc. My father was kind of taken with the idea.

Ring: *. . . How do you react? How would the children react?*

They closed the pre-release house indefinitely to save fuel. Therefore no private room and no comfortable bed. No seven letters a week and four visiting hours a month.

My mother saw *Born Yesterday* and said Judy Holliday was as good as was expected. She hoped Holliday would prove her ability at some other sort of character but even if she didn't, she said, *the girl's great. So she's not as versatile as I am. . . .*

Tuesday.

Frances: *Sixty Nine days and that's not bad. . . .*

No California season ever produced the sudden switches in temperature that existed around Danbury, reported my father. Yesterday it was warm and springlike, with the last traces of ice and snow all washed away by a pleasant rain. Then temperatures plummeted, the rain turned into a blizzard, and the next day— *colder than the bosom of the heroine of "Bell, Book and Candle" before her conversion,* he explained.

Feb. 8.

Ring: *And as for the frustration on change of quarters . . . I can still absorb in stride what is known in local circles as 66-and-a-getup.*

Friday—Feb. 8.

Frances: *. . . The Detroit thing would have been just wonderful* [convertible or not]. *. . .*

But my mother didn't know if it could be worked out. The car situation had changed considerably since she began making inquiries and she was told dealers couldn't make the Detroit sort of arrangement because there was a shortage after all.

Frances: [B]*ut if it doesn't work—we'll have our trip after you get home—if it's only a long weekend. Darling—please consider the convertible idea terribly seriously—I know it's hazardous, but after all Joe was just about the age Jim will be when he first had me drive him around . . . and I was much more jittery then. . . .*

For one of the really pleasant things, said my mother throwing caution to the wind, was the business of driving around in the sun. Since she didn't anticipate our finding a house with bathing terraces, and since Joe and I also felt very strongly about having a convertible, and since, as my father put it, the whole question of a car was really a luxury, she was for shooting the works and getting what we all wanted.

Frances: *I love you and so do all the children & Polly. . . .*

Feb 12 (62—see below).

Ring: [S]*ince even a day gets to seem important at this stage, it is pleasant to report that I will leave here Sunday morning, April 15th instead of the 16th . . . "meritorious good time" having been recomputated. . . .*

It was too bad there were such complications to the Detroit idea, wrote my father, and it did seem pretty impractical in view of them.

Ring: *. . . As for the convertible issue, you must have known you had me licked when you enlisted the children (or they volunteered) on your side. . . . only hitch . . . now . . . you may well find you can't get your choice of model in a scarce market. . . .*

Well, it turned out the Detroit idea was still uppermost in everyone's minds—and all hands were concentrating on its fruition.

Sunday.

I had a sort of pleasant evening yesterday, wrote my mother.

Louise Losey took off for Palm Springs with the Howard Koches, and Joe Losey invited her out to dinner and the Golden Gloves tournament. She hadn't sat through so much boxing in years and although, she said, a great deal of it was boring, she enjoyed the whole business. She said the fight crowd was a lot friendlier than other sports enthusiasts. And she had a fairly good time, even though she questioned the usefulness of the sport.

Frances: *Polly is in fine shape and seems to have returned to her tasks with renewed energy and will. I'm very floundery at this point because of no work, but will probably be considerably perked up next week when the rewritten version of "Skid Row" is given me to read.... I only hope something comes of it. I need to work ... the problems of the interpretive artist are countless....*

The only acting exercise my mother had was reading to us. We were a very enthusiastic crowd. And old enough now for her to really witch up the witches.

Even Joe, wrote my mother.

Frances: *Remember when he couldn't bear hearing about Bambi's mother? He's still as sensitive, but has made himself get tougher—growing up, I guess.*

Jimmy has a cute new trick, he adds our last name on to everyone else's now, so that the world is filled with Lardners.

The second bridge tournament concluded with my father and his partner finishing 450 points behind the winners and about 3,500 ahead of the rest of the competitors. And more important, he was granted his request for the private-cell house basically intended for night workers. The new quarters lacked human-being beds, but they promised the advantages of solitude, a window, radiator, toilet, and sink in each cell. My father hoped under these conditions to focus his remaining two months on a film story. But if he didn't get anywhere with it, he would return to the book, the first twenty thousand words of which had already been delivered to the authorities for review.

Granny dropped by in a reddish dress she was afraid was too loud for midwinter prison visiting. But in the course of the visit she offered to help finance the car.

A Dodge-Plymouth dealer in Glendale said no problem arranging Detroit delivery deal so long as a definite order was placed by mid-March for an April 16 guaranteed delivery. He'd allow $750 on the Ford. A convertible in Detroit with no extras was going to cost about $370 more than a four-door sedan.

Wednesday.

That's a large difference for the convertible, said my mother. *But wouldn't it be nice, honey.*

My father hadn't intended to write again that week because he had nothing to say in addition to his letter of the previous night. But then my mother's of Wednesday came and he wanted to let her know that he was excited she could swing the car deal. He was now in sympathy with her fondness for convertibles and promised permanent acquiescence if she decided it was the best idea.

Feb. 16.

Ring: ... *The first thing Monday morning, April 16th, seems to be the time for delivery. If it turned out to be considerably easier for you to get a night plane and arrive Monday morning, I would take the train and do the same. But I'd rather spend Sunday night with you than in a Pullman berth and if you could arrange to get there Sunday afternoon or evening, I would contrive to fly and do likewise.*

Frances: *But, I do think that there's enormous pleasure to be had from a convertible for all of us.*

Housing, however, was the big problem, said my mom. We couldn't continue on in our little house after my father got out. But we'd worry about that later. It was just that thinking of car costs led to housing costs, which led to housing needs. And the unfurnished-houses-to-rent situation was as bad as ever. Well, *Lah dee dah!* she crooned.

[But] *to get back to* [the] *car.... * [A] *black convertible or ... a grey one ... ?*

Frances: *Shall I meet you on the morning of the 16th in the main hotel—at the airport—at the Plymouth factory—where? Do we wear red carnations?*

... *Did I tell you Poll's been going around with a nice guy named "Brother" who is a cousin of Paul's (her former swain). Anyway Brother (who is a great friend of Katharine & Joe's) and Polly have gone off with K & J horse back riding and Jimmy and I are keeping each other company. It's very sweet of Poll—but she's gotten herself into this by "promising" and once you "promise" you're cooked. Apropos of nothing at all Katie needs a great deal of love and ego bolstering for all her lazy ways. She's far too much like me. I've said that before.*

MONDAY—FEBRUARY 19—55.

Frances: *My dear dear Ring Lardner Jr.... Will you stop worrying about the amount of work you'll be able to do. You'll ... get some done or you won't, but I don't want you feeling pressured—not yet anyway, honey! And now that I've decided that you mustn't be pressured—about how many pages are 20,000 words? ... [S]omehow you've got to have a chance to write because you want to, and* <u>not</u> *because it's going to bring home the bacon.... Ring I think you ought to develop a more artistic temperament and stop being such a mathematician! Oh Lord—I sound like the fellow who told Sylvia J. that she ought to stop stuttering....*

Frances: *Darling—I'm sort of against plane rides that are uncertain. I don't know how long it'll take you to get to Detroit, but I want it to be as fast as possible after your release....*

It seemed a possibility existed at other places, and my mother wanted my father to check on it. If a member of one's family were there to pick up the inmate—he could be released at midnight the night before his regular release date. At least she knew it existed at Trumbo's place.

Feb 19 (55).

Ring: ... *Tell Katie and Joe that I love them and miss them and that even if they give permission for us to make a slow return together, I will see them by the time Joe is seven years and ten days old.*

As for the release situation my mother mentioned above—there was no such custom at FCI Danbury because the town was fairly accessible to the metropolitan centers from which most of its inmates descended. And a large percentage of them were whisked away by relatives when the time came. My father said there would be midnight exits nightly under the system my mother heard about.

Twenty thousand words can range from forty to eighty pages of a book. It depended on how the book was set up.

Thursday.

Frances: *Your generosity of the car matter is overwhelming. ... Are you sure you won't really be wild at me for being extravagant? The difference in payments a month will be about $25 ... between the convertible and the cheapest 2 door coupe. The $750 we'd get for the Ford will be exactly right for the down payment.*

... By the time you get this it'll be 50 days and that's practically nothing. ... I'll be in Detroit on the 15th if you can be there then. ...

Feb 25.

Ring: *Regarding our rendezvous seven weeks hence, I don't think you should undertake too blithely to make it the 15th until you have checked the schedule, with the necessary switch at Chicago. ...*

My father was afraid of my mother having to make a night trip and find herself with a wasted Sunday.

Ring: . . . *Anyway, let me know sometime soon when you might sensibly and conveniently arrive and I will try to synchronize accordingly. I'll find out in the next week or so definitely but I'd guess that the earliest I could make it would be around 5 P.M.*

I'm perfectly aware that all this detailed planning is rather ludicrous at this point and I do it in the teeth of the predictable letdown that will set in when everything's arranged and there's still a grim waiting period. But . . . I ask your indulgence. You'll have to be very gentle and tolerant with me these next 49 days—and very likely for a few weeks thereafter. For my part the only thing I can promise is—

MUCH LOVE—RING

. . .

DEAR KATIE AND JOE,

It's beginning to get a little warmer here which makes me feel good because I know that soon it will be spring and a little more than three weeks after spring starts it will be time for me to start home.

I want very much to see you and Mommy and Jimmy and Polly. It seems like about three years since I saw you last but I guess that can't be right. If it were right, then you would be 10 and 9 years old and Jimmy would be 4½. And gosh, Pete would be almost 15 and Ann would be almost 13. I don't think I want you all to be that old yet.

LOTS OF LOVE,
DADDY

There was plenty of excitement at our house with Jim requiring stitches after running into the coffee table, thereby cutting his chin and bleeding all over the place. *A terrifying specta-cle,* declared my mother.

Those stitches! she wrote. *By now I'm so tough to it, that I was able to stand by and be of some use to the doctor, but I know I could never have watched it before the accident. . . .*

It took two nurses, the doctor, my mother, and some mummy wrapping to hold Jim still for the few minutes' "cauterizing." He was kind of knocked out with sedatives but fine after the whole or-deal, with the sutures and a bandage way more than was necessary.

Horrified, I watched the slop of his morning oatmeal dribble into the gauzy thing hanging from his chin, advancing toward cohabitation with the wound.

Tuesday—47 days.

Oh he's wonderful, wailed my mother. *Wait till you see him. Did I tell you that now that he's caught on to this talking business his use of it is just spectacular?*

Frances: *. . . All right, my darling—if you want a grey con-vertible you'll have it—even though I certainly hadn't made up my mind by any means.*

Wednesday—46 days.

Frances: *I'll be gentle and you too, please. . . . If you're mak-ing fun of me when you ask for gentleness and understanding, and are simply using my too often repeated words as a mild re-proof—it'll get you nowhere. I don't think you really are. . . . It's just that you used to be tempted to do so. . . .*

Ben Margolis (the attorney) wanted final approval from my mother to go ahead with a suit against the woman who ran into her and she couldn't decide to do it. It could wait until after she had a chance to discuss it with my father but, Margolis said, he'd never run across so much reluctance in his life.

Saturday—43.

Pretty shocking news about Gale and the other people called by the committee, wrote my mother—*especially Gale....*

Four actors—Larry Parks, Gale Sondergaard, Howard DaSilva, and Sterling Hayden—and four writers—Richard Collins, Waldo Salt, Paul Jarrico, and Robert Lees—received subpoenas.

Frances: ... [I]*t's so terribly cruel and unnecessary. It's so pointless.*

There wasn't much about it in the local papers, but the town and especially the studios were humming with speculation about future events.

March 4.

Ring: *I wasn't making fun of your appeals for gentleness and understanding.... It's just that this place occasionally gives one the feeling that by God, people had better treat one with some appreciation of what it means to be shut up for a long time—which is basically nonsense ... what I want most of all is to get back to normal living ... and I'm sure I'll very quickly find myself wishing people would hit on other topics of conversation than what it's like to be in jail.... I don't anticipate any serious problems of personal readjustment.... What does frankly concern me more is the problem of what I incline to call professional adjustment though you would be more apt to use the word "artistic" and I'd compromise on a term somewhere between the two if I could think of one.*

... I've become convinced that through inheritance, circumstances and my own bad judgments, I got to be something of a public figure before becoming a writer instead of the other way around, and I propose to make a belated effort to restore the proper balance. Since one manifestation of this resolve will be a firm refusal to make any public appearance or take any public

political action until such time as my own estimate of my professional (or artistic) standing seems to justify it and although this is at least as much a reaction to the popularity I have achieved in certain quarters as it is to the unpopularity I have achieved in others, it may be regarded by some as a cautious retreat in a time of panic. So be it.

More serious is the relatively late start I am making in book writing. This does have its advantages: There is little chance of my writing a really bad book at this point, and none at all of starting out with one fine effort and never being able to equal it—as happens often with the young writer whose first novel is an autobiographical outpouring. But there is a likelihood, even a probability, more hazardous at 36 than at 23, of my mastering the craft slowly and doing a couple of only fair jobs before I produce a good one.

I think I would have abandoned movie writing by now even if I hadn't been pushed out of it. One reason I clung to it was that I couldn't accept the stock formulation that movie work was all prostitution in contrast to the virtuous respectability of "serious" writing. I still don't accept it. But the catch about Hollywood is that you have to be extremely good at it (and it helps to possess subordinate talents such as directing) in order to surmount the restrictions and limitations. And I was never, nor I think could be, better than a fair screenwriter, though money success and a natural hesitancy to face facts obscured this realization for a long time.

There's nothing wrong of course with continuing to be a moderately competent movie writer, as so many of our friends do, if it is pretty clear that you wouldn't accomplish anything constructive in any other line of work—any more than a short order cook should seek a new trade in despair because he realizes his talent is on a lower level than that of Escoffier. But in my case, as of now, it isn't clear to me, and can hardly be to anyone else, that I *can't do something rather good in the special sort of book I want to write. It's also possible that I might be able to turn out a play of merit but I have less confidence in that direction and will probably never try it unless something happens to provoke a more persuasive impulse.*

And now, to draw on the gag file, let's talk about you for a change. What do <u>you</u> think of my performance?

LOVINGLY,
RING

March 5, 1951.

Dear hibiscus blossom—The pen with which I started this became contumacious and had to be retired . . . , wrote my father, whose absorption with a single theme made it necessary for him to write immediately again. Mainly he'd omitted a comment on my mother's question about suing her adversary in the West Hollywood crossing duel of last December. He thought she should proceed if Ben Margolis felt it was the sound thing to do. However, this green light was not a sign, he said, of blanket trust in the professional man. His sentiments toward the medical profession (never tender to begin with), for example, had hardened recently due to what looked like a misguided experiment on his face. Any surgery was going to leave you wondering about the conspicuousness of the residual scar, he admitted, but this one threatened to leave the scar *and* the original condition intact. Instead of a bump there was now a bump with a crater in it *like an extinct volcano in miniature.*

dear DaDDY—, Joe began. The rest he dictated to my mother. *I miss you and school is fine*, etc. Westland had gotten a new bicycle. And two friends tried to crash into him whenever he got on it. *The new byke is so fast that only about once they crash into me. . . .* The rest of the message was about a fire station being created in woodwork, an activity my brother favored over block play because with blocks he was told to clean up. And Lola—his new teacher—was nice. *So with our swings and our school ladder we make big contraptions. Contraptions are real slick . . .*

In the meantime, there was quiet concerning the new investigation. The only story in Hollywood about the people subpoenaed came from Bob Kenny's office, and not the committee, although the committee ran an original piece in relation to Larry Parks and Edward G. Robinson about two weeks before.

The New York Times, Friday, February 23, 1951.

The House Committee on Un-American activities has sent two investigators to Hollywood armed with subpoenas for at least ten movie figures who may testify in a new inquiry into communism in the film capital.

One subpoena names Larry Parks, star of "The Jolson Story." The others name writers, directors and producers....

Representative Bernard W. (Pat) Kearney, Republican of New York, has identified Mr. Parks as one of the witnesses he wants to question in connection with the case of Edward G. Robinson, film actor....

Edward G. Robinson appeared voluntarily before the committee in December to deny that he ever was connected with subversive organizations.

There was much speculation, but nothing concrete. The subpoenas ordered the witness to appear in Washington to testify on March 21. But the date was subject to change. There was a lot of talk about the remainder of the original nineteen witnesses being recalled, as well as new people. My mother said the whole thing was disgraceful. She couldn't see what they hoped to accomplish.

Frances: *Oh baby—what an eternity—forty days from tomor-row. How's your cheek? I love you and can't wait—What a thing to say to you.*

FRANCES LARDNER

IT SO HAPPENED that whenever Grandma Marie in New York City got a letter from my mother in LA, she phoned Granny wherever she was—New York or Connecticut (Granny spent winter months in a Manhattan hotel)—and imparted all the news the latter had already heard, because my mother tended to take care of her two obligations in a single outburst. Well, such a call took place, and in the course of it Grandma put forth her idea of hopping a bus to Detroit in April in order to see my mother there. This, my father indicated, was about as delectable a scheme as had come to his attention in a long time. And it was up to my mother, he said, to scotch it. Bring the matter out into the open, he declared, by mentioning his New York visit for three or four hours on the fifteenth and, though he would be lunching with a couple of his codefendants and seeing his brother, he would work in *a quick session* with her.

Friday, March 9.

Please tell Joe that I like his letter [which Mom penned] *a lot and. . . . Maybe we can work out some contraptions together at home. . . . Don't tell him, because I don't want to wound him, that he shouldn't have spelled 'bike' b-y-k-e.*

Ha!

Much love to Polly, Katie and J.M. [*M* stands for "Mark."] *I love you.*

RING

March 11.

Ring: ... *I'd like to make a couple of things clear on the transportation situation, and then ... go ahead and do what seems most sensible. ... One is that I don't want you to subject yourself to any serious inconvenience or ... likelihood of arriving a wreck in order to save ... money.*

On the other hand, my father said, there was something very satisfying about economics. [E]*ven if ... dissipated by later extravagances.* Also, his proposal for a Sunday-night rendezvous was based on the fact that it would be a nice thing, but not one to sacrifice any other important considerations for. My father pointed out that there was also something to be said for them having a day together and then a night. And the train would be at least as easy, maybe more so, for him to work than a plane.

He said he worried that my mother hadn't worked in a couple of months and had voiced no complaints about it. It concerned him more when she didn't mention it. He wondered if it looked like a blacklist situation.

Ring: *Tell Katie I thought her drawings were very good, especially the one of the girl with the one green eye. She's beginning to show a better sense of what people really look like, along with some special touches of her own. And say to Joe that I love his letters but right now I have to go take a big, fat shower before it's too late. ...*

My mother had the flu. The same old flu that attacked most of Los Angeles made it hard for her to concentrate. But after an irritating series of encounters with the dealer from whom she was supposed to get a special discount, she finally made arrangements for the car. She said she just wasn't cut out for bargains or vice versa. Anyway, the car was ordered from a reliable man. A gray Plymouth convertible—gray top.

Her inclination at the moment was to take American coach

to Chicago and transfer to Detroit, getting there Sunday night. But there was still time for all that.

Frances: [A]nd if all the children don't catch "the thing" from me we'll be in great shape for your return. . . .

. . .

March 13-1951.

Dear Daddy
I am having lots
of fun in school.
I thought Mom-
my was going to
write the letter but
I wanted to do it.
Oh about the big
fat baths I do not
like to take a big
fat bath I hope
you feel good.
I know the letter is short
Love
Katie
Please write.

My father was soon going to be down to what was known in local parlance as a drunk's bit. *Bit* was used for a sentence of any length—as in *a three-year bit*—and subject to a variety of quaint modifications.

He said it might be highly premature, but here were things my mother should include and not include in her luggage. He would be equipped with the items he'd left home with. What he lacked most was informal attire: slacks, shorts (outer) and perhaps two shorts (inner), and two or three informal-type shirts. He didn't arrive with a coat and should be able to get along without one if the weather was reasonable, but if my mother could conveniently carry his old gray raincoat over her arm, it might be a worthwhile precaution. The one indispensable item was his driver's license.

Granny was assigned the task of preparing maps with alternate routes because of her experience (as my father put it) in the transcontinental touring field.

Now, he said, there was practically nothing to do but *wait out this infernal month.*

My mother's flu was hanging on so the doctor came and shot her full of penicillin, but cheerfully allowed as how he didn't think it would do any good.

Wednesday.

Darling, about my spelling, began my mother, obviously wounded by the byke incident—*did I tell you what a terrible thing has happened?* A biography she was reading about Fitzgerald stressed his inability to spell properly and she was afraid it had its effectiveness.

Frances: *Maybe your return will prove to be a counter balance and I'll look things up again. It's so nice sometimes though to say with Pop-Eye—"I yam what I yam and I like it."*

My mother made a tentative reservation on the Saturday-night flight on the unscheduled.

Frances: *There's no questioning the fact that at worst I can save about $30 going unscheduled.... I'll see you Sunday night.... *<u>However</u>* and this is a big one—I prefer to take a day time flight—for a number of reasons.... They have so few planes (on the unscheduled) that even with fare being paid there is the possibility of a flight being delayed as much as a day or two.* Thus making it impossible to plan on a definite connection from Chicago to Detroit.

Frances: *I'll let you know. Of course you realize that I've practically talked myself into making an Amer. Coach reservation? You are please to go ahead and let Ellis or John make a plane reservation for you (because as we *<u>both</u>* know, once I've been stuck by a notion of yours—I can't bear to change my mind about it) and because it's important to remember that a new car can only be driven about 35 miles an hour for the first five hundred miles (with hourly rests of five or ten minutes or it'll be wrecked for life) which means that we ought to get started some time on Monday—which means that I can't wait to see you on Sunday the fifteenth . . . oh darling—the sleeplessness is starting up real bad again. Oh and while I think of it—please don't try to make me do without nods immediately. I'm really an addict and it would take months of readjustment and as I've always said I can hear everything with them anyway....*

Down Holly Drive they were making the new freeway, and it was fun to watch because of the tractors involved. On Sundays when the men weren't working we went down there to play. We mounted the tractors. Across the street there were pipes and we got on them, too, and jumped from one to another. And back across the street were nine pipes in a row. Big ones. We got down by sliding on the end pipes. The kids on the block held a contest of who was the prettiest lady and everybody chose my mother. They also indicated she was the sweetest and the nicest to the boys, which she insisted wasn't true.

Wednesday, March 14.

What do you know? I'm completely overcome by the honor, wrote my mother, *and I must say both Joe and Katharine are terribly impressed and sort of look at me in a new way—but don't you believe it—pretty mean a lot of the time.*

March 16 (drunk's bit).

Ring: ... *Your letter of Wednesday came today and about planes you seem to be making sense. About cars, though, I hope you aren't. ...*

My father was certain the thirty-five-mile-per-hour limit was a thing of the past.

[W]*e can seek expert advice on starting and abide by it. I've been figuring on a full week ... though maybe Polly will favor a more rigorous schedule. My training in early rising may create a problem and a possible solution to this and making mileage might be for you to do your last couple of hours sleeping en route every morning. Naturally you would be transported from bed to car without so much as the dislodging of a nod.*

Ever since my father had turned the pages of the book over for scrutiny (four weeks ago), he'd been expecting to report that it was on its way. (It had been approved for export.) But, he said, the process might not precede his departure so he was probably going to be leaving with both that and whatever he completed on the movie story, which, he said, wasn't going badly.

Granny visited my father and expressed the view that she had been grateful for the opportunity the last eight months had provided of seeing him more frequently than usual.

March 19.

Ring: *... Dear Katie and Joe, Your letters came Saturday and I was very happy to get them, along with Katie's pretty cat picture. ... I think it was a good contest you had on Holly Drive.*

My father would have voted for my mother as the prettiest lady on the block, too.

Ring: [A]*nd I know she has been sweet to the boys all her life.*

It was beginning to be a little bit like spring at the prison. But my father kept thinking how much nicer it would be in California. He wished he was there *climbing on tractors and jumping from one pipe to another.*

My mother, over the flu siege, went to dinner at friends', only Polly telephoned at midnight to say she wanted to step out. A "quack" who'd seen her on Thursday had her all worked up over some internal disorder so she couldn't sleep. She was generally gloomy, groaned my mother, and suddenly said she wanted to go someplace. My mother commiserated, though, and was soon going to take her to "a reputable lady doctor" to check on her troubles. She only hoped the outcome would put Polly in a better frame of mind.

She wrote the Book-Cadillac asking for a room with a double bed for April 15, and felt very forward, never having written for a reservation before.

Sunday.

Frances: *You mean you don't want the Auto Club to chart us a trip? O.K! The car will have a black top after all.*

Monday—27 days.

Frances: *... Poll was her <u>best</u> happy pulled together self today. ...*

About Olivia [Olivia Polly Garland]—*She had been told by* *that idiot doctor ... that she had an internal cyst which needed immediate operating—but today's good humor and general niceness was there <u>before</u> this afternoon's visit to a highly reputable medico ... who not only contradicted the other diagnosis, but said she was in fine shape generally. <u>Doctors!</u> Anyway the result of all this good news was that Polly said without prompting from me that maybe the next time she ought to go to a "head doctor." So of course everything's peachy with us now. But I know it's only temporary. Next week there will be another catastrophe. Ah well—*

March 21 (25).

Ring: *In case you haven't yet reached a decision on the plane matter, I have only the not very important point to contribute that if you did get into Chicago at 9:30 A.M., you could wire me in care of John and I could probably, if a seat were available, get to Detroit by midafternoon. . . . [I]t looks as if I will have to go the most costly way (about $34) in order to get there at some reasonable hour on Sunday. . . .*

I didn't mean at all that you were forbidden to do route planning ... simply that you didn't have to if you didn't want to. . . .

Only in order to lay out a route they had to decide which of the main ones they preferred and what the most important considerations were: speed, climate, scenery, minimum altitude crossing the Rockies, and so on. As my father saw it, there were three choices: *(a) through Illinois, Iowa, Nebraska to Denver, and thence thru Utah and Southern Nevada; (b) same to Denver but then south to Albuquerque and through New Mexico and Arizona; (c) to Saint Louis and then through Oklahoma and Texas Panhandle to Albuquerque, thence same as (b).*

Spring arrived. Only in Danbury, the very next day—there

was a fresh blanket of snow. But soon after, when no longer in evidence, my father optimistically began counting on a mild spell for his remaining three weeks.

By way of a footnote to the routes he already submitted, he had computed that the southernmost—via St. Louis—was definitely the shortest, by between 150 and 175 miles.

Ring: *Not all that much in a total of 2500 to 2700 miles.*

But then there was the even more southern way of about the same length through Toledo, Cincinnati, Cairo, Little Rock, southern Oklahoma, northern Texas, New Mexico, and Arizona.

At the very stage when my father's boredom with Office of Classification and Parole duties had become extreme, the place was inundated by a swell of spring business. And he said it looked to him like a close finish between his breaking point and release date.

. . .

The New York Times, **Thursday, March 22, 1951.**
LARRY PARKS SAYS HE WAS A COMMUNIST

Larry Parks became the first Hollywood witness to admit ever being a Red. He'd drifted into the Party in 1941 and drifted out again in 1945.

March 23.
I don't know when I have been so moved as by the news reported here that [actress] *Betty Garrett was in a state of collapse following the revelation of Larry's testimony,* wrote my father.

In Hollywood Mr. Parks's wife, Betty Garrett, was ordered to bed by Dr. Leon Belous, physician, the *Times* said.

It's appalling, continued Ring, *that John Wayne and the M.P.A.* [Motion Picture Association of America], *various columnists and the committee itself all had a better advance briefing on what he was going to say than she* [Betty Garrett] *apparently did.*

Larry Parks begged the committee not to force him to "crawl through the mud to be an informer" on Hollywood friends. But when Parks was threatened with contempt the hearing went behind closed doors, where according to a committee source he "came through in fine style," supplying the names of about twelve movie actors whom he had once known as fellow Communists. The actor said he never had been ordered to try to influence American thinking along Communist lines through his screen or stage roles, and added: "If you go to the movies, it is almost evident that this was not done."

The New York Times, **Thursday, March 22, 1951.**

Mr. Parks... born in Olathe, Kan., grew up in Joliet, Ill. .... acquired his beliefs and convictions from his home, a Protestant church and the public schools.

. . . [H]e is opposed to anti-semitism and believes that "every Negro child has the same right to food and shelter and education and opportunity and dignity that was granted me at birth."

According to his attorney, Parks himself was now "sick of heart and sick in bed."

MY MOTHER FINALLY decided upon the North American flight Saturday night and, she said, the Book-Cadillac confirmed for the fifteenth. With three weeks to go she was in an enormous state of excitement about my father's upcoming release. She just hoped she'd calm down when the time came. Why did he

(Dad) have to get mixed up with a "hyper-tension type," she moaned, instead of someone with a more "phlegmatic gland system"?

She would wire my father from Chicago, care of Uncle John.

Frances: *Oh—before I forget—I finally have a radio show for next Thursday—Suspense . . . I haven't any idea what I'll be playing, but judging from past performances on that show it should be a fairly important part. . . . The part in Skid Row is completely out . . . and another possibility in a Hecht picture has collapsed because the star's girl is going to play it and I can't compete with that.*

My father said he could hardly object to my mother being excited over their reunion except it might be open to criticism on the grounds of prematurity.

March 26 (20).

Ring: *Three weeks is still quite a stretch of time, especially in view of the present inflated scale of time units; . . . for instance . . . 90 of last year's seconds don't even make up a full minute. . . .*

Now that my mother had resolved on a policy of economical transportation, he was feeling guilty about the fact that his was going to be extravagant. He hadn't been able to achieve any compromise with the Federal Bureau of Prisons. It would pay his basic coach fare to Los Angeles if he were going there by train or the same to Detroit. But the bureau would not contribute a nickel to plane fare.

Ring: *In accordance with your letter of Saturday, I will instruct John to reserve me a seat on . . . American Airlines . . . leaving N.Y. at 2:55 P.M. and arriving at 5:45. . . . [I]f you get to Detroit even as much as an hour before I do . . . go on into the hotel and, depending on your mood, relax or prettify yourself, ei-*

ther of which activities are to be preferred over waiting around an airport.

My mother was leaving the travel route up to my father. But she was inclined toward the warmer parts.

Monday.

Frances: *The children are terribly happy and very sweet about the trip—and they understand that it may be a week or ten days before we actually arrive home—and the only thing I've promised is that we'll telephone sometime during the week.*

Oh—did I tell you about the job on "Suspense"? I think so, but in case I forgot to mention it—it's on Thursday—CBS.

There was absolutely nothing new on anything, she said.

Frances: *My goodness—I never knew things to be so <u>static</u> except for your homecoming.*

At the Hunters' Easter party on Sunday, my brother Jimmy consumed more candy than anybody. And somebody accidentally ate out of Joe's basket, so Ian made it up to him with the result being that he got more than any of us girls. Susan and Mary Butler were also there.

Katharine is very happy these days. It's very good for her to play with a child [Susan Butler] *her own age and Joe is Joe—* wrote my mother—*sometimes a great hero and other times such an irritant that you have to squash him! Did I tell you that Jim is going through the "no" stage already and I'm miserable that you've missed his sweetest period. . . .*

Frances: *Oh . . . darling—what a fantastic waste this . . . has been. Now that it's almost over we dare to say it. . . .*

MY FATHER SAID he also desired a warm climate. Therefore the southern route was best. It was the shortest, he said.

March 29.

Ring: *After seven days of driving, four hours difference may seem relatively as important as two weeks meritorious good time after 9½ months.*

Tell Katie and Joe that except for the fact that I love them I haven't any messages . . . that won't wait till I see them in about three weeks. . . . You might also tell Jimmy that I love him and am thinking of him, though I'm afraid a father is a pretty abstract . . . concept in his young life. And by all means include young Miss Garland [Polly] *in the distribution of my affection.*

My mother was back in bed with her lingering flu, proclaiming it had to be cured in time for her radio rehearsal the next day. And Joe had decided he didn't want a real birthday party until after she and my father returned. Settling for cake and ice cream and a few little presents on the actual day, he was going to have his boys over when they got home.

In Danbury it rained two days in a row—and my father informed us that his prejudice against eastern weather had been immeasurably fortified during the year.

March 30.

Ring: [G]*ood to hear your voice last night again after so long, though the program as a whole . . . pretty hard to take. Apparently radio is determined in its dying years to go to the grave without making any amends for its sinful life.*

One of the horrors of the place, my father said, was there wasn't a moment outside of working and sleeping hours when the sound of the apparatus wasn't in your ears. And his earplugs had been confiscated on admission.

Polly went off to an Elks dance and borrowed a dress from Kate Preminger, which my mother shortened and ironed for the occasion.

Saturday.

I think she's pleased, wrote my mother, *and . . . in a lovely mood . . . so I'm a bit more cheerful. Dear Poll—when she's fine, she's such a lovely person and we're such good friends—and I guess she thinks the same of me—I mean that when I'm fine I'm sort of all right too. Oh Lord,* my mother sighed. *What a time to be Chekovian. . . .*

Frances: *Darling—of course you'll have to fit Marie in—I thought that was decided weeks ago. As a matter of fact I received a letter from her . . . in which she faced up to the fact that her idea was a pretty silly one, but although there was no mention of* expecting *to see you I think she'd be miserable if it couldn't be arranged, no matter how briefly. . . .*

Ring, my dear, dear Ring—this part of it's almost over—just two weeks which are interminable . . . I want to hear you talk!

Granny visited my father, which was fortunate because he'd broken the right lens of his glasses in a handball game. It never could have been replaced in time for release through institutional channels. Although such a thing was strictly against regulations, my father was able to arrange for her to take the glasses into town for repair after he made it plain that he couldn't do his job without them.

He never meant to suggest he had any intention of not seeing Grandma Marie (in New York)—or *S.M.* (for "sainted mother"), he called her. The only place he was unwilling to see her was in Detroit.

Ring: [E]*n menage a trois. Plans are already under way to provide her a place in the safari to La Guardia Field, probably just behind the champagne and dancing girls.*

The coat or jacket could be scratched from the list of previously suggested items. It turned out the government was going to supply my father well in that department—for either northern or southern routes.

He said he was going to take a stab at getting to the end of his film story on the upcoming weekend in order to turn it over for censorship on Monday. This would allow five days to concentrate on thoughts of freedom.

Concerning travel routes, my father had just discovered his unfairness to the North in mentioning only the way via Denver, when in fact there was a slightly more northerly route via Omaha, Cheyenne, and Salt Lake City.

MY MOTHER RECEIVED two letters in one day, one written on March 30 and the other—April 2. The thirtieth one got waylaid to Booton, she wrote, puzzled.

Friday.

Frances: *Where is Booton? I can't tell from the postmark whether it's New Hampshire or New York.*

April 9.

Booton [is] *a mythical community in Postal folklore,* remarked my dad.

Frances: *Anyway—I'm distraught at not having come through better this week ... but it's been a busy one ... largely occupied in spending money—isn't it shocking?*

My mother now had two new dresses, a suit, and a gold velveteen coat.

Frances: *But ... I've justified my behavior on the grounds that you had urged me to do it and that everything was just "a wonderful buy." You won't see too much of this finery until we get back home, because it's kind of glamorous and not right for travelling, but oh boy wait till we're home—I will dazzle you—if that's what you want of course.*

Ring: *My dearest love—Unless I think of something urgent to say to you tomorrow . . . this will be my last letter . . . from here. . . . This is the moment then, when we synchronize our watches and make a final check on plans. . . .*

I'm sorry that I didn't do well . . . in letter writing last week but I was trying to finish my story, which goal I reached in a manner of speaking. . . .

[L]ets not ask people over to the Book-Cadillac next Sunday.

DEAR JOE AND KATIE,

It's very nice of you to let Mommy go to Detroit to meet me. Thank Polly for me too. I'm also glad that I get to be at Joe's party. I love you a lot and I'll see you in less than two weeks.

DADDY

In anticipation of my father's return we pumped Jimmy full of Daddy talk and old Jim laid on us what he thought was a huge joke, which was that Daddy was a bad boy. The idea thrilled him and he roared at the idea of a daddy being a bad boy. My mother informed him that my father was a good boy. But then, she said, let him find out for himself.

Frances: *I love you and it's practically immediately now—*

FRANCES LARDNER
2048 HOLLY DRIVE
HOLLYWOOD 28, CALIF.

Coming Home

When my father said good-bye to prison he was given an overcoat at government expense—a navy officer's black winter coat with a detachable lining and some slight imperfection, and whenever he wore it he remembered leaving the place. Granny and Albert were waiting at the gate. They drove my father to Uncle John's apartment in New York City and after a while Granny, visibly happy that my dad was over the whole ordeal, indicated she wanted to return to New Milford. What a relief for her not to have the strain of those visits anymore, thought my father. They said good-bye not knowing how long it would be before seeing each other again. From Uncle John's on West Twelfth Street my father went to East Tenth, where Dalton and Cleo Trumbo were occupying half of the house belonging to the writers Donald Ogden Stewart and Ella Winter. An old brownstone with large rooms, high ceilings, chandeliers and fireplaces, and a small garden out back, in the heart of Greenwich Village. Trumbo had been released from his institution the week before, and Cleo came from California to meet him. The three of them had midday drinks and talked about the uncertainties of the future. The whole situation had gotten much worse. Senator Joseph McCarthy had appeared on the scene. The Rosenberg case had been tried and the general anti-Red feeling was more or less at its height. The hysteria was much greater. There were all sorts of black-market jobs available before the men went to jail. But after, it was an entirely different atmosphere.

My father did see Grandma Marie, and friends Sylvia and Julian Rochelle wound up buying my father an early dinner and taking him to the airport to catch the plane to Detroit to finally implement the plan my mother and father had worked out by mail. My father's destination—the fabled Book-Cadillac Hotel. The largest building in the world when it opened in 1929, the Book feted several U.S. presidents, business moguls, movie stars, and sports figures. Babe Ruth, Spencer Tracy, and Harry S. Truman all partied there. Automotive pioneer Henry Ford and his wife, Clara, often square-danced in the hotel's ballrooms. It was the place selected for my parents' rendezvous. The next day they picked up our new Plymouth convertible from the factory (two-door, light gray) and began driving it the rest of the way across the country. It had a cutout plastic sailing ship under clear plastic on the dashboard, which must have been the *Mayflower*, the ship that delivered the Pilgrims. I think the dashboard was light blue. They didn't force the pace. It so happens that is all I know about what took place then.

After leaving Danbury it was a full week before my parents stopped off in Newport Beach to see Peter and Ann. "It was shocking how gaunt he looked," my stepsister said, recalling our dad in a black trench coat with sunken cheeks. Then it hit her, she said. "My God, he was in prison," she exclaimed. From there my parents called Holly Drive and learned Uncle John was trying to reach them. Upon contacting him, my mother and father received the sad news that Granny, alone in her bedroom, had had a stroke the evening of my father's release. Another one occurred a few days later in a New York hospital. My father didn't know if it was pure coincidence that she had had one that night. But seeing him in prison bothered her a good deal, and maybe she was holding herself together during the visits. "So there could have been some kind of significance," he concluded. "The relief of the tension," he said. "Maybe having it all over with led to the stroke."

As for me, I'll never forget the day my father came home from jail. What sticks in my mind is standing on the side of the playground waiting and waiting the whole day for his arrival at the Westland School ... then seeing him pull up in the Plymouth. I remember this feeling that he was *finally* home, and all the people standing around witnessing the momentous event.

In June when the lease was up on the Holly Drive house we moved to a bigger one on Cory Avenue just south of the Sunset Strip. The new house had a white ball hanging from a pole we could punch. We didn't stay in it very long. My parents couldn't get work. I knew my father couldn't get hired in Hollywood anymore. We left town for Mexico City, where it was cheaper to live and where we joined a community of blacklisted artists trying to make a living in the Mexican film industry. We would have more time there, reasoned my mom and dad—the same money that would last a year in Mexico would last half that somewhere else. The Butlers and the Trumbos paved the way.

HUGO BUTLER HAD BEEN living with his family in Ensenada in Baja California since the spring of 1951. And actively avoiding a subpoena since the day two U.S. marshals turned up at his home in Los Angeles. His wife, Jean, was having dinner with their four children when they arrived. Hugo, suspecting he might be summoned to testify in the new HUAC inquiry, said to her that morning, "Look, maybe I won't come home tonight. We're invited out for dinner. Come if you can or call if anything happens." When the doorbell rang at supper time, Jean knew with certainty who was outside. She looked through the little peephole and saw two guys wearing hats. She said she could tell they were from the East because no southern Californians ever wore hats. They were looking for Hugo.

"He's not here," she informed them.

"Where is he?" they asked.

She said she didn't know.

They asked her when he'd return. "We had a little disagreement," she said. "I don't know when he'll be back."

The two guys looked at each other and one said to the other, "What shall we do?" But the reply was something Jean didn't catch. They then thanked her and left.

Terrified, Jean returned to the children. Next began the elaborate business of vacating the house and finding a phone without being followed. "Honey, you better get on your horse," she told her husband when she reached him. After her mother-in-law arrived to take charge of the kids, she joined him at the restaurant where it was arranged they'd go to the Hunters' for a night or two. Jean was without toothbrush and had nothing to sleep in but a slip, and she didn't hit home for about four days. Hugo never crossed that threshold again.

In early November that same year, at the risk of getting caught, the Butler family crossed back over the border and hooked up with the Trumbos in a San Diego motel parking lot. And in three cars with luggage, a sheepdog, a Siamese cat, and seven children, the two families set out for Mexico City.

. . .

A couple of months later the five of us piled into the Plymouth and said good-bye to Polly Garland and Polly (the teacher) and the Westland School, where I was rehearsing the part of a Hopi Indian. We took off for El Paso, where we planned to pick up the Pan-American Highway and cross over into mainland Mexico. I liked the Westland School by the time we left. I loved Polly Garland and I remember her friends fondly. There were other housekeepers and a chauffeur and the man she married—Chad Hicks. *Brother* was his nickname. Just before we left he was picked up by the police and beaten. A case of the wrong man.

As for the car trip south of the border, despite occasional skirmishes over the two prevailing map-reading techniques (my mother's method was freestyle), we generally had a good time. We kids were mostly in the back with our feet on duffel bags that filled the floor space between the front and rear seats. The exception was my three-year-old brother Jim—sometimes perched on my mother's lap. One bag was square and gray, the other—cylindrical and adobe-colored like a giant hot dog. Being a convertible, our car didn't have a very big trunk, so we just loaded everything in. Along the way I took in the little villages and adobe huts, barefooted Indians, and—the farther south we got—tree-shaded plazas called zocalos. My mother doled out treats from her purse. I also contemplated the multiplication tables. Having relied heavily upon the friendliness of the little Westland store for instruction, my math skills (my parents concluded) were lacking. Joe and I were going to attend the American School in Mexico City along with other political expatriate kids.

The Trumbos found us a two-story furnished house in Las Lomas that was airy and light with lots of rooms and a backyard. We had a cook and a housekeeper because these services didn't cost much in Mexico. My parents said the pressure of the blacklist and the pressure of having been in jail was put aside for a while. They were with some of their closest friends. Shortly after, the Hunters joined us.

Living in Mexico was hard. I felt fat. In fact the entire matter—the whole six-month residency—owing to several gloomy recollections is better left alone. For one thing, I turned nine just after we arrived and was thrown a birthday bash with a piñata to celebrate. Pounding the papier-mâché creature filled with goodies to release its contents was a blast but, when the blows turned on yours truly, the merriment came to a halt. I was held down by the Butler and Trumbo kids (primarily the older ones whom I had known only briefly in LA) and spanked in the name of birthday.

And I don't remember when I started dancing. Sometime in California. I have a memory of choreographing a little number to Les Paul and Mary Ford singing "Mockin' Bird Hill" on the radio (Joe associates the tune with Polly so he assumes she also liked it) and loving *The Red Shoes*, the movie. But I can recall a dance class in Mexico City where Michael Butler called me *Katharine Lard wears a leotard*. How was I to know then that Michael felt like "one of nature's factory seconds," as he later revealed. He was a hurtful little shit, he added (as a phrase of remorse). He only hoped (he said) that his defects (which inspired the rhyme) had been tempered somewhat in the crucible of time.

Then there was the evening of strip poker.

I had hoped to round off this section with some amusing reminiscences relating to a game that took place. But because the occasion seems to have slipped the minds of the other participants, my memory of losing, being too chicken to drop my slip, and taking refuge in a closet is all I can offer. Here are some of the remarks of those I swear were there. "I don't remember that we ever played," said Michael Butler, recalling only a round with two girls named Nancy and Diana—in '57 or '58. "Zero memory," echoed his sister Susan, though she wondered if somehow it was connected to her brother's floating poker game. Chris Trumbo also drew a blank. At least he admitted it sounded like a Trumbo escapade and probably something he and his sister Nicky engineered. Then Chris wound up saying that I wanted to play so badly, I fantasized the event. "It is odd," he said, "that the loser is the one to shed clothes when the game itself is nothing but an excuse to go naked. No wonder adults seldom play strip poker but get right down to the fundamentals with a minimum of shuffling."

Well, dear reader, I'll leave you with this reflection but, as you can imagine, in light of the offending alias I obtained during dance instruction, at the time I wasn't into clothing divestment. And I'll close this chapter as we shuffled off to Granny's farm in Connecticut, which we did (after six months) when the money ran out. We were broke (there hadn't been the movie work those blacklisted guys expected in Mexico) and my grandmother Ellis had had a stroke. But at least my grim thoughts were ripening in some lovely surroundings. In Mexico there were the bike rides through the Bosque de Chapultepec, the donkey ascent to the volcano Popocatépetl, the "floating gardens" of Xochimilco. And also, there were burros loaded with firewood walking by.

New Milford

My paternal grandmother, Ellis, lived in a pre-Revolution farmhouse she purchased in 1934, the spring after my grandfather died. It was a combination dairy and tobacco farm when she bought it, with no running water or electricity, and the house had been known a generation before (by the previous owners and their friends) as "the place with eight rooms and eight fireplaces." Granny paid seventeen thousand dollars for it and nearly two hundred acres, and put that much into it for improvements—adding on a porch, the kitchen, a pantry, and quarters for the help. She bought a couple of horses, cows, pigs, and chickens and raised quite a bit of stuff that was useful during the war when eggs and butter were rationed. My grandmother didn't need all that acreage but she liked the idea of nobody being able to build anywhere close.

Her sons John, Jim, and Ring were all working on newspapers in New York, and David had just started attending the Taft School—a boarding school not too far away in Watertown, Connecticut. My grandmother was forty-six at the time and thinking of a future by herself with visits from her sons, and the isolation didn't bother her. Albert Mayer lived with her to drive and take care of the outside. He had been with the family for a couple of

Grandmother Ellis

years as the chauffeur—first when they lived in Great Neck and then during their last years in East Hampton, before my grandfather died. In Great Neck, Albert had also taken care of their cow and pig. He occupied one of the rooms off the kitchen.

David took my mother there for a weekend along with their mutual friend George Woodward in the summer of 1941. They had met several weeks before at a going-away party for Jack Kahn. E. J. Kahn Jr., a staff writer at *The New Yorker*, had been drafted into the army, and a party was given for him at the Village Vanguard. My mother was wearing a black fitted heart-shaped dress and a big felt hat with a brim and a black veil that tied under the chin. David was standing at the bar in a tweed suit. He was just under six feet, had broad shoulders and, according to my mother, the kind of looks you didn't notice right away. He wore glasses. "Like Superman when he's a reporter," said my mother, referring to Clark Kent. By all accounts, he was easygoing. "There was nothing fancy about him," she said. "Or putting on an act, or showing off or being important—so you liked him. You just met him and you liked him. You couldn't help it. Everybody did."

They talked for a while at the bar and then David, who was taking over the "Tables for Two" column for Kahn, invited my mother to go nightclubbing with him. She'd often gone out with Kahn and earned the unofficial title "New Yorker night-club date" because of the previously mentioned piece Kahn wrote sparked by my mother's resemblance to Constance Bennett for the anniversary issue in 1940: "Constance Bennett and Me." David was twenty-two when he inherited this package (the column and my mother—which Kahn considered an outright gift, he told me, when I met him many years later). But my mother, then twenty-six, thought David was older. "He was an amazing, strong young man," she said, citing an incident between them soon after they married. It was late at night and they'd had a fight. "I don't remember what the hell we were fighting about," she said, "but I said I'm getting out. I'm leaving. It was wonderful the way he handled it. He just took me by the arms, held me against the door, and said, 'You're not going anyplace.' " It impressed her so, she said. It took the wind out of her sails. "And at the same time, it was loving and protective." My mother said he knew how to behave. "It was amazing how smart he was for a kid."

As for George Woodward, he was a charming, attractive sort of guy who had aspirations toward being a writer. His family had a little money and he was a friend of everybody on *The New Yorker*. For a while my mother had a crush on Woodward, who was ten years older.

"My whole life was such a fantasy existence," she said when I asked her what it was like seeing the house in New Milford for the first time. "You know, if I were to write my autobiography, I would call it *I Made Myself Up*. I was the little daughter of all the

Russians. I was the royal princess. We weren't poor. We were this wonderful noble family who had money," she said, "and who..." She corrected herself. "Money we didn't have. No, money we didn't have. But money didn't matter because money was dirty and only common people ever talked about anything like that. See, I never felt poor little girl in rich surroundings. I always felt this is my due. I never felt I didn't know what fork to use. Even if I didn't know what fork to use."

My mother was born in Russia, and her father's father had had a title of sorts. It was the kind that got conferred upon you by a ruler, she said. You didn't pass it on. And she didn't know how he happened to have it—but to her the thing spelled royalty and translated as kith and kin to the czar. She lived in Odessa with her parents, Leon and Marie, in Marie's father's big apartment until the revolution broke out and then the family moved to Sevastopol, farther south on the Black Sea. Leon's heart was with the revolution, explained my mother, but he didn't do anything about it. He decided leaving was the smart thing to do. Get out while the getting's good. Before they got killed or something. The goal was to get to America.

In Sevastopol Marie had a miscarriage. She never got pregnant again. In Odessa there'd been an old Russian nurse but in Sevastopol there was just the maid, Lisa, a Russian peasant girl, whom my mother loved. And it was in Sevastopol that Frances began getting all worked up over her mother. Marie was jealous of anybody who was around her and could (if so inclined) spew forth something sickening—i.e. racist slurs. And she'd act superior. They lived in Sevastopol for a year while they still had money.

From Sevastopol they went to Constantinople and Marie sewed jewels into her dress—a gray chiffon and purple taffeta gown with pleats on the hem. She stitched her gems inside the pleats so they'd have something. The jewelry would have been taken away. In Constantinople my mother went to an Italian convent school. It was the first school they put her in. Leon and Marie did everything they could to try to earn money. It was around that time, said my mother, that she began finding out about what she dubbed her "strange background."

"You know how kids don't put things together," she said. My mother had fasted with her father on Yom Kippur and gone to synagogue with him on high holy days and liked it but never put anything together. She didn't know what they were. She hadn't thought about it, she said. She was five years old. And then one day, this woman, this friend of her mother's—an old Russian Greek Orthodox woman whom Frances said was crazy about her—invited my mother to her house for tea. My mother went and the old lady acquainted her with the story of the crucifixion. She told Frances about Jesus Christ being nailed up on the cross by these terrible people—the Jews.

Frances wept buckets, thinking it was the saddest thing she'd ever heard. "I guess she was a religious woman," she concluded about her fan. "I don't know what she was. Can you imagine telling a little girl, for entertainment, that story?" And when Marie showed up at the end of the visit, my mother began conveying to her the wretched thing that happened to this wonderful man. And Marie said, "Feynichka ..." Grandma Marie didn't say much more then, but when she got my mother the hell out of there and into the open air she said, "Now, Feynichka, you know this couldn't have happened because Mamachka's Jewish. The Jews couldn't have done this because Mamachka's Jewish."

"That's all I had to hear," said Frances, who often referred to her mother as a thorn in her side. "That sealed it. That made it absolutely certain they had done it," she said. But in any case, it was the beginning of my mother finding out that her mother was Jewish.

"I didn't know what Jewish was," she said. "Maybe I should have known but I didn't. It was a secret. I wasn't told." From then on my mother began putting together small things she heard here and there. Little pieces of information came out.

Like the thing about her Greek Orthodox great-grandfather's so-called title, for example. And his son falling for and marrying a Jewish girl (in Poland or Vienna) and her father (Leon) being considered a bastard, etc. This was before the revolution, and intermarriage wasn't recognized in Russia. Leon's mother's name was Lipetz. My grandfather's name should have been Leonid Vladimirovich Offcherenko after his father, but it was Leonid Vladimirovich Lipetz and it became Leon Lipetz in America.

"The thing about her always," said Frances in reference to her mother, "was that she was such a big heroine. She would do stupid things and then be such a big heroine." Grandma Marie's stint as a cook in Constantinople was an example. My grandmother got a job as a cook for a Russian folksinger when she really wasn't cut out to be one. Her family had servants so she hadn't been trained to do anything around the house. As my mother put it, Grandma was very carefully reared. So there she was gallantly sewing stuffing into a chicken neck or something, only she parked the needle in her dress for safekeeping. "And of course," said my mother, "it pricked her in the breast." Then there was shrieking and carrying on about this terrible thing that had happened.

And once, when Frances was little, using a double-edged razor to sharpen a pencil, she got it in her finger and there was this finger dangling off. "Then she was wonderful," said my mother. "She'd snatch you up and run to the doctor screaming and yelling." But my mother said she was filled with terrible embarrassment even if her mother was doing something wonderful.

"The same thing happened on our trip from Odessa to Sevastopol," she recalled. "My mother was the heroine." All the Jews were told to go down into the coal bin. It was terrible, she said. The sailors threatened to throw them overboard. (Actually the family didn't have to comply because Leon was carrying a Polish passport stating that he wasn't Jewish, which would have protected them—but he said wherever the Jews were going, they were going. "That's the way he was," said my mother. "That's why I loved him so much.") So the three of them went below and Marie would escape, posing as an officer's wife (or so she claimed) and saying they were right to put those stupid Jews down there, and then she'd nab food and bring it back with her. "I believe it," said Frances, "because she was crazy and fearless in many ways."

Finally my grandparents got the necessary papers for America, only then my mother got nits in her hair, which caused a delay. But ultimately they made it. And Marie went to work in this country when my mother was nine, taking Frances with her (as interpreter) to help land her first job. She found employment in a nursing home and then worked for a doctor in the Bronx. Grandma Marie became a nurse without ever having gone to school for it. She took a practical nursing exam and passed somehow. She always wrote badly in English.

"But it was terrible," said my mother, "because you see, the terrible thing about her was if you could think of me at my worst extended about a hundredfold then you'd sort of get a picture of what would happen. The reason I have survived in this world, despite behaving badly at times, is that I have a decent nature underneath and I'm always sorry if I've done something rotten. I want to fix it. Whereas Grandma really operated on an eye for an eye and a tooth for a tooth. And I don't believe an eye for an eye," said my mother. There were scenes as far back as my mother could remember. My grandmother was always leaving. Regularly departing. You'd have to go and beg and plead and carry on to get her to come back. Or she wouldn't talk to you for weeks.

My mother moved out when she was seventeen, when she went to the Neighborhood Playhouse School of the Theatre. Leon and Marie lived together until then. When my mother was accepted at the playhouse she lied and told her parents she couldn't get a scholarship unless she moved away from home. She had a hunch that if she left, her father would leave, too. She felt sorry for him. "I loved him very much," she said, "and I didn't realize that he had done her damage or anything like that. I only saw it from his point of view because I would see her bad behavior and he'd make me feel good and she would make me feel terrible."

There were rumors that Leon had been living with or having an affair with another woman. And Marie was very much in love with him. But the separation didn't last long. Less than a year. Leon died the following summer. He got pneumonia and died, and my mother said they probably were going to go back together. "Grandma was pretty powerful. She was always bailing him out. He'd get paid by his grocery men." Leon was selling wholesale groceries then. "They would pay him and he would juggle the checks. He'd run short of money and cash a check and hope to pay it back." He was a weak man, my mother said. Weak in character, and he was a drinker. "Maybe a little drinking. A little gambling. Maybe a little showing off with women. I don't know. I don't really know. Poor soul. He was so young. He was forty-three when he died—God—and the poor little life snuffed out."

. . .

That weekend Ellis put Frances in the downstairs guest room and David and George Woodward slept upstairs. When my mother got up the next morning, Ellis was in the study having breakfast in a lovely rose-colored dress. She was so pretty, said my mother. Ellis had Albert bring in another tray and they talked for hours while the two men slept. My paternal grandmother was born and raised in Goshen, Indiana. The second oldest of seven sisters and brothers—she lived there with her immediate family, a grandmother (a direct descendant of Peter Brown, who came over to Plymouth Rock on the *Mayflower*), two maiden aunts, and a seamstress, until she attended boarding school in Massachusetts. Then in 1905 she went to Smith College.

Her father was in the lumber business before he retired (when my grandmother was fourteen) to become president of a bank.

My mother fell in love with Ellis, the house, everything. "It was everything I never had but should have," she said. "It was like *Little Women* had come to life. Except that Granny was more sophisticated than the characters in *Little Women*," she said. "I loved it all." Her father had given *Little Women* to her when she was little and that's the family she wanted to be part of. That's the mother she wanted. The only warmth my mother could remember was her father carrying her when she was five years old and putting his cheek next to hers. "If I hadn't had my father," said Frances, "I would be a raving maniac. I would be a complete lesbian." (Don't ask.) "I don't know what I'd be."

When David died the person my mother really wanted to be with and share it with was Ellis, but Granny told her almost immediately that her pain was too great: Her husband had died in 1933 when he was forty-eight. Her son Jim was killed in Spain as a member of the Abraham Lincoln Brigade during the Spanish civil war in 1938, and now David. My mother had to respect my grandmother's grief.

So she said her idea of how to cope with "this terrible pain that was so horrendous that she couldn't bear it" was to go to Tim Costello's and hang out there, where she and David had been together. Hang out in the saloon. And as previously mentioned, she returned to work right away. "My life was cut short like *that*," said my mother, energetically slicing one hand with the other. "It was as if I was just cut like *that*. Finished. This beautiful life which we had . . . One of the things a friend of mine once said to me that she would never forget was that she came to see me and I said to her 'I love my life,' because she'd never heard anybody at the moment of having it saying 'I love my life.' Well *I love my life* got cut off. Finished." Frances and David's brief "storybook" marriage, so called by my mother, had come to an end.

My mother had her work in radio and was busy with it all the time and David had his, and their social life was all David's work at America's most sophisticated popular magazine, *The New Yorker*. And it had been such fun. David was considered remarkably good and he did a variety of things very young. My mother was doing two shows. One in the morning and one in the afternoon. She wasn't on every single day but was a great deal of the time. She would get through working, come racing home, get dressed, and out they'd go. There was always something they had to go to: a sporting event or a nightclub or a movie or play. "I tell you it was paradise," said my mother. "I mean what could be better?" This was before Joe and me and after. They had a very gay life, she said. "It was really very gay."

When Frances went to see Granny (after David was killed), she'd try to keep everything on an even keel. They would occasionally say things about him—remembering things—but not right away. My mother was afraid of saying something that would cause my grandmother greater pain. "I mean how much was this poor woman supposed to take?"

My mother said, "I never dealt with the fact that this was my husband, the father of my little babies, and it was terrible. It was just plain terrible. I was always covering up what I felt."

She saw Granny several times a week. (My grandmother had just moved from New Milford into New York to a hotel for the winter.) They would just sit in her hotel room—the two of them—and try not to intrude upon each other.

My mother stayed away from Grandma Marie for three days after the news of David's death. But then she went to her mother's apartment, taking her friend Sylvia Rochelle along, and when the two women walked in my grandmother's first words were, "Aie, Sylvie, everything happens to me."

There were cows in the fields when we arrived at Granny's. They belonged to Mike Smiersky down the road. My grandmother no longer had any of her own. Besides Granny there was, of course, Albert, whom I guess you could call fiercely loyal, and for a while a woman named Eva who had cooked something special for the occasion. She didn't live there. We arrived in the summer and there was fresh corn from the garden and strawberries, and eventually we had cats—maybe there were some already—and a dog named Licky, and Albert would make macaroon mounds he called beetle cookies.

Three children ages nine, eight, and three might not have been exactly what the doctor ordered up for my grandmother, but my father said the obligation she felt not to inflict her gloom on us kids brought back some measure of her old good spirits. The strokes had left her with some paralysis and a few other impairments—lousy peripheral vision is what I remember. She wore blue-tinted glasses a good deal of the time. And the weather affected her breathing. If it was humid she had difficulty coming down from her room upstairs. I don't think my grand-mother ever gave up cigarettes but she surrendered to filtered ones, and it was practically a pastime to prevent her from plac-ing the unfiltered end in her mouth or watch her clip the singed tip with scissors if she did.

It was on the occasion of naming our dog Licky that I learned that my father and his brothers also arrived at ordinary pet handles when the situation arose and that my paternal grandfather shared their loser selections with his readers in his column "In the Wake of the News." This was the daily *Chicago Tribune* column he took over in 1913 and continued writing for six years.

> Well I told you a few weeks ago how we got hold of a milch cow that was jet black and we leaved it to the kiddies to give her a name and after they had only thought a part of one day they all of a sudden hit on Blackie just like they was inspired. Well we give our little boy Jimmie a parrot for his birthday and the bird could not have been in the house more than 2 hrs. and a ½ when all 4 kiddies was calling her Polly.

In the New Milford setting, too, I was introduced to *The Young Immigrunts*, the story of my grandparents' automobile trip from Chicago (where they had lived) to a new home in Green-wich, Connecticut, as told from the point of view of Ring W. Lardner Jr. (age four). With a preface by the father. My father, the so-called author, in describing this trek east, talks about their exit from Manhattan (which he calls the Bureau of Manhattan) and somehow "getting balled up on the grand concorpse." After which the following exchange takes place.

Are you lost daddy I arsked tenderly.
Shut up he explained.

Well, I laughed my head off when I heard those lines at about age ten. And recently it occurred to me that they conveyed (in a nutshell) the family reticence—the uncommunicative nature frequently alluded to. My father and Uncle John, for example, were called "the Indian" by some friends mainly in reference to their taciturnity. And there was the story about their pal Lizzie Wheeler, who saw the four Lardner boys throughout her girlhood, and who said she was fourteen before she knew small boys could talk. And the word *lost* (delivered by my father) in my grandfather's bit of dialogue also had great meaning. I'm referring to the fact that sometimes everything seemed vague, fuzzy, and sandy to me—like getting caught in a giant wave in a rough ocean on an overcast day. (I experienced the wave thing when I visited my cousins during the summer at their beachfront home on Fire Island.) Uncle John claimed he was part Indian. And although he didn't include anyone else in the tribe, I wanted to join the act. This was an urge sparked (despite my pale complexion) by Sonseeahray (Morning Star) in *Broken Arrow*— the film I saw during the penal interlude.

I remember that first summer Albert drove us into town to do the marketing. I don't know who actually secured the produce but my mother eventually did due to a sense of responsibility and gratitude she felt for being given a home and food. She felt she had to give back. She even learned to cook. I remember sitting in the back of Granny's Buick, however, with Albert at the wheel, with books from the town library and his newspaper. The paper, probably the *News*, had a headline declaring Stalin dead. But that would have been in March '53. And even though my parents were in the middle of an extended reexamination of their political views, my father was still pro-Stalin from the sound of it. Or at least I deduced from the talk that was going on in the car that Albert was on one side and my parents on another. Albert, the German man-of-all-work who had driven Granny to visit my dad in prison all those times, was probably anti-Russian in general. Whereas my father (as previously mentioned) had been very impressed by the Soviet Union when he was there in the summer of 1934. Russia seemed to be the only country that was serious about fighting fascism.

My father could have been laying that on old Albert and more. In any case, I wouldn't have put it past him to have been offering up something of a challenging nature. This would be in keeping with a tendency dating back to his youth: As in East Hampton in 1928 he got into difficulty after trying to persuade a neighboring child who was a couple of years younger that there was no such thing as God. (Naturally the kid took the matter up with his parents and it got back to my grandparents.)

Then shortly after, at Andover, there was the alarm-clock-placed-in-lectern-drawer-during-lengthy-chapel-service episode. And breaking into one of the secret societies at night just because nonmember entry was forbidden. Plus an accidental plunge from a fourth-story window ledge. (My father said he was always doing something to call attention to himself—or expressing some opinion that other people would find outlandish.) Being drawn to the goodies sent by the family of a fellow student, my father wound up in a Boston hospital with a fractured pelvis and shoulder. He had thought it would be amusing to enter through his neighbor's window and nab the stuff. However, a slim overhang from window to window had to be traversed, and while he was holding on to a shutter that wasn't firmly hooked to the wall, disaster struck.

. . .

I was a regular at the library on Main Street. Borrowing books by a neighbor down the road—Phoebe Erickson—who wrote in a log cabin about families. They were probably regular preadolescent fare—and then, I don't remember when or how, I discovered romance novels. Junky love stories written for teenagers, and I sneaked them to my room thinking I should probably be aiming for something more profound. I do remember reading, maybe later, maybe when we were just summering in New Milford, *Anna Karenina*, however, sprawled out on the little wooden bridge that crossed the stream. Purple and white lilacs and dogwood in view, and willows by the pond. I think I was struck by the beauty of the place. Definitely a brightness I hadn't known before. There was a flower garden, too. I don't think I worked in it. I loved watching Mike Smiersky and his men shape hay into bales on Granny's farm. I liked the activity and the smell. I remembered the scent of the house long after we didn't have the house anymore and I liked the slanted wall in my room. I would lie on my back and put my feet on the wall and drive it like a car. I loved the wood floor and the sheepskin rug in the bathroom. I think I even remember coming to New Milford before I was three, before we moved to California to marry Ring. I liked picking raspberries out of the garden even though we weren't supposed to (it was practically a sin) because there wouldn't be enough for dinner. I liked swimming in the pond although it was cold as hell, and going to Candlewood Lake where the water was warmer and there were other kids.

New Milford is where I got my period and I spent the evening in bed luxuriating over the event. For a reward Joe gave me a family of little glass skunks. I think I began discovering my brother Joe in New Milford. I spent my ten-cent allowance on glass critters in California. I don't know if I was still investing in them in New Milford. I put the skunks on my bedside table. I wondered if they knew at Candlewood Lake I had gotten my period. I felt grown-up. Maybe I liked the family's respect. My parents were clear about sex and sexual development or at least what they wanted me to think. Menstruation was good. It should be called *period* or *menstruation* not *on the rag* or *falling off the roof* (like Aunt Hazel called it). They said intercourse was beautiful and when I was seventeen my father mentioned a diaphragm. I'd been making love (without him knowing) since I was fifteen. I don't think I'd given any thought to a diaphragm, but went to my parents' friend, Dr. Pleshette, and got one. I remember when my father brought it up. He was putting shelves in my room. I liked that he was paying attention to me and I probably thought he was hip. My mother said nothing on the subject. She told me about masturbation, with which I was already acquainted. I used to wear underpants with my nightgown. Wearing them produced the desired result: warmth when the thing rode up on me in the night. But then there was my mother's interpretation: I was wearing them so I wouldn't masturbate. And masturbation, she said, was okay.

I loved visiting Phoebe Erickson in her log cabin on the dirt road leading to our house. It was where she went to write. She and her husband lived elsewhere, farther up the hill. I don't remember any writing of mine in New Milford. I do remember using a typewriter, and Uncle John visiting from New York City calling me a fast two-fingered typist. He was, also, he said, and he was one of the most respected journalists in America. Uncle John didn't talk much, Granny said, but when he did everyone listened. I liked school. I made a scrapbook all about Abraham Lincoln because he supposedly freed the slaves, of course. But my mother let it be known she was partial to Jefferson. He had done more, she said, referring (I think) to the Declaration of Independence. And Joe followed suit (he and the president shared the same April birth date). I felt slighted that we weren't all one in our allegiance. I have lots of memories of this two-year period in New Milford. The order may be askew.

There's a photograph of me running with Joe outside. I am wearing shorts and my shirt is hanging out. My hair is cropped short and I am much larger than my brother. He was already skinny. My hair had been chopped off by a barber. I can't imagine why my mother took me, and when I returned I could tell Granny didn't like my new do. However, later she changed her tune. I figured my mother said something to her. I always knew my mother thought I had a good face.

I was a sneak eater in New Milford. I liked the cocktail hour. There were pretzels every night. We'd gather in the study. Sometimes there would be stories about my grandfather and F. Scott Fitzgerald and Granny when she was young and all Granny's boys when they were young, including my real father. A life-sized portrait hung in the study of David with unshorn curls, a homemade middy blouse, and a golden velvet short pantsuit. A portrait painter had been hired to preserve the cherubic look. The painter came to the house in Great Neck, his wife in tow. They occupied a large guest room and used one downstairs for a studio. Grandpa didn't like the wife (she talked too much) so he hurried the process along. The portrait of David is mine now. It was left to me by my grandmother. And I have David's Bible.

Also in the little study, behind the love seat by the window on the side that Granny sat, was a pencil drawing of my uncle Jim and it was to that image that I attached all that I heard about him.

. . .

Jim was slighter in stature than the rest of the boys and he had the most regular features. The best-proportioned physique. He was clearly the handsome-hero type, which got him cast as the romantic lead in Uncle John's American version of *H.M.S. Pinafore* (written when he was fourteen), called *U.S.S. Skinafore,* and the other theatricals performed in the Lardner living room. And occasionally he tested his strength by seeing how quickly he could pin my father's shoulders to the ground. (What I was told about his agility and strength reminds me of my brother Joe.) At Harvard, besides writing songs, Jim became New England intercollegiate wrestling champion in the 145-pound class, and he could tear a Manhattan phone book in half. Like Granny, he loved puzzles and calculations of all kinds. When he made up his mind to do something he stuck with it—like dispensing with overcoats the day he concluded too many had been lost. Going coatless from then on. I learned also that he died in Spain.

Jim had traveled from Paris to Barcelona with Ernest Hemingway and Vincent Sheean, who were covering the war. After a few trips to the front lines—talking to the people in the brigade—he decided to enlist. He'd been there only a couple of weeks when he decided writing about them wasn't enough. He was the last American volunteer to join the Republican army and one of the last to be killed. He was twenty-four. This information I affixed to the picture on the wall. All that, and a bird (mentioned earlier) named Polly.

In Great Neck, Zelda and Scott Fitzgerald lived just a couple of miles away. During the year and a half they did (before the Fitzgeralds left for the south of France), it was with the Fitzgeralds my grandparents had their closest ties. There was a porch on the side of the Great Neck house facing the home of Herbert Bayard Swope (legendary editor of the *New York World*), and my grandfather and Fitzgerald sat there many weekend afternoons, drinking ale or whiskey and watching what my grandfather described as "an almost continuous house party" next door. The location of the Swope house, I learned, was just right for the view of Daisy Buchanan's pier across the bay. It was Fitzgerald who told my father to go to Princeton. And here's what my father said about Zelda (who left on him the deepest imprint), although he wasn't yet nine the last time he saw her. Zelda was twenty-two when they first met and my father would have preferred it, he said, if she'd stayed behind when the kids and grown-ups parted company. Free and impulsive in saying or doing whatever she felt like, that's where she belonged, he said. And my father also said, he never saw a photograph that captured her beauty.

In 1934 shortly after my grandfather died, when my father was nineteen, he went to an exhibition of her paintings with Granny. Zelda was in an institution then, but Fitzgerald was there and Granny asked how his book (*Tender Is the Night*) was coming along, and Fitzgerald replied that it was finished. Just three months' worth of corrections, he said. Well, this startled my father and the incident stuck in his mind, he said, because that was a long time, he thought, for what Fitzgerald was talking about—a little last-minute editing. So he concluded Fitzgerald must be a slow writer.

There was drinking every night in New Milford. I sneaked pretzels and peanut brittle, and there were sit-down lunches in the summer but, between you and me, I didn't always feel I deserved to openly partake of the stuff that was served. Like chipped beef and cream sauce (one of Granny's favorites) or other fattening grub that was laid before me. And sometimes I wouldn't be dining at all. I was dieting. Stranded out in the garden sucking on a tomato or something. I was weighed by my father on the big railroad station scale on Sunday (I think it was for baggage, for God's sake) so I could check my progress. It was large and I imagined everyone could see. Sometimes I would weigh in at the stationery store where we bought the Sunday newspaper. This was doubly treacherous. There I ran the risk of bumping smack into people exiting church, which meant not only being viewed on a scale but dressed in goddamn blue jeans, signifying heathen upbringing (on the day of rest). I didn't like being in town in my informal attire risking an encounter with my friends in church gear. I knew it was better to be Jewish, which was uncommon enough in New Milford, because of Karen, a popular girl who went to synagogue. I was asked once what religion I was and I said, "Guess."

People have said that it's strange, this business of being plunked down on a weighing device, but I swear I was under the spell of my father's logic. The number on the scale determined success or failure in the weight-dropping endeavor. And I wanted to lose weight, I must have declared to humor the home team who'd indicated there was value in slimness.

The town was for Eisenhower, and my parents were picking us up at school and tearing ass home to listen to the McCarthy hearings. My mother cried when the Rosenbergs were executed in the electric chair at Sing Sing. And, of course, my father had been in jail. I didn't know what I felt. I just kept this part of my life apart. I didn't talk about it anywhere.

My brother Jim's friend at the end of the dirt road believed in God. His brother was a priest. I remember my father debating the subject. I hope not with Gregory who, if I was ten, was probably five. (My father's beliefs on the subject have already been made known.) I don't think Granny liked me as much as she did

Joe. I loved her. I thought she was the way to be. Elegant and smart. She did double-crostics and knitted and crocheted and she read. *Pride and Prejudice* was her favorite book.

I know now it must have been a rough time for my parents. My father was concerned about work and remained so throughout the blacklist, but he found release, he said, in writing the book he began in prison (*The Ecstasy of Owen Muir*) and even though he didn't expect that it would solve any money problems he did concentrate on it pretty hard for most of two years. In New Milford he only took time off from it to try a couple of things to make immediate money. One was a television series somebody wanted to do of my grandfather's stories. My father did two adaptations on spec and my uncle John put his name on them, but they never got made. The other was a magazine article that never sold. A writer friend of my parents put her name on that. My father was worried about the fact that we were living off his mother. She provided the basic expenses of housing and food. He felt that he could get established in some other form of writing even if the novel wasn't a bestseller. There were some other things he knew he could write books about, and he figured he'd be able to build a name that way.

My mother said living in New Milford was the worst time for her. The hardest thing, she said, was doing the family marketing. "I know this sounds dumb," she said. "I just wasn't used to any of it." In California there was always Polly. My mother tried to earn our keep by conquering homemaking. And she'd drive Granny around—take her on little outings. She said it was a miracle that they survived it and remained friends. In New Milford she would do the shopping for a whole week so she could go into the city and try to find a job, and by the time she'd complete the task and hit Railroad Street on a hot sunny afternoon, "I swear

I'd think I was going crazy," she remarked. "The fatigue and marketing. I didn't have my work. I didn't have any sense of security about anything," she said. "As a woman. As a mother. I was living in somebody else's house without a pot to pee in." (We didn't have a cent.) "I don't know how I survived."

In New Milford my mother said she would get pains in her stomach. She couldn't be who she was. "I couldn't give vent to the angers which I felt," said Frances, "which maybe isn't such a good thing to do but it's better to give vent to it than keep it all under wraps."

From New Milford that first summer my mother got a lead on *Philco Television Playhouse* in *Holiday Song* by Paddy Chayefsky. She said, "I'm going to get a job. I don't care what kind of blacklist they've got—I'm going to do it." The show got good reviews and my mother was singled out in the press. But after that, nothing happened. There were no calls for anything. She kept trying. She got frantic about it. Finally she landed a job covering for Maureen Stapleton in a play and was happy to be involved in the theater in New York even though she wasn't doing anything except understudying. My mother came home to New Milford on her day off. Then Paddy Chayefsky wrote *Marty* for *Philco Television Playhouse* with her in mind. "You can imagine the excitement," she said. "God, it was so wonderful." The salary was set. She was to pick up the script and see if she thought it was okay. "Script approval!" exclaimed my mother. "I would have crawled on my hands and knees . . ." She went into New York the next day. She was to contact her agent before going to the office. She phoned and was told to try in an hour. They had to get back to the producer. My mother called back in an hour or two and was told to try later. They kept her calling until finally in the late afternoon they said they were so sorry. A terrible mistake had been made. The part was cast. My mother strongly suspected something had happened but she wasn't sure whether it was the blacklist or what, until the following September when *Holiday Song* was repeated and another actress was hired to play the part Frances originated. Everybody was cast in the same roles except my mother. The producer was very forthright in admitting that the other cast members had said they'd quit if she wasn't included. He was with them, he said, and understood how they felt, but had informed them that their protest wouldn't do any good. All that would happen was—they wouldn't have jobs, either. Then my mother really knew why she hadn't gotten *Marty*.

She felt awful for years. The thing that was particularly bad was that she couldn't talk about it, she said. She'd go up for a job and get asked: If you're so good, where have you been? Why haven't we seen you before? My mother said she would just talk fast about raising her children, etc. But never in all that time could she come out and say, "I'm blacklisted."

Joe and I meanwhile were being introduced to household responsibilities. We took turns drying dishes, setting the table, etc. I learned the Gettysburg Address wiping the plates with my father. My other association with this activity was busting Granny's Spode gravy boat with the pattern Billingsley Rose by accident. There was a risk to my grandmother's more fragile and valued possessions with us in the house but only once did I hear her say anything like she should have smashed her antiques before our arrival. My grandmother didn't raise her voice.

I remember my father picking me up at dance class. The sun was setting. My mother did the makeup for a recital. I liked a boy named Jerry. I guess he liked me. At least we sat together with his little brother Tommy at the movies on Saturday afternoons. I really liked Paul who lived in a shacklike dwelling at the foot of Long Mountain Road and who was older. I can't imagine what he saw in me although briefly (for a day or so) I possessed his school ring, which added up to something.

I loved the movies. I loved westerns and musicals and listening to *Wild Bill Hickock* and *Sergeant Preston of the Yukon* and *The Shadow* on the radio. And the Academy Awards every year. My father had won one. I guess I knew that then. I loved Charlie Chaplin and went to Westland with his daughter Geraldine. Being crazy about Chaplin was something else not to mention to my friend Sally because his politics were suspect. I liked Sally and Mary Alice and Karen. They were good friends to have. I remember thinking I was going to be famous when I grew up. I didn't know at what. I remember Valentine's Day and the stash of Valentines at school and wondering how many I'd get. *How many* mattered. I was picked up after a party by my parents following several rounds of a kissing rendition of musical chairs. When the music stopped you laid one on the person seated in front of you. Only everyone involved had zoomed by my location. Therefore I was miserable by the time my parents fetched me. I think I even told them. I hardly remember ever telling them any of my feelings.

They knew I was deeply troubled, though, when I pulled lousy board scores in high school in 1959. They must have known. I cried my eyes out. It was humiliating. Low scores. They concluded I was unhappy two years later when John, after taking me out a couple of times when I was eighteen, sat there at the Diamonds' puffing on his pipe, surveying the scene rather than talking to me. My mother indicated later that it was cool that I dived into the Diamonds' pool (as if I were immune to the boy's seeming lack of interest) and went for a swim. I sure didn't know what else to do. I think my mother, a nondiver, also admired my manner of exit. But Joe could tell I was brokenhearted and followed me up to my room to be with me when we got back to New Milford, where we were staying for the summer. He knew I was upset. I wrote a story about John later to erase him from the picture. I wanted him to like me, though. He was a blind date recommended by the Hunters—my parents' best friends. My parents knew him. I cut my hair, became more sophisticated and thinner, but he didn't get the message for over a year.

I wanted Granny to like me. Everyone was crazy about her. One time—it must have been right before Christmas—my friend Vivian, who had one blue eye and one brown, and I went through my grandmother's drawers for a preview of upcoming loot. Granny was wise to this endeavor, however. And onto the fact that someone other than her had shut those drawers because they weren't flush the way she liked them. We were all interrogated and I lied. I knew Granny believed Joe (not me), who clearly had nothing to do with it. And I was positive I wouldn't be able to see the Doris Day movie in town that night, which was where my focus lay (for one thing, the investigation was eating up a lot of time). I did, though. The one in which Doris Day sang "Once I Had a Secret Love" atop her horse. But my lie lingered like a tormenting ghost.

Eventually I would put friends through a measuring-up process in my head, filtering them through my version of the family lens. I did this particularly years later with men, especially in the beginning. My father, drunk one night, let me know in his way that a serious boyfriend of mine lacked humor. So I chose John, who giggled; though, like certain family members, he didn't speak much. His parents knew my parents; their political thinking was allied or at least in the same ballpark. This took pressure off me. Later we married.

Ballpark brings to mind baseball and baseball makes me think of Granny. She liked the Dodgers and would listen to games on the radio. She taught me what she knew. Sometimes the family traveled to Ebbets Field. I got attached to baseball, too, and collected pictures of the Dodgers and tacked their images to my wall. I liked the stories I'd hear about my grandfather traveling with ball clubs and my grandparents' lengthy courtship. Almost four years. I think I knew that my grandfather was a drinker. Drank a lot, then would go on the water wagon. But generally speaking he didn't write while he was drinking and made quite a concerted effort to conceal his drinking from his boys. Occasionally my father saw the bootlegger with a sack over his shoulder and he knew liquor was served. And he knew in a vague way that something was wrong with his father (which he associated with drunkenness) when he came home several times at seven or eight in the morning. There was some reason why Miss Feldman—the formidable trained German nurse in charge of the boys—didn't want them to go to him. But at the time my father thought it was just occasional heavy drinking.

Ring used to call himself a responsible drunk, which meant he never really forgot his obligations either to work or to the household. "You know I never really goofed off for any period of time or got into any real trouble," he proclaimed. Maybe that's what my grandfather was. I don't remember being aware of drinking on my father's part until we hit New York after the two years in New Milford.

I felt shame doing something I truly cherished. Reclining on my bed reading and eating because I got the idea that food consumption, at least mine, met with disapproval. In New Milford I started the practice of holding back at meals and indulging (later on) in goodies stashed away for the occasion in the privacy of my room. I don't ever remember being very successful at the railroad weigh-ins. By the time we lived in New York I was resolving every New Year's to lose weight and my parents were offering rewards for poundage lost. At thirteen or fourteen I was taken to a doctor who said "no wonder," which was an expression of sympathy (I thought) for the details I told him about the two fathers, and he loaded me up with pills. I reduced rapidly and was congratulated on my success.

There was quite a scene, as I remember it, over my reading *Bonjour Tristesse* by Françoise Sagan, who was barely eighteen when she wrote the thing in a month. By this I mean I knew how Granny felt and how my mother and father felt. Especially my father. I was enjoying the book, which received a huge volume of international publicity. It satisfied my urge for love and beckoning melancholy and clearly they had all read it. It wasn't my usual garbage (adolescent narratives of desire, etc. for kids that they'd never touch). I proceeded with the story conveyed in a style so coolly sensuous about a young woman (Cécile, age seventeen), summering in a white villa on the Mediterranean with her widowed father, on the verge of her first love affair with a twenty-five-year-old law student named Cyril. Although that's putting it mildly. For in fact the relatively mild events of the summer get turned into a melodrama of a high order instigated by Cécile and result in tragic consequences. Cécile may have adopted a cynical attitude toward love that made her fond of repeating to herself Oscar Wilde's line: "Sin is the only note of vivid color that persists in the modern world." But I mainly tracked her fiery ambivalences and fixed my gaze on the teenage heroine's romantic utterances. Like: "It seemed to me," she said at one point, "that love was the only remedy for the haunting anxiety I felt." The book is also, I might add, about a slightly amorous friendship between a father and daughter. Well, Granny thought I (at barely thirteen) was too young for this. She might even have concluded it was trashy in content. But my father didn't discriminate about my reading.

Lying on my bed and reading was so predictably soothing. I think my parents wanted me outside more, though—running around, jumping up and down—whereas I relished board games and the card game hearts, which, along with poker, was a family affair. My father photographed me at the dining room table slouched over so I could see in black and white what lousy posture I had. My father was practical.

Am I finished with New Milford? Granny church no church blue jeans outside not running around hair cut short spin the bottle Paul McCarrol's ring picked up at school rushing home McCarthy hearings the Rosenbergs and Mom cried and Pop had been in jail too fat privately devouring food sneaking books Jerry and Sally and we bought a winter coat with a belt I must have looked round I wanted Mary Janes when I lived in Santa Monica but the strap wouldn't make it around my ankles.

We left New Milford after two years at the urging of my mother. "I wanted you to grow up where you had some sense of rubbing up against the city," she said, "and being with other people who were going through the same thing you were." Also she needed to get out of the town for her own peace of mind. "Oh God," she exclaimed, "it's a wonder we didn't all go crazy."

New York City/
The Early Years

We lived in a hotel until our apartment was ready and I
went to Joan of Arc Junior High and was put in a class
where they offered (as an elective) modern dance. I didn't make
the accelerated academic program called "rapid advance." I got
lost the first day returning to the hotel and landed on the wrong
floor. Eventually we moved into our new home.

The beginning is blurry. But I remember writing a story/
diary of a pioneer girl traveling around with her family in a covered wagon who nabs a charging bobcat between the eyes with a
shotgun. And a poem called "Neighbors" honoring our seventh-
grade course of study—housing in New York City—which got
printed in the school magazine.

There were lots of different kinds of kids. Puerto Ricans and
blacks and a girl I knew in a gang with a knife. The Junior
Emanons. This spelled *no name* backward, the weapon-bearing
lass informed me. In my class almost everyone spoke English. I
don't know how it was set up exactly but some classes were less
bright. And in some the inhabitants hardly communicated in

English at all. The principal made announcements over the loudspeaker or intercom that came blasting into each classroom. "Dr. Sweeting speaking."

Friends emerged. My best friend was a girl named Alice. Jewish. I had a Jewish grandmother. I briefly wore a Star of David around my neck. I went to a Quaker camp. I wondered if I should become Quaker. There were dances with Alice at the synagogue on West Eighty-ninth Street. We counted the number of times we tripped the light fantastic at the temple. Me hardly at all. We boogied together with our girlfriends after school. I laughed a lot. Once I threw myself on the floor and cried and cried. I was pretending. Pulling a fast one on old Alice, who was impressed. We went on a double date. I don't know where we dug up the boys. I was shaking from trepidation when the guy picked me up. He and I rowed a boat around Central Park. I wore lipstick on the street and to school, afraid I would bump into my mother and get caught. I was not allowed. I got my first bra at the five-and-dime. I had asked for the smallest. In pain, I lay under my parents' bed watching some movie my father and Ian were screening. The bra was too tight. I returned the thing, this time with my mother in tow.

My father wrote for television on the blacklist. It was his main source of income during the fifties. He and Ian wrote pilot films for American television shot in England. The first one they did was called *The Adventures of Robin Hood*. There were several others. They got a whole bunch of other blacklisted writers involved, because it was much more work than they could handle. The producer, a woman named Hannah Weinstein, knew when she hired them that they were blacklisted. She was an American who went to England and started producing films there. Hiring blacklisted writers was actually part of her purpose in setting up the company, partly out of principle and partly because they were less expensive. The stories were written in New York and sent by mail to London. Fake names were placed on the scripts.

We couldn't tell anyone that our father was writing one of the most popular shows on television (*The Adventures of Robin Hood*) because Weinstein sold the series through a distributing company, which sold it to the CBS network, and CBS would have canceled the entire thing if they knew. But my brother Jim, to win their affection, told everyone he could at Camp Onas. I was also in attendance and denied the whole thing. Probably because I'd been taken to task for a similar offense. Once in New Milford my parents were sitting around with friends. I was with them and said something about *Robin Hood* and my father followed me up to my room and said I'd better not. I thought they were friends. I thought it was okay with friends.

"My memory is so hazy," said my brother Jim when I brought up the ghastly affair wondering if he recalled spilling the beans at the camp. "I mean, for example, Camp Onas," he said. "Essentially my sole memory of the place is the fact that there was this terrible skin disease."

"Did you have it?" I asked.

JIM: I don't remember if I had it. I had the beginnings of it. But, no I basically didn't have it.

ME: Do you remember that you told kids?

JIM: I don't remember particularly doing it at Camp Onas. I remember that I was guilty of this on occasion.

ME: You weren't very popular at Camp Onas, and in order to get the kids to like you, you told them, and I told them it wasn't the truth.

JIM: Oh, that must have made them think I was very peculiar, but then I guess they already thought that.

ME: It was a hard secret to keep. That was a pretty appealing thing—that Dad wrote the *Robin Hood* series.
(pause) Even though they told us we couldn't tell anyone because he was writing under a pseudonym.

JIM: Yeah.

ME: I'm sorry I did that.

Some other time I asked my brother if he felt at all like an outsider because of the blacklist. "Yes," he said. "Oh, absolutely. That was the whole story."

In 1956 my mother got a little job on a daytime soap, *The Edge of Night*. They liked her, she said, because she was funny. So they kept writing the part in. She was on and off that show for nearly ten years. My mother said, "They kept it quiet, of course." It never became a contract part. "It was just something they'd slip in." It wasn't until 1963 (when she was forty-eight) that she got a legitimate job on a nighttime television show called *The Defenders*, but time had gone by. She was no longer that twenty-nine-year-old charming whatever. She wasn't a girl anymore.

I didn't come up with a boyfriend at school. I liked a boy named Joel at camp. He liked me. This didn't amount to much. I wore his baseball cap. He was a catcher. I danced close with Cecil Rogers. He was black. He became my boyfriend. I liked the Sunday meeting at Quaker camp. We sat on the grass. A clearing in the woods. Anyone wanting to speak stood up and spoke or read. I liked Vespers Sunday night. I liked dancing close. I was drifting into my first year of high school. Thirteen. I also became attached to a counselor at Camp Onas. I definitely had a crush. I used to talk to him by phone about my father's drinking when we got home. I think I did this to draw him closer. But my father's drinking upset me. My father standing at the door to my room, slurring his words. My brother Joe and I didn't like eating out with our parents at Wilby's. It was a bar and the light was dim.

Mrs. Jacobi, my eighth-grade teacher at Joan of Arc, really liked me. I took dance classes at the Neighborhood Playhouse where my mother had studied acting. Taking two buses every Saturday morning for the crosstown trek. A Saturday when the mothers were in the audience—mine wasn't—and I sprained my ankle and some other mother helped me. I was moved ahead at the Neighborhood Playhouse. I left because I wanted to go to movies Saturday afternoons. I wish I had kept on dancing.

Second year at Joan of Arc I took the test for the High School of Music and Art. My parents couldn't afford a private institution. My mother told me I was good with my hands, and I was given painting lessons with a woman who helped me prepare for the entrance exam. I took the test and got in. Music and Art was good for me because there it was no longer a secret that my father had been in jail. He was kind of a hero for standing up for what he believed.

I don't think I considered becoming a painter. There were kids there much better than I. It didn't occur to me they'd been doing it longer. I wrote some. I liked carrying my story idea around with me. This was for a class in which we had to produce something weekly. I worked on the school paper. I didn't contribute much. The only thing I actually remember was an obituary for a classmate who'd fallen off a mountain over summer vacation. I did two things—a watercolor of a crow and a conté crayon drawing of a woman—that stand out in my mind. They were hung at home. We had to keep sketchbooks. They were checked and graded regularly. The drawings added up. I remember once staying up late writing. My father standing at the door wondering why I was still awake. My story was taking longer than I thought it would. "They always do," he said.

My papers for school were never finished ahead of time; I was always rushing at the last minute. My parents said work should be done at a desk not sprawled on the bed. I never sat at the desk and felt whatever I did couldn't be all that good being executed at the wrong location. I remember dictums—not a whole lot of actual help. Still, when I was in trouble in math my father worked with me on algebra. I got to like algebra. He also helped me with my paper on Communist China. I did my best, however, my sophomore year when I was in love with Ben.

The Castle on the Hill

"I knew very little about many things," explained my mother one day. "I didn't know how to open a Coke bottle, for Christ's sake. Do you realize that? I didn't know a lot of things."

"I didn't either," I said in a friendly manner.

"You knew more than I did" was her reply. "You went to bed with somebody at fifteen, didn't you? I didn't," she said.

"It was a different century back then," came my helpful response.

Ben

"No, it wasn't a different century," my mother shrieked with accuracy. "It was the same century. And you know what? I had the same feelings . . . No I didn't," she recalled. "I was frozen. I didn't have any feelings. I didn't feel anything."

"You didn't have a dear person." I gestured amiably.

Kate, Jaimey, and Ann

"What do you mean I didn't have a 'dear person'?"

"You didn't have Ben Koenig."

"I didn't have Ben Koenig. But I had somebody who loved me and whom I loved and who would make fun of me for being a virgin."

"At fifteen?" I asked.

"At sixteen, I think. No, you were lucky. You were lucky to have nice sweet Ben Koenig. But you wouldn't have found him if you hadn't had me for a mother. No question of that."

BEN AND I MET at the High School of Music and Art, or the "Castle on the Hill" as it was known. I can't recall if it had crenellations and merlons at the edge of the roof. Typical medieval fortifications. I kind of think they were there and that they were straight-edged—not dovetailed. In any case there were about 125 steps leading up to the place. Outwardly we were so different, Ben said to me, reflecting back. Ben came from a secular Jewish family and lived in the Bronx near Van Cortlandt Park in the Amalgamated, the oldest limited-equity housing cooperative in the United States. We lived on West End Avenue in

Manhattan. By his own admission, he had read very little, knew little of life; his family was cultured, he said, "but not overly so." He had odd interests. Steel pans, for instance. He loved the vibrant, loud, offbeat sound of those fifty-five-gallon oil drums. And calypso music. Even before Harry Belafonte, Ben was loving the lilt of it and appreciating island songs about social issues.

Jane

He was acquainted with all the union songs— "Union Maid," "We Shall Not Be Moved" (originally a gospel song), "Gotta Go Down and Join the Union" to the tune of "Lonesome Valley," "Joe Hill," etc.—and leftist music (songs that put the people first) that seemed to come naturally to him. He sang these songs with great conviction, prompting a classmate to remark one day that he was so deep and introspective that he was clearly the most sincere Communist of all our friends. Ben didn't say much in response because he knew something she didn't. He didn't really know anything about politics and could barely define Communism.

Before we met, he hadn't heard of Ring Sr. or Jr. Or he confused them with the detective-story writer Erle Stanley Gardner because the last names rhymed. As for the blacklist—it was just a vague idea floating in the air. The Hollywood Ten—a complete unknown. But Ben knew about Joe McCarthy. He'd spent a summer in Great Barrington, Massachusetts, with his aunt Rose and uncle Bob (both Republicans) watching McCarthy on TV. And in the sixth grade he'd stood up for a fellow student who'd provoked the liberal teacher by confessing that her parents supported the senator. His defense before the horrified teacher was that his classmate and her family had every right to their opinions and the teacher was wrong for picking on the girl, Birdie, in a McCarthyite manner. The teacher agreed and quit her harangue. This was Ben's first First Amendment victory. From his mother, a school laboratory assistant, he inherited some general feelings about social justice; from his father, a lawyer, ideas about legal and civil rights and civil liberties.

Through his friendship with me, he began to be more aware of other forces at work around him. Though I didn't tell him much, I told him some things about my family's situation and the blacklist. Once I said I was going to the opening of a movie my father wrote but I was sworn to secrecy and couldn't reveal where or what. In fact, I never told Ben any of the projects my father worked on. Occasionally our friends would allude to how well-known or important my family was but he said, frankly, he was more interested in me than he was in my family.

In the sixth grade Ben also discovered folk music and the guitar. Not like it was out of the blue or anything. He was already picking out songs by ear on his Arthur Godfrey ukulele. Now he wanted a four-string tenor guitar because it was tuned very much like the ukulele. It was a natural transition, he reasoned. Instead his father took him to the music department at Macy's and bought a Stella, which the great blues and folksinger Huddie (Leadbelly) Ledbetter played. It was the cheapest model, however, with six strings (Leadbelly played twelve-string)—more strings for the money, said his dad—and painful to play. But though he developed heavy calluses, Ben persevered.

Meanwhile, his older brother Bill introduced him to hootenannies at the Pythian Temple on the West Side of Manhattan. That's when he began imitating Pete Seeger. That's who he wanted to sound like. In the packed Pythian, Ben sat on the floor in front of the folding chairs as close up as he could get to Seeger standing onstage—looking up at Pete thumping away at the banjo. Pete used it to get the crowd singing. (Ben also eventually acquired a banjo.) Firing them up. Leading people, through song, to believe they could do something positive about the conditions of the world. The working class (which meant working with your hands—untrained workers doing hard backbreaking work), strikes, singing songs about miners—all these things occupied Ben's mind. He was just learning about Pete Seeger and Woody Guthrie, who were out with striking autoworkers in Detroit. Or wherever things were going on, they'd be there. "I Don't Want Your Millions, Mister." Ben wanted to be Pete Seeger. He was already kind of dressing like him. Work shirts, suspenders, and jeans.

Soon after he began taking guitar lessons with Jerry Silverman, who was just completing his first book about the blues. And through him, Ben upgraded to a Favilla. Steel strings. Nice sounding, it was made with care. Not just slapped together the way cheap guitars were.

Ben would rise in the morning and start strumming. School was merely an interruption to his playing. He'd go to PS 95 on Hillman Avenue, which was just one block long (he lived on the north end—the school was on the south end), return for lunch, but mainly to play. His kitchen window had a fire escape that opened onto an area facing the other apartments in the six-story development. On pleasant-weather days he'd sit at the windowsill with his feet on the fire escape and play and sing—his music echoing throughout. He loved the outdoor city acoustics. For him, it was like singing in a canyon somewhere. It was just another place to practice, but other co-op dwellers stopped him on the street to praise his concerts. After school Ben would pick until supper. Then, after supper, all the way to lights-out. At age fourteen, in the fall of 1956, astonishing no one, except perhaps himself, he entered the High School of Music and Art.

My path to that establishment you could call a horse of another color. When I learned about the New York City specialized public schools, for example, I wanted a writing one and, if one existed, I would have applied. I also considered the High School of the Performing Arts in acting but, casting aspersions on its location (on West Forty-sixth Street), my mother wouldn't hear of it. Instead she was gearing me up for M&A, enrolling me in Saturday art classes to learn a thing or two while stockpiling works for the required portfolio. When the time came, I arrived at the entrance exam with a mammoth red canvas affair. Thank God I got in. I was accepted at age thirteen (as an art major), the same time as Ben. We met the following year.

I began eating lunch with him in the cafeteria with two friends, Jaimey and Ann. Jaimey, Ann, and I were a threesome. Julian the magician ate nearby. Also Chuck, a fellow alumnus of Joan of Arc—his father was the famous social realist painter, Joe Hirsch—and some others. Julian, having studied in Union City, New Jersey, with a very old vaudevillian, was accomplished at sleight of hand.

Ann was my best friend. We liked each other a lot. We had fun together and were good pals. It's amazing how generous we were to each other considering we weren't really well trained in the complicated reciprocities of love. It's not just a matter of being loved, it's knowing how to love somebody else, and when you're not trained to love yourself, to figure out how to love others is very difficult. I think we were very caring. We met freshman year in French class. Lauterbach, Lardner—we were next-door neighbors in the seating. One day I leaned forward, tapped her, and told her who I was. I thought our parents had known each other, I said. Both our fathers were writers and knew each other, perhaps, like all the left-wing arts intellectuals knew one another one way or another. But I also remembered meeting her father before he died, while mine was in jail, at the Stewarts' house on the West Coast. In Santa Monica at the corner of Salka Viertel's Mabery Road. Ann was ultimately allowed to know about my sleeping with Ben because, besides being my dearest friend, she was the person with more experience than anybody in my world. There was just this sense that she wasn't shockable.

Ann and I liked thinking about people and talking about them. We talked a lot about people. Not just teenage stuff. We concentrated on personalities and ways of being. It was part of our trying to find our footing. She recalls that I liked being in so-cial settings and that I worried about my weight. She was aware of this, she says, because my weight was also something my mother worried about. Ann knew this even though I hadn't told her the gory details—like the TB invalid decree my mother laid on me. "Do just the opposite," she'd instructed me of the pre-scription for the tubercular invalid. While it was better for them to stand than walk, sit than stand—or, better yet, they should lie around—it would be advantageous for me (in terms of benefit-ing my exterior) to reverse their rule of thumb. And every year, when resolution time rolled around (as already mentioned), my parents promised money if I got slimmer. What Ann remembers is standing in front of my mirror with me in my room during a dress-trying-on ordeal. Maybe they were dresses for some dance. The yellow and the green. She clearly remembers that. She thinks there was a scene where I really got upset about how I looked.

Jaimey was in the picture very early because of Ann knowing

her from the neighborhood on the Lower East Side of Manhattan and her father having some kind of flirtation with Ann's mother. Possibly even an affair. Ann's home life was so scatty. So roiling. It just sort of came unstuck altogether. Her mother was an alcoholic. Her father died of polio when she was eight. They had to move from East Eighteenth Street to West Eighteenth when their house was torn down. They would never do that now, says Ann, because it was an incredible house. Then her mother left, at the end of Ann's junior year, for Amagansett, to be with her lover (a Danish seaman), and Ann resided briefly with a family on the Upper West Side. Then everything got out of hand largely due to a whole imbroligio with their teenage son. Ann was trying to figure out how she was going to go to college and be vice president of the GO—attempting to make a life in some kind of way—and it was really impossible.

She and I were altogether serious about our romances. Love was some kind of magic wand. If we could just find the right guy everything would work out. I remember her room way up at the top at West Eighteenth. Her sister was already at college by the time she and her mother, sister, and brother moved there. The house was a narrow little jewel: three stories, with the kitchen below the ground floor. The first floor was the living room, the second had two bedrooms and a bath, and the third another two bedrooms. Ann's mother's bedroom was on the second floor, when she was there, which wasn't often, and her little brother had the back bedroom on the third floor. Ann's was in front and this handsome older boy from our high school named Paul came up to that room. Ann had this enormous crush on him. It was incredibly exciting. A seduction of the first order on Ann's part. It was all sort of set up. Paul was given the keys. She was in bed waiting. He ascended the stairs. It was Victorian in its calculations, but nothing came of it. Ann was determined, however, to get his attention. She had to change her style. Like me, she had been wearing dirty Keds and black tights. And, almost always, olive green and black. Her favorite combination. But she made a concerted effort to have things look a little more collegiate.

Gradually Ben and I got closer. I was a terrific flirt, he said. Also a bit stuck up. He said I corrected him if he slurped soup (at his house no one cared) and he remembered a lesson on chewing without being heard. But he was so taken with me he rarely complained. In reality, as hard as it seemed, he said—he felt he had something to learn from me. Art museums were there to be enjoyed, for example, not just some torturous thing that you did on a school field trip. "It was a Woody Allen experience," he later explained: "Bronx boy crosses into Manhattan."

Then sometime in January, cold but no snow—a walk in Riverside Drive Park—sitting on a bench, slightly awkwardly we kissed for the first time. Soon after, Ben gave me a silver ring that his brother Bill had made and we were going steady. He was teaching Jaimey the guitar at the time and told her about the ring. It crossed my mind that he could just as easily have gone for either her or Ann. And, he said, it was probably true that it could have gone in any direction. But there was only one of us, he said, who had any real sex appeal and "that fact alone left the competition in the dirt." He loved my look. "A bohemian/artistic/leftist type." (Although you had to be from Bohemia to be Bohemian, instructed my father.) The style was artistic. I wasn't too fat or skinny in his eyes. I began letting my hair grow long. Dark opaque stockings and dirty sneakers with holes. Pierced ears. I was an art student so there was usually a little paint somewhere. My father looked askance at the piercing but sent me to the office of a doctor he'd met in jail to have it done.

This inmate doctor administered his physical in prison and Ring told me this about him. A prisoner, who had been around awhile, was talking to a recent arrival who'd undergone a checkup and was grumbling about something when it was over. To which the veteran remarked, "Well, you should have been here last summer. We had an inmate doctor who did the physical. He was really good."

"Inmate doctor," the new fellow queried. "What was he in for?"

"Drugs, I guess," replied the old hand.

"That's not really the case," declared my father, who was standing by eager to impart the relevant news. And he proceeded with information about the Joint Anti-Fascist Refugee Committee, its refusal to turn over a list of the people it helped out of Franco's Spain, and contempt of Congress, while the two fellows listened politely.

Then: "I guess it was some of that and drugs, too," concluded the experienced resident.

The doctor in question, Jacob Auslander, had fallen victim to HUAC in the Joint Anti-Fascist Refugee Committee case. As one of the leaders of the committee, he refused to give records (really lists of names of Spanish loyalist prisoners whom the Joint Anti-Fascist Refugee Committee was helping) to the Un-American Activities Committee. He was afraid members of HUAC would give the names to Franco's fascist government. So he refused.

As for ear piercing, Auslander was probably a neophyte. He was Viennese and very cultured but the holes on my lobes are a little low and what I remember is that he took several phone calls between punctures.

We were all increasingly conscious of creating a look, said my friend Jane who arrived at Music and Art as a sophomore, fleeing the tough Junior Emanon girls of Joan of Arc. They scared the shit out of her, she said. They were particularly tough with Jane

because one of their boyfriends liked her. One of the pack came
after her. It wasn't so much that she was scared of getting beaten
up by them as she was scared of being like them. And those same
girls were headed for Julia Richman, the alternative for Joan of
Arc girls who didn't make it to one of the special schools. Jane
remembers being very surprised she got into Music and Art because it was like winning something, she said, and she never
thought she could win anything. I shared the sentiment. The only
thing I ever won was a third-place ribbon in a swim race that contained just three participants.

Adopting a Parisian thing early on, Jane always dressed in
black stockings and turtleneck shirts taken out of some movie
she saw. (We were both regulars at the Thalia, the venerable art-
house cinema on West Ninety-fifth Street. European films edu-
cated us about life. American films certainly didn't.) And
makeup that took up half her face. The eye makeup was very important. Jane painted almond-shaped eyes. Her long hair was
sometimes braided. "Okay, so who's the goddamn Indian," bel-
lowed family friend Zero Mostel (blacklisted at the time) sitting
in our living room one day when she appeared. "So glamorous,"
she thought. She'd seen him as Leopold Bloom in an off-
Broadway production of *Ulysses in Nighttown* for which he'd
won an Obie. This encounter was a mark of achievement for her.
Jane was looking for looks.

The first time she saw Greta Garbo, for example, in *Queen
Christina* wearing leggings, high boots, and a sort of nineteenth-
century blouson jacket, she proclaimed, "I am going to dress like
that my whole life." It was the androgyny that appealed to her.
Garbo had that, and Dietrich. Jeanne Moreau came later.
Moreau looked weathered, like she'd just rolled out of bed with
someone and the cigarette and the kind of beaten-up thing. Jane
just hoped by the time she turned thirty, by the mere wishing of

it, she would open her mouth and French would come out. She wished so hard because it was the only way she thought she would ever speak French. As Jane said, powerful wishing was such an incredible part of her life.

Her father had been a Communist and she recalls coming home from grade school and seeing her parents galvanized in front of the TV during the McCarthy hearings; and being cautioned about what she said in school. She couldn't say anything about her family. That they were Russian Jews. Or anything about their politics, or what they believed in. The way Jane thought about it then—they believed in all the good things. You know, rights for blacks. Whom we didn't call blacks. Negroes. All the democratic principles. Which is funny when you think of what happened regarding her boyfriend whom Jane probably didn't mention to her parents was six-six and black. Her father first laid eyes on him when Marcus picked her up for a date. But her father didn't say a word or indicate his displeasure then. Not until later when they got home and were entering the apartment. Then her father grabbed Jane and pushed Marcus back, slamming the door in his face. Jane was dragged to the bathroom, lifted into the tub, and the shower was turned on her. "I know what you're up to," said her dad, seething.

They had gone down to a coffee shop in Greenwich Village, said Jane, who was stunned by her father's racism. (Her parents weren't just Communists, she said. They were crazy Communists.) She and Marcus had sat there talking the whole time. "Who knows about what?" she said. "About life. I don't even remember what we talked about." After that, they saw each other secretly, at school (Marcus was a senior at M&A), sitting in the subway a lot, or going down to the Village. Jane didn't know how much racism he had been exposed to before, but he really came up against it that night.

"If you can think of Emmett Till three years before," she said, reflecting back on the mangled and decomposed body she'd seen in the newspaper and her parents clucking over it. The whole idea was so frightening. That was one of those things that made you think about how you were going to spend the rest of your life. You weren't ever going to be that way. You were going to fight for that never to happen. "It fell in the same category as the Holocaust stories that informed all of our lives," said Jane.

"The issue around it was sexuality," she said. That's why the episode with Marcus and her father made her think of Emmett Till. "He sees a tall black guy and that's what they've got to be doing. The only reason I could ever go out with this guy is I'm hot for his dick. And that's why he threw me in the shower."

A short while later, while visiting at her place (Jane lived across the street), what happened with Marcus became fodder for dealing with what I perceived as a perilous situation. Jane flew past me crying out, "My father's after me!" "Run, Jane, run!" I instructed. While Jane fled through the door and down the back stairs, I remained to deal with her dad, who appeared roaring like a goddamn dragon. "Your daughter is a wonderful girl," I uttered, hoping to detain him. And Jane made her getaway while I blocked the brute.

From then on she spent as much time as she could at our house; she felt safer there and she went home as little as possible. (Not that our establishment was a bed of roses.) Her parents weren't too happy about this. They thought Jane was telling tales on them, which, of course, she was. And they referred to me as Katie's Korner Klinic. KKK.

Jane said I was very vocal about my mother. What a pain in the ass she was. Critical, etc. "There was just this sense of disappointment with you," she said. "You weren't respectful enough." (This earned me the nickname *Miss Snipit* from my father.

Snip for short.) And Jane witnessed Joe and me taking off on our mom not quite behind her back.

I documented one such exchange between my mother and Joe. My brother's testing limits had established that our mother, for the moment, was in a good mood. When he had told her that the tongue (the leftover meat from some meal) was terrible, she agreed. He said it was really horrible. "Horrible!" exclaimed my brother. And again our mother concurred. Joe took it further. "This tongue tastes like shit," he said finally. To which she replied amiably, "Well, Joe, I don't know as much about that as you do." Thus: "Mommy was in a good mood this morning," concluded Joe.

I could go on about my brother Joe here and even insert him more in my chronicle, but frankly he'd rather I didn't. He doesn't want to be written about. In fact, he's pretty touchy on the whole subject. He says it's not that he's shy about appearing in someone's book. He actively opposes the idea. But I've got to tell you about the time the two of us were sitting around listening to Dvořák's *New World Symphony* in our living room. We were both so moved by the thing. Joe sat and looked at the books in the bookshelf. Swayed by a powerful feeling, to put a lid on his waterworks, he read aloud the titles of the books on our parents' shelves. I sat and listened. I then told him about school; about things I had felt and done. I hadn't seen him for a long time. This was during my freshman year at college. As I was talking I thought of what I was saying. I thought of repeating these things again for effect. (I was phony as hell. Just as I loved running down a hill and it was important not only to do the thing but also declare I *love* running down a hill to the world to make an impression.) As I was doing this I began to cry and Joe said, "I knew you'd break before I did." We were both goners when it came to that music and we knew we would be. I swear we were that close.

I used to lose my temper easily with my mother and cry most of the time when I didn't get my way. I would cry or exclaim the F word, etc. My mother was afraid of me. "It's funny how one can feel so full of hate when they are mad," I told Ben. Sometimes she wouldn't talk to us for days. Joe claimed he liked the silent treatment. I didn't but I would have died rather than admit it. And often I wound up in my room. Either banished there or retreating voluntarily, slamming the door and leaving behind a trail of expletives for my parents. I could say the meanest things, but much of the time what I really felt in my mother's presence was awkward and lonely as hell.

I wrote about one of these incidents to Ben. I'd begun the day happy, but following an encounter with my parents about summer plans, I plummeted.

June 27, 1959

. . . I want to know where the hell and when we're going to be this summer. I keep saying that I want to be near the city— expressly to see you. Daddy keeps saying "I don't want negative ideas." Okay so the first time I happened to express my wish thusly. "I don't want to be far from the city." What a nut—Jesus Christ what this family won't do for an argument. So I changed my desire so it would seem more positive for the old man . . . I wanted to be able to tell you where to write. That's when it all began. . . . Perhaps a few letters will have to be forwarded. This is what I got so upset about. It's funny (weird funny) what happens to me—I get lonely, afraid and perhaps confused and definitely feeling sorry for myself and I cry. Today I was selfish—I was happy, loved people, was fun, was sweet charming Katie all I'm sure because I felt pretty. Ben, are other people selfish? Why do I cry?—I must like to cry. Am I always selfish? I want someone to

answer me. Why can't I be answered? I think Mommy might send me to an analyst in the fall. I'd like that . . . Don't pay any attention to me I'm feeling sorry for myself. I want you to hug me.

"And this too will pass." Isn't that wonderful, Ben whenever something is sad—"And this too will pass." It's wonderful for it is true. True for me and true for everyone. "And this too will pass."

I don't know how the phrase came to me but I kept saying it.

Jane was impressed as hell we could talk back to my mother. But she also found her entertaining. There was an element of performance all the time, said Jane. "I mean she always came across as a little girl. There was nothing about your mother that was adult." Jane was delighted with the whole bunch of us. Jim was too young to take seriously but there was a liveliness about all of us, she said. "We're not talking about Ring, now," she confessed. Though she liked him, "he was not the most gregarious. But he had a certain twinkle." Anyway my father had the sheen of celebrity, she said. He could sit there next to his Academy Award, as far as she was concerned. She'd seen his golden statuette (though it wasn't displayed prominently) and—having practiced receiving one for years, wrapped in her knotty white chenille bedspread, before actually holding it—the Oscar held tremendous magic for her. "Ring didn't have to do much. He was sort of aristocratic," she said. Jane read my grandfather's short stories before she met me in junior high. And she still has the copy of my father's book he gave her—*The Ecstasy of Owen Muir*—and in it he wrote, "With love and avuncular blessings." She had to look up *avuncular*.

With Ben I discovered the music and freedom of the Square. He heard about the Sunday-afternoon sings in Greenwich Village's Washington Square Park, and in the spring of freshman year he prevailed upon his parents to help get him there. After

they drove into Manhattan and dropped him off, he approached
the musicians standing around the fountain picking their instru-
ments. Eric Weissberg, who was a couple of years ahead of us at
Music and Art, and Marshall Brickman were picking banjos.
There were a few guitarists and a fellow playing a washtub bass.
Ben took out his guitar and began playing along, but since he
was shy and never spoke to anyone, he never got to know any of
them very well. They were kind, however, and never criticized
him or told him to take a hike. Many of the songs were familiar.
Ben had a very good ear for chord patterns, and it was simple for
him to join in. When he began to sing no one stopped him. But
the one thing he didn't know was the etiquette of playing in a
group. Ben thought the words were important. They had to tell
him to stop singing so that an instrument solo might prevail.
Being a quick study, however, he never made that mistake again.
Then his parents began to trust him to get to the Square by himself. He'd take the D train and get there when he could.

After a summer break as a counselor in training at Camp Willoway, Ben returned to the Village music sessions in the fall. Pete
Seeger would sometimes show up, and Pete's half brother Mike
played fiddle. Mary Travers must have lived nearby because she
was often around and no one could ignore her sexy, electrifying
personality or her blond hair. This was before the Peter, Paul &
Mary days. Roger Sprung was a continuing presence with his
crisp bluegrass banjo playing. Ben heard Sprung play "Lime-
house Blues" on his five-string and never forgot it.

On rainy days the music moved to Izzy Young's Folklore
Center. They'd all crowd into the place and the music, bouncing
off the walls, would bring out the passionate kind of group
singing that later went out of favor, when the music turned introspective and personal and people started listening rather than
singing along.

When the weather turned cold, the group headed indoors to a gym in the Labor Temple on Fourteenth Street. It was there Ben first heard a guy with an incredible gravelly voice and a unique guitar style. Dave Van Ronk. He couldn't believe his eyes or ears.

Ben took me on the subway with him and his guitar. I remember getting off the train at the West Fourth Street station. Only soon after, he stopped bringing the guitar. Who wanted to carry around a guitar when he could put his arm around me, he said. Greenwich Village was the bohemian part of New York. It felt grown-up.

Actually we were on the cusp of bohemian versus beatnik. Bohemia had been sort of dying out since the twenties. The poets started reading in New York. *Howl,* the foremost poetic expression of the beat movement, appeared and Ben wrote a paper on Allen Ginsberg for English. Grabbing hold of the line (from *America*) "Go fuck yourself with your atom bomb," he delivered it as an oral report. Jane walked around barefooted and at sixteen got hired as a waitress at the Village Gaslight where the owner, John Mitchell, cautioned, "Don't fuck the cook, he's mine." The Village was the center of cool. At the Gaslight poetry was offered along with pastry. This was in the Beat Generation days, predating the folk "tidal wave which later rolled in with Joan Baez and Bob Dylan riding its crest," as journalist Al Avonowitz put it.

I meanwhile was busy striving to represent the underdog in Dr. Barnett's social studies class or at least be on the case about getting the whole story told. It seemed to me he drew a map of Europe in which Russia became a goddamn ocean. I resented this for some reason. (I learned years later that my brother Jim had a similar experience with the disappearance of Russia in the fourth grade at Hunter College Elementary School.) I couldn't count on old Barnett to get it right about Communism, or the Soviet Union (which we were studying), so he parked me up in front of the room, to fill in the gaps, after I told him so. I was eager to ward off anti-Communist talk and misinformation. (Both Jim and I—from really early on—felt obliged to argue with teachers about Communism or anything like that. We would sort of speak up and make a spectacle of ourselves.) Look what it had done to my father, for God's sake. I always believed in what he'd done. I never had any second thoughts about whether his being in jail was a disgrace. I didn't feel it was a disgrace. As far as I was concerned, he had done the thing that was heroic. He, however, didn't think of himself as heroic. "The alternative to doing what we did would have been to cooperate completely with the committee, as some subsequent witnesses did, and that was a very degrading thing. Because once you acknowledged that they had a right to ask those questions then the next questions they asked were who else was in the party or in such and such a group. And then you had to talk about a lot of other people who may have been involved quite innocently and whose reputations and livelihood you'd be threatening." Anyway it was extremely distasteful to do that, said my father. So according to him, the only alternative was to challenge the committee and hope that they would win in the courts. "I say it's no more being a hero than if you're walking along a fast-running brook and you see a child caught in the current. You either just walk on and pay no attention or you make some effort to save the person and that's not really heroic."

Actually Ben said the whole "folk revival" practically started at the Square. It didn't just happen when Dylan arrived on the scene. The Weavers were recording best-selling hits in the late forties. They may have been almost hounded out of existence by the Red-baiting fifties, but Pete Seeger and some like-minded souls kept their folk songs alive in New York City and elsewhere. Some of it was leftist-political, he said, but it was always combined with music of the American folk and other world cultures. To this was added some country and western (Hank Williams, for example), and it coincided with the rise of bluegrass, which also was becoming a big influence. Southern ballads and a bit of bluegrass is what Ben heard when he first went to the Square and joined the little group near the Washington Arch. There weren't many people then but there was plenty of enthusiasm. By the time we were ready to graduate, however, the Square was packed and you could hardly get near the groups to join the music making. The love of the music had grown.

Smoking for Jane went along with eye makeup in adopting things to be adult. We had to be older to be taken seriously. Trying to smoke like Bette Davis in *Now, Voyager*, where she's exhaling out of her nose and mouth, Jane saw eye to eye with Charlotte Vale, the Bette Davis character. Charlotte was from an aristocratic Boston family so there were some leaps there. But she was involved in a messed-up relationship with her mother, which caused Bette to puff up a storm. Jane identified with her. Bette/Charlotte was held hostage. Bette's mother really didn't give a shit about her and wanted Bette to keep her company. This, for Jane, was all too familiar.

Compared to Jane's mother—an obvious witch—my mother was a veritable dreamboat. About Frances, Ann said, "She was energetic. Almost to the point of exaggeration. Very vain," she said, "and her vanity went out in all directions toward others and in relation to others." Like Ann and me. (Old Ann expressed things eloquently and passionately. She knew and could articulate how you felt, then and now.) When you came in the door my mother would look you over and make her pronouncements about what you were wearing, etc. There was this thing about how you looked. And she set great store by manners. She would correct your speech. She was very judging. Or at least you felt she was. And to Ann she seemed stagy. There was something about her gestures and the way she smiled that Ann found enthralling. My mother was very warm to her, however. They would sit together in the kitchen and talk. Ann remembered being grateful to her for being interested. Sometimes she felt guilty or confused because she got along with my mom so well and she didn't quite understand why it was so difficult for my mom to get along with me or me with her. I seemed to be wonderful, said Ann. And on the whole, she thought my mother was wonderful. She didn't always think she was wonderful, but at that point she did. (It was okay with me that she talked to my mom, I later told her. I had someone to talk to—Ben. I'd found someone who gave me so much love. And Ann needed her. She was practically an orphan, for God's sake.) There was a side of my mother, she said, when she had her glasses on, that was less actressy and more engaged with some other part of herself. When she was busy reading scripts in her bedroom. Reading something. Manuscripts of one kind or another.

But the household itself was so peculiar, she said. Like this fantasy house. The house she didn't get to have. It felt like it was busy creating mythology about itself at all points, Ann said. And that she found exciting, too. "But at the same time," she said, "myths are about a certain kind of impenetrability. So people weren't really allowed a full access to anything or anyone because the myth was the thing that was important. Centered around Ring, of course. And Frances—very busy trying to cope with and at the same time protect him and very interested in their social life." She remembers the two of us doing homework and my parents getting dressed up and going out a lot and the boys often behind the closed door of their bedroom. And some-times Ann would arrive in the afternoon or evening and find some kind of soiree going on.

The thing that was most affecting about Ring, she said, was the kind of amusement he seemed to take in things generally.

My father was funny. I thought he had just the right kind of sly sense of humor.

"Although I'm not sure that wasn't a certain kind of mask," said Ann.

It's true sometimes it was hard to know if my father was really there, even if he was in the room with you. Sometimes I was afraid to be alone with him—partly because I was in awe of him. For one thing, he was almost never wrong about his facts. And, as previously indicated with the account of the periodical peddler, at times I didn't know what to say. On those occasions it was as if it were my job to utter the things that were going to be of interest or up to snuff. I mean there wasn't going to be a ques-tion from him to you: how's it going, or what are you doing, or any of those things. You had to kind of design the way. My father was so hidden; I didn't always know how to make contact with him.

He was sort of courtly, said Ann, continuing, and perfectly nice to her, and a few times they actually did have a conversa-tion. She remembered feeling quite honored that he would spend any time with her but she thought that was after she was in college and coming back and visiting and sitting and having a conversation with him in the living room.

"They were very self-involved—your parents," said Ann, reflecting back. "They were in another realm." She never really had a sense that they were present, she said. "I mean, they were there but their preoccupations or their minds and hearts seemed to be somewhere else. You could almost say they were bewildered by being parents.

"There was such a strong current in that house of things not spoken of or not addressed," she said, sighing. "A kind of secrecy that was quite palpable." And it seemed to her, when she got to meet the other players in the Lardner constellation, it was ubiquitous. It wasn't just our household. To tell you the truth, she claimed everyone she met in the family had the same sense of being in some kind of aura. "Being in an aura," she said. "Having some kind of aura. Or wanting to have an aura or giving themselves an aura." What Ann was speaking about here was the notion of entitlement. She is interested in endowments of privilege and how they are related to, as she says, "some skewed notion of heritage as opposed to actual achievement although at times of course they are both. (Ring.)"

I know this isn't necessarily a good thing but I liked being in an aura.

Ben vividly remembered my parents, too. Especially the tense times with my mother. We were always fighting, he said. It was one of the things I confided in him. Crying at times, which I could do with him. He remembered the paper tacked on the bulletin board outside the kitchen listing all the allowance my brothers and I were losing because of our behavior. At the rate we were going, he said, we wouldn't receive any for the rest of our lives. It was always in the minus numbers and it seemed to him that my mother was at a loss as to how to control her children. On the other hand, she had a leading role for a while and received good notices as a chic lesbian at a theater on Bleecker Street in Ben Hecht's play *Winkelberg* about a Village poet, Maxwell Bodenheim. Bodenheim drank himself insensible and finally got killed in a sordid row with a sailor. And each day dur-

ing the run my mother went to work when most of the people
Ben knew were coming home. She would get on the subway to
go to her off-Broadway gig. The idea that one would travel by
public transportation to become a performer by night was exciting to him.

My father drank too much during various dinners Ben
shared with us. He slurred his language. His drinking was always a source of contention between my parents. My grandfather's drinking was a problem in my grandparents' marriage
from the beginning but there never was any fighting. They had
separate bedrooms. Granny told my mother once (or implied)
that it had to do with my grandfather's drinking and the hours
he kept. My grandfather used his bedroom basically as a workroom, but he slept there most of the time. My mother was told
by Granny's friends that she never said or did anything about
her husband's drinking. She just acted like it didn't happen.
This, however, was not my mother's way. She was inhibited in
my grandmother's house in New Milford but once we moved out
there was plenty of screaming and yelling. My mother's screaming and yelling.

My father's drinking began at age fourteen during his second
year at Andover. He would convert hard cider into a form of ap-
plejack by hanging it out a window in winter to freeze, then boring into the center of the ice to recover the still-liquid part where
all the alcohol created by fermentation was concentrated. Also,
there were expeditions to speakeasies in the nearby city of
Lawrence or Revere Beach where no proof of adulthood was
required. He said on weekend days these forays had a cloak of
legitimacy—you could get school passes to a museum or a concert in Boston or to visit a relative in the area. Other times they
took place at night and the drinking youth left their dormitories

by window, either with a simulated body in their beds or after the
10:00 P.M. room-by-room inspection by the housemaster.

During my father's first year and a half at Princeton, the
handiest speakeasy was reached by a bus ride to Trenton, where
you could buy bootleg booze to conceal in your room. On January 1, 1934, the repeal of the Prohibition amendment went into
effect; in Princeton the old bar at the Nassau Inn was reopened,
and in New York the Artist and Writers Club (known as Bleeck's),
where my father had been joining his brother John and his
newspaper friends, was opened without a password to any reasonably grown-up male. Bleeck's was a *Herald Tribune* and *New
York Times* hangout on West Fortieth Street. *The New Yorker,*
then on Forty-fifth Street, wasn't far away. Also a number of theater people frequented it. Bleeck's had been a speakeasy named
Artist and Writers Club. As a legal establishment it became Artist
and Writers Restaurant—*artist* singular and *writers* plural. That
was the way Jack Bleeck who ran it just happened to write the
sign, but my uncle John said Jack Bleeck only knew one artist. It
was a custom, among the newspapermen particularly, to play the
match game to see who paid for a round of drinks.

When my father went to work the following year for the *New
York Daily Mirror,* Tim Costello's was his bar of choice, and most
of his five working days ended up there. James Thurber was a
customer and a friend of Costello's and Costello decorated the
walls with Thurber drawings, which Thurber drew right on the
wall in pencil. A man in the art department at the *Mirror* went
over the pencil in india ink. My father said he was careful, however, to limit himself to two or three double scotches if he was
going to a bridge club in the vicinity to supplement his meager
income. He had discovered that he could raise his twenty-five-
dollar-a-week income an average of ten dollars by two or three
evenings' diligent application to the game.

His days off, he went to Granny's newly acquired house in New Milford, where he would conform to her one drink before dinner and most of the time, he said, none afterward. Possessing at that time a respectable capacity to hold his liquor, he was rarely visibly affected by it with only occasional lapses, he said, into more or less deliberate drunkenness. And that continued to be his general drinking pattern for the next twenty-five years, with his ability to hold the stuff diminishing over the years so gradually as to be almost imperceptible except in retrospect. I refer the interested reader here, as I was referred by the recipient himself, to a letter in the Dalton Trumbo collection *Additional Dialogue* that described my father's symptoms during the latter part of this phase.

Los Angeles, California
October 28, 1945
DEAR RING:

About two years ago I was having dinner and a few drinks at the Players with Hugo [Butler], and he happened to mention that you looked sallow, and I said you weren't. I told Hugo flatly that I thought it was a hell of a thing to say about somebody you were pretending to be friendly with, and that I had never thought you were sallow, and that a lot of people who were running around whispering and giggling about how sallow you were could occupy their time much better by staying home and paying their bills. I also told him that I was your friend, that I didn't care whether you were sallow or not, and that sallowness was something like having a club foot: if a man had it he had it, and it didn't help matters any by going around and blabbering about it behind his back.

I also pointed out that even if you had seemed to him to be sallow, that wasn't any sign you had always been sallow or would necessarily continue to be. I told him for example that liver trouble might cause a man to be sallow, and that a little spell of clean living generally fixed a liver up, and what the hell business was it of Hugo or anybody else about the state of your liver. I likewise told him liver trouble was no joke, with a lot of pain attached to it, and anybody who had it deserved more pity than censure. We parted friends, but that night I got to thinking about all the things Hugo had said, and I sent him a note by hand in which I repeated everything I had said to him just for the record. I'm glad now that I did, too.

About six or eight months later I was having dinner and a few drinks at the Players with Lester Cole, and quite suddenly Lester said to me wasn't it a shame the way Ring was running around drinking himself to death and ruining his liver and not paying his bills. He said that Hugo said that I had said that this was because you were so callow. Lester said this, for him, hit the nail right on the head. I saw right then what was happening—in fact, I foresaw this whole situation coming up as far back as that—so I set Lester straight right then and there. I told him I'd much rather have a dirty mind than a dirty liver, and that if you wanted to drink yourself to death, who had a better right?

I also told him that when your eyes slide up under your forehead like they do sometimes when you're goat drunk, why it wasn't intentional because it was something you couldn't avoid under the circumstances, and probably didn't come from the liquor at all but rather from a sudden fit of depression. I also told him I didn't know anything about your bills. I said you were my friend and your not paying your bills didn't lessen my liking and loyalty one iota. I denied that I ever said you were callow. I said you were young, naturally, but has a man got to be callow just because he is young? I said your callowness had never made the slightest difference in our relationship, and that you would straighten up as soon as you had broadened and deepened, and that in the meanwhile I didn't want to talk any more about the matter. That night I wrote him a note by hand and delivered it myself to make sure he got it. Now he probably still has the letter, and if you want to get in touch with him one reading of it will clear a great deal of our current misunderstanding, and perhaps show you who is your true friend.

Now not so long ago I was having dinner and a few drinks at the Players with Bob Rossen, and Bob said he'd been talking to Lester, and that Lester had said he believed I had doped Lardner just about right when I said that he was too shallow to care whether his liver rotted away and his bills were paid or not, and that all this boozing and liver trouble had given him fits. Bob wanted to know whether it was epileptic fits or just kind of stomach fits. Naturally I denied all this, and went into a great deal of detail to get the story straight again.

I said to him, how should I know what kind of fits they are? I said you were a friend of mine and I didn't like everybody in town talking about your having fits. I told him I saw no connection between you being shallow and having fits, and I named him eleven people who are shallower than you and don't have fits at all. I also told him that epileptics are normally harmless if you just stick a piece of rubber or something between their teeth to stop them from biting their tongues off. I told him if I didn't mind fits, why the hell should he? I said that regardless of what kind of fits you had, dieting and a wholesome life would steady them down quite a bit and maybe even eventually cure them entirely.

I got so sore about Bob talking like this about a friend of mine that I didn't even wait to get home to write. I grabbed two menus and a pen and wrote him a letter on the spot. Now I don't know whether or not he still has it, and I didn't make a carbon, but I'm writing him a note by hand tonight asking him to send it to you by hand if he still has it, and after you've seen what I really said, you can drop me a note by hand if you still care to keep me as your friend.

Now I suppose a lot of this has got back to you, twisted and distorted as usual, and that you are sore. Paul Trivers [a playwright and screenwriter] wrote me a note by hand saying you had written a note by hand to Ranald [MacDougall, a

writer and director known for such films as *Mildred Pierce* and
Objective, Burma!] asking him to stop writing falsehoods
about you. I've written Randy a note by hand asking him to
explain himself, and I expect an answer by hand before evening. Now I'll send you a note the minute I hear from him, together with a copy of my note to him and Trivers and Trivers'
note to me, together with any other notes that may arrive in
the meantime, and then maybe we can compare notes and try
to straighten this thing out. Until then, I don't see any reason
for you getting so hysterical about it as indicated in your note
by hand of yesterday.

On the other hand, maybe you don't want to straighten it
out, and if you don't, why that's okay with me too. The goddamned doorbell is ringing all hours of the day or night, waking the kid up every time it rings, and the kid is bawling and
notes are coming in by hand from people I never even bothered to make enemies of, and I think you might remember
once in a while that I've got a job to take care of and a wife
and children who are dependent on me. Or I guess maybe you
figure I've knocked out four novels, three short stories, twenty
motion picture scripts, and speeches and pamphlets too nu-
merous to mention by just sitting around writing notes in your
defense. Now I want you to understand this very clearly:

When this whole thing first came up, and Hugo said to me
you were sallow, I knew goddamned well you were sallow. You
may have thought you had deceived me, but you didn't. I
thought you were sallow from the first day I met you. I have
often said to Cleo, "Christ, he's sallow!" It was only my loyalty
to you that caused me to deny something that every loose-
lipped son-of-a-bitch in town has been talking about for years.
Now if this is the reward I get, then okay.

About your bills, why hell, they're not my responsibility.
But just to stop your yapping, I'll pay them if it'll make you
feel any better. Just send them into the Roberts office and I'll
see they're taken care of so we won't for Christ's sake have to
hear any more of your talk about them.

About your liver, I don't see how you can hold me responsible for its condition at all. *I* didn't teach you to drink—you were a dipso long before I met you.

About your eyes the way they roll up on you, why I haven't known whether you were looking at me or the inside of your forehead for seven years, and now with the attitude you're taking, I frankly don't give a good goddamn.

God knows I've tried to be a good friend, and loyal, and stop all the talking about you. But I may as well tell you that I think you bring a lot of it on yourself by the way you go around acting all the time. And while I'm at it, I might as well tell you that I'd rather you didn't drop by the house all the time anymore. If you have anything to take up with me, just drop me a note by hand. I don't mind you being around, and certainly Cleo doesn't, but I'm not going to have you scaring the kids half to death in one of your goddamned fits.

SINCERELY YOUR FRIEND,
DALTON TRUMBO

I think this letter would make anyone want to drink.

Trumbo was my father's closest friend among the nineteen Hollywood personalities subpoenaed to appear before HUAC in the fall of 1947. He was smart and funny and deeply concerned with what was going on in the world. He loved to talk, but, my father said, unlike most people with that tendency, Trumbo was almost always worth listening to. "His writing was almost as facile as his speech, and he turned out an incredible quantity of material, especially during the blacklist, when his price was drastically cut," said Ring.

It seemed to my father that most of the people he knew who were drunks were writers. And he read somewhere a reference to Nobel Prize winners in this regard. (He was interested in doing research about writers and drinking because of his father, and himself, and a few other people he knew.) He said he investigated and then realized that every American Nobel Prize winner (this was before Isaac Bashevis Singer and Saul Bellow) except Pearl Buck had been a heavy drinker or an alcoholic including Eugene O'Neill (he quit at age thirty-seven), Faulkner, Hemingway, Steinbeck, and Sinclair Lewis. He also did a compilation of hard-hitting twentieth-century American writers. Between 30 and 33 percent of a list of names he pulled from some almanac of twentieth-century writers fit the definition. And my father said he probably missed a few. Growing up, as he did, among writers and living his adult life in Hollywood and New York, he met a large number of them. So in many cases his knowledge was personal. Others he knew about from books. He said he thought probably more poets have been drunks than in any other field of writing. "One recalls," said Ring, "Robert Burns, Verlaine, Swinburne, Poe, Dylan Thomas, James Whitcomb Riley, Edgar Lee Masters, Edwin Arlington Robinson, Dorothy Parker, Conrad Aiken, John Berryman, Hart Crane, Randall Jarrell, Delmore Schwartz, Wallace Stevens. There are a great deal more," he said.

He assumed the fact that writing was an occupation that didn't require specific hours, where the individual sets his own hours, was a factor. "You can go on a bat for several days and then stay on the wagon making it up, doing a lot of work at a time you don't have to show up at an office," he said. "And it's probably because it involves frustrations and alternating good periods." My father believed writers were more subject to anxiety than a lot of people simply because they got themselves into holes either through some kind of block or just laziness or something. "You suddenly realize you have to make a deadline," he said, "whether it's self-imposed or something else. And you get anxious about it. And even if you know the fear is going to go away you use it as an excuse to have a drink. 'That'll calm me down.' " My father said another reason was "the loneliness that is involved in the process of writing and the frustrations of wrestling with creative problems."

Here is part of a conversation I had with my dad on the soothing benefits of the stuff. I didn't know if he was willing to talk about himself.

ME:	Did you think for yourself . . . Did you observe that alcohol loosened you up in some way? As far as writing?
RING:	At least for the thinking. I have on a number of occasions gotten good ideas . . . I never really tried to write anything while drinking. But sometimes something has been sticking, and something I haven't been able to think of—a funny thing, or how to solve a particular problem—has come to me. But it's really only after a first drink or two that some good thought seems to strike. If you begin to get very drunk that doesn't continue. And I think the fact that you spend more conscious hours with the problem when you're not drinking, whatever the writing problem is, probably makes up for those occasional inspirations.
ME:	Well, what did drinking do . . . Or what does it do for you? You seem to be . . . Tell me if you don't want to talk about this.
RING:	No . . .
ME:	You seem to be a very different kind of drinker now than you used to be.
RING:	Yes, I don't ever drink now . . . I don't get drunk.
ME:	Well, I think I've seen you drunk.
RING:	Well . . .
ME:	. . . in Connecticut within the last couple of years . . . One night.
RING:	That's possible but generally speaking when I do drink, it's apt to be either some wine at dinner or a stiff drink just before going to bed.
ME:	Yeah, why do you do that, Dad?

RING: It helps me sleep.

ME: Do you have trouble sleeping?

RING: Yeah.

ME: Does that do anything for you? Just a little?

RING: Yeah, it relaxes.

ME: Well, do you know why you drank? I mean besides the physical?

(long pause)

RING: There was a whole difference between when I drank in my twenties, thirties, and forties and later . . . I did get drunk quite a bit, but I didn't drink every day until . . . I think it was 1960 . . .

The change began, in my father's eyes, in 1960. In January a woman for whom he had cared deeply for twenty years died of accidental drunken self-immolation, and then in February his mother suffered a fatal stroke. And before the end of March his brother John died of a heart attack at forty-seven, leaving my father the sole survivor of what had been a family of six. (Right after my uncle John died was the only time I ever saw my father cry. I was alone in a room with him at the time and at a loss as to what to do. I remember embracing him, hoping it would help.) As a result of these deaths, my father said his drinking pattern significantly changed. Alcohol just made it easier to forget things, he said.

And no abstinent period in the years that followed lasted the full ninety days my father gleaned was the AA-designated crucial minimum but, he said, they lasted long enough to persuade him that he had the demon under control. However, as he said in his memoir (*I'd Hate Myself in the Morning*), on a couple of occasions, "desperate to lick the problem," he committed himself to strenuous detoxification programs only to find himself unable to maintain the permanent sobriety they were after. Then he tried to stop (and this is what really gets me) drinking on his own. On the second day of this attempt my father was having lunch with a publishing executive when he blacked out. When he came to, he found himself strapped to a bed in a hospital alcoholism unit. Again he went through the detox process and after some AA sessions (so called by my father) he said he was judged ready to continue his recovery on his own.

In the last decade of his life, after starting a "wagon" stint a couple of times but always finding some reason to cut it short after a day or two or three, he would embark upon other schemes (even documenting them for his heirs or anyone interested in him or in the subject of alcoholism) to deal with the drug that was a significant part of his life for so long in an attempt to reassure himself that he had the addiction under control. What he was after was recapturing what he had decided was a fairly successful method (during the previous eighteen years) of controlling his addiction. Consuming no alcohol at all except an occasional glass of wine or a single beer until fairly late in the evening—within an hour or two of going to bed. Then knocking back two stiff drinks surreptitiously in fairly quick succession, *stiff* meaning three or four ounces of eighty-proof vodka, usually with some form of mixer. He said that this on most nights put him to sleep pretty quickly and quite soundly. He varied this pattern now and then, up to three times a year, with a period of total abstinence. This seemed advisable to him, "perhaps essential" to prevent a return to his former "more extreme addiction." But as I said a little while back, my father kept finding reasons to cut these periods short. (He also took an occasional single drink before dinner besides the nightcaps.) And he was determined to overcome that block.

Meanwhile my mother had embraced the ideas of AA,

which she first absorbed in meetings of its spin-off group, Al-Anon, as the solution. She came to understand that alcoholism was a family illness and that changed attitudes could affect recovery. She tried to deal with the effects of the disease in her own life. Alcoholic attitudes were in her genes, and they affected and afflicted the way she looked at life. She had gotten to be very controlling. She worked on reacting less to drinking and its consequences. (This was after I moved out.) She chose to look after her own life and recognized that it was her responsibility to do so. To find out what she needed, what she wanted, what she wanted to pursue, what would make her happy—what was best for her own being. But she threatened to leave forthwith a couple of times after she caught my dad in the act, which she did either by taking a sip for herself of what she assumed to be a soft drink, or by deliberately deciding to check up on him, or after running across a hidden supply. (My father claimed to have been fairly ingenious about hiding places.) In each case he would confess to a temporary lapse and my mom would make a flat declaration that she was leaving for good unless he pledged permanent abstinence. My mother ultimately stopped drinking. But she never left.

"Do you know I love him very much," she proclaimed on more than one occasion. She also said: "I'm very lucky that it's ended up the way it has. That we've got each other." And my father loved her. He even told me so when I was probing the matter during my investigation of the launching of their life together. I asked him what Frances was like when they met. "Well," he said, "she was very charming and full of vitality. She had and always has had a very engaging personality and an ability to get along with people and make talk and say what's on her mind. Sometimes without thinking too much about it. Very articulate. I was in love with her," he kind of mumbled. He repeated it. "I was in love with her."

"I don't understand it," said my mother. "The person he was in love with was that fucking so-and-so," she shrieked (when I shared this with her) in reference to my father's dear friend mentioned earlier. "Oh I hated her. No, she burned up, poor thing." In 1957 while my mother was understudying Kim Stanley in *A Clearing in the Woods* at the Belasco Theatre on Broadway, my father moved out to a hotel for about a week. My mother asked him to. She said I couldn't recall this development because he used the excuse that he was working on a script. He said he was staying away to work. And also, my mother said, because he came every day and emptied the garbage. "She was beautiful," she said of her nemesis. "She was like a lady spider. There was something so charming and adorable about her and she thought of herself as this muse to writers. She would encourage and inspire the writing. Well," said Frances, "I never thought of myself as the muse or the inspiration. I had my own ideas for myself. I wasn't going to be anybody else's muse."

But my mother said she thought she would die when this happened. She was so unhappy. When my father considered leaving her, she said he couldn't because that other person wasn't good enough. The spider wasn't "the pure in heart." She and Ring were "the pure in heart."

I once asked my father if he was familiar with any of the research that had been done on alcoholism in the family, and he said he knew that there was an inherited tendency. "A susceptibility," he said. "I am reasonably sure that it has an effect on the family and children so I'm pretty sure it would on mine. But as far as figuring out what are the effects of my drinking as opposed to the effects of other environmental influences . . . I don't know. I can't tell specifically."

. . .

My father drank too much on various occasions in Ben's presence, but Ben mostly recalls that my dad was quiet and a bit shy toward him. And that he gave my brother Jim a typewriter for his birthday or Christmas and Ben always thought of that as a major difference between our families. It would never have occurred to his parents that he would even want one. A typewriter spelled exotic to him. He'd never met a family of writers before. The typewriter stays in his mind to this day as an intellectual message to a kid—no one was sending such messages in his family. Ben was fascinated by the library on West End Avenue. He'd never seen so many books in one household. To the left of the fake fireplace in our living room all of them were on Catholicism. Ben only had a vague idea about my father's book *The Ecstasy of Owen Muir.* The book he began in prison. He finally read it as a senior in high school, but it had never occurred to him that someone would do all that research just to write one book.

One day while poking among our books he found, to the right of the fireplace and behind the volumes on the bottom shelf, a loosely wrapped package. He unwrapped a statue that turned out to be the Oscar. Ben couldn't believe what was in his hands. He called me over to convey his excitement, not quite comprehending why it wasn't out there for the world to see. (Actually what I remember most is its function as a doorstop. Later when my father got another one—for *M*A*S*H*—they shared a spot on a shelf in his workroom.) He claims he perceived nervousness on my part about what he'd done but maybe my father had forgotten about it, he said. Or lost track of where he put it. He says I told him to put the thing back. Reflecting back on it, Ben imagined how angry my father must have been at the industry that could so easily give and take away. But at the time, it was one more thing about the adult world that he was beginning to suspect was more complicated than he'd imagined.

After January, over the months, Ben and I began to make out more extensively. It was a mutual learning experience, with neither of us pressing the other to go further than what felt safe. Over time we found refuge in the various nooks and crannies of my family's apartment on West End Avenue—the little room off the kitchen, the sofas in the living room, my bedroom. We visited Ben's apartment in the Bronx and did some experimenting there.

Sometime in the early spring of 1958 when not everything was in bloom, Jaimey's parents took a small group of us to a leftist colony in New Jersey. We spent the night on the floor in a cabin. Jaimey was there, of course, and my brother Joe, and Ben and me. Jaimey's parents slept elsewhere. As the others slumbered near us, we began what was natural. Ben's hands began to roam a bit along my body and eventually he touched my breasts. Although it excited him terrifically he immediately felt he'd overstepped his boundary. He was apologetic, nervous, and excited at the same time. It was then, he said, that I showed my true colors. I gently whispered, trying not to wake anyone, and coyly suggested that it would be okay if he touched me again as long as he didn't try anything else.

Then on the car ride home we both said it was a onetime thing. We would never do it again. But we felt so grown-up and of course we continued to make new discoveries. Boy did he love me for my willingness to help our experiments along, which we continued over time. Ben's hands roved farther, and I became more adventurous. Several times we came close to making true love. Once Ben visited the Donnell Library and took medical books off the shelves so that he might learn some anatomy. But the clinical pictures only confused him. Learning by doing ("the Dewey approach," he said) was more to his liking. I, meanwhile, got my hands on some book dealing with the sexual responsibility of a woman. And in June, shortly before we were to part for the summer—Ben to Camp Willoway as a waiter on Lake Tiorati in Bear Mountain, New York, and me to the Vermont Creative Work Camp (VCWC) in Putney—upon a smallish couch in my family's living room we consummated our relationship. We were virgins no more. No protection. We were lucky.

I remember nights that followed. But that was after the summer. The two of us often in my room with the door open waiting for my parents to retire. When they finally went to bed, we also went to bed (in my room or in one of the little rooms off the kitchen) and Ben would leave between three and five in the morning. His trek home was a lonely one. He was tired, of course. The subway system was often tending to repairs during those early-morning hours. He would either have long waits for a train or be standing there at the station with a train parked for a long period of time. When he finally reached the Bronx he had to walk what seemed a great distance, often in cold weather, to get to his home.

Then there was the time his departure coincided with my father's reemergence for a nightcap and Ben's hasty retreat to the couch in front of the window, its back facing West End Avenue. He dived behind it, remaining supine there as my father headed for the kitchen to fill his glass. Scared out of his mind, he tried to be very quiet within spitting distance of Ring, who was now seated on the sofa nursing his drink and reading. Ben stayed hidden until my dad called it quits.

Ben left for Camp Willoway before my departure for VCWC.

I called up Ann that night. She wasn't there but her mother answered the phone. I told Ann's mother how I had just seen

Ben for the last time. Before his two months in the army, I said, exaggerating the facts but not my sense of loss. Or eight weeks, I said. It sounded shorter. She listened sympathetically. She told me she felt sad. I asked her why. She had no future was the gist of it. I wanted so much to make her feel good—to hug her and tell her not to worry and that I liked her. I hated it when people were unhappy. I didn't want them to be sad.

... *Well, I cried ALL RIGHT!* I told Ben in a letter. *I bet you never knew you could be missed <u>so</u>, you big fool....*

We corresponded practically every day that summer. Ben loved the way I wrote. I seemed to do it effortlessly, he said, finding my dispatches exciting to read. They were animated, he said. "Lively and filled with dashes." He claimed he even tried to copy my style but, according to him, his efforts felt labored and heavy. Whereas mine were light. He could feel me in the writing, he said.

Jane made me feel much better—she kept telling dirty jokes and about her brother who has a mania for throwing things out the window ... , I wrote.

6.25.58.

I went to a house today that you would absolutely hate: Jane's house. I sat on the arm of the couch in their living room. Her mother started yelling—"no, no—sit on the chair over there." She was afraid I might dirty her beautiful sofa as Jane explained.... Her mother is so fond of that damn sofa that when she discovered it was too big to fit in the elevator she had it pulled up and taken through the window on ropes—their apartment being on the eighth floor.

... We're having watermelon for dessert.... I don't want to eat it 'cause it'll remind me ... of you and that makes me sadder. Woe is me!!

Dear Ben,

... I ... have a problem. I'm telling you ... because you want me to be honest ... and I want to be anyhow. Kit [whom I met through my friend Gerry and who escorted me to a New Year's party pre-Ben] *arrived in New York today. I saw him for a few minutes. He still likes me and I don't want him to. When I see him next I'm going to tell him about you. What do I say—I'm in love with this boy (meaning you) and I have no desire to like anyone else but let's be friends—or maybe something else just as corny. How do I tell someone ... without hurting them? ... I'll let you know what happens. ...*

My parents noticed me sitting in here (living room) writing you this lengthy letter. They want me to do likewise for them. Ha! You come first old boy. ... They feel that they deserve long letters because they have loved me and been on my side all my fifteen years. By the way did you get my postcard on your day of arrival—today? They were sort of joshing?!

June 27, 1958.
Dear Ben,

This letter will probably be written in two shifts. ...

I had a long talk with you last night. Your picture, you nut. I started crying again. ... I don't want to and I know you don't want me to. I remembered how you made me laugh just before you left and said that it wasn't going to be that long ... you made me feel so much better. I promised you last night that there was to be no more crying. Something else is bothering me though. I felt funny about the way I told you about Kit. I don't know if I just should have skipped the whole thing ... but I have decided that there is really no problem what-so-ever. I am going to tell him all about you and it will probably turn out that I'll have a good friend. I don't know what the big fuss ... is. ...

The city is so hot and sticky.... My hair is getting ... long! But it's hot.... I'm going to cut it—no please.... [M]ake me promise not to cut it ... I would do the same for you!

END OF FIRST SHIFT

Hi! I'm back.

... Guess what? I saw a woman walking down 59th Street without shoes. She was walking her dog. I guess that accounts for no shoes. ...

June 28th, 1958.

... This train is ... squeaky. [This was written on the train headed for camp.]

... I'm wearing that skirt that you think looks like a typical Russian peasant and a white blouse, red high socks, red belt, old sneakers and my red velvet ribbon. ...

We've discovered about nine kids ... who are headed our way. [Joe was with me. Also Gerry—the friend mentioned earlier.]

Dear Ben,

... We arrived here about an hour and a half late—hot and sticky. ...

No, your handwriting is not so bad!

... I just checked the date of your letter (I received one) and it only took two days.... Hey ... I'm going to have quite a reputation in this camp: Miss Katie "Hot-Lips" Lardner. ...

If I live through this summer I think I'll be as strong as an ox. Between the walking hikes and bike hikes I'm bound to.... I have to go and finish unpacking. ...

June 29, 1958.
Dear Ben,

... Most of the kids are 15 or 16.... It's so funny to hear some of them sit around asking if they know so and so usually for-

getting so and so's last name, "Do you know Norman from New York?"

I spoke to Kit last night. [He was a fellow camper.] *Joe made some comment like, "I guess her letter's from Ben." Kit later asked him ... what relationship we had. Joe said "steady." Kit and I got talking (as I mentioned) and he asked me if I was going "steady" with you. I said "yes." I started in with the fact that we didn't like the word "steady"—I told him that it was hard to explain the wonderful relationship we have, but that I would like to try sometime. He wants me to. I told him how I felt every time I heard someone play the guitar.... He also wants to talk with me about communism—he heard my father was a member of "The Hollywood Ten."*

June 30, 1958.

... The regular session started.... I am going to be so strong. Dancing (modern) every day and hikes....

Weekdays are better calling days in this joint—so when you call me try to make it on a weekday....

Camp's livening up—I don't think it's going to be so bad....

Kit's playing the guitar—attempting it anyway. I can hear him from in here—in where? My cabin of course. He was just playing Jamaica Farewell. He envies you—I didn't overplay you either—I just told him exactly what you were like—he envies you for being so talented—He likes you and he hasn't even met you. I talked about you without prejudice feelings slipping in—it was hard but I did it.... I love you.

P.S. I'm not pregnant!

Dear Ben,

... I'll try to give you an idea of what this place looks like although I'm not too sure myself. The boys sleep in a barn sort of cabin up the hill from the main house.... The girls occupy the

main house and a little cabin which contains four rooms. I sleep in the front room, which contains two double-decker beds....

Joe came to breakfast with his Camp Timberlake sweatshirt on.

Last night before falling asleep I was lying in bed thinking of you and feeling rather lonely. I...remembered that Gerry and Joe were here and it made it so much nicer. I dreamt about you. You were carrying your guitar and some other instrument around. You also kissed me outside of school in the park—but the park was different somehow and most of the kids were my old friends from Joan of Arc. Some of them were talking about Alma Martin (a girl who left school due to pregnancy) and they said ... she now had two kids!

Who knows—I have the craziest dreams, man!

I love you so much.

The American
Middle East

ᘐᘐᘐ

Ben says even now it's hard not to think of me when he looks at the cover of *The Freewheelin' Bob Dylan* album—at the Village downtown; snow on the ground. "Don't know what street it is," he says, "but it looks like Dylan's walking south. . . . Cold in a jacket that's not quite keeping you warm. Well, it's hard, even now, to look at that picture and not imagine you on my arm. Being cold and having a warm soul."

It was over for us, however, when after an on-again, off-again period, I took up with Dick (a class ahead of me) the middle of my freshman year at the midwestern college I was telling you about when I began this tale. I was in Granville, Ohio—the American middle east, my dad said it should properly be called—at Denison University. A CHRISTIAN SCHOOL OF LIBERAL ARTS AND SCIENCE was written on the wall at the entrance to the place. My stepbrother had been a Denison graduate, and I think it was one of the handful of institutions that accepted me. The place reeked of Republicans, but the faculty members were predominantly Democrats, I concluded. Even though I achieved some happy moments there, I was forever planning my exit. For the first couple of months though it looked like I might not even make it out for Thanksgiving vacation owing to lack of funds on the home front. Nothing had ruffled the calm of the ménage since I'd left, my dad reported, not even an offer of employment. The "Hollywood thing" he'd been expecting to hear about was not entirely dead, but the symptoms, he said, looked fatal.

The "Hollywood thing" reminds me that the previous year (March 1959) I was allowed to say that my father had gone to California to write a movie. Maybe someday I would be able to tell him what movie, I said to Ben at the time. Also at the time I'd seen an article in the *Daily Mirror* that went something like this: Dalton Trumbo, once banned by Hollywood studios for being pro-Red, was doing the new script for *Spartacus*. His fee was fifty thousand dollars. In addition, the director Otto Preminger announced to the newspapers that Trumbo had written the screenplay of *Exodus*. It was still hard to get jobs and renew contacts and it was two years after that before my father was able to get a job with Otto Preminger. (The first picture he had his name on was called *The Cincinnati Kid*, with Steve McQueen, in 1965.) But various chinks seemed to be appearing in the blacklist armor so things weren't looking so glum.

"The terrible thing about the whole business, really," said my mother, "was what it did to people. It made the victims of the blacklist suspicious and fearful." My mother got an important job in a Broadway play (*Seidman and Son*) in 1962. She said, "I was so crazy when I was doing it. My understudy dressed in the same room with me and I thought that maybe she was from the FBI."

As for the Thanksgiving weekend, I was instructed to make a plane reservation with the understanding that the trip might have to be abandoned as a dispensable luxury. However, what wound up getting abandoned were all the projects my father said he had in mind for strengthening my character during the holiday recess. I got a car ride to New York, but he had to go to California for a "movie job of sorts." He was especially sorry, he said, to miss seeing me in the transitional stage of becoming a typical Ohioan. By Christmas he probably wouldn't recognize me. "Wear a carnation or something." For the Christmas holiday I took the train out of there.

Dick said he found me in the "baby book" at Denison—the collection of freshman photographs the upperclassmen went over with a fine-tooth comb. I had long hair and a solemn look, he observed, and I was from New York. He descended from nearby Short Hills, New Jersey. He also must have seen me on campus, he said. He called and proposed that we hook up after the Christmas break. We met, however, on the ride home and sat together and talked the night long. Probably my head rested on his shoulder. He loved my hair hanging down my back. Pierced ears were pretty new then but he was ready for new. They looked sexy to him and a bit exotic. My dark clothes made me mysterious. For Dick, New York was our common denominator. He had attended summer school in Manhattan. Before we met he pulled out a piece of his patella from somebody jumping on his back (horsing around in the dorm) from a double-decker bunk, which led to flunking gym and classes at The New School. And in high school Dick had gone into the city. He therefore considered himself more sophisticated than other kids from Short Hills. We were both easterners in Ohio. "Ohio was our wasteland," he remarked. One of our first dates was a hayride. We both had to pee, so we jumped off and did so within yards of each other, laughing and pissing at the same time.

In early January I was still telling Ben I loved him. I had no desire to see anyone else. In fact, the whole idea kind of made me sick, I gushed. And in the middle of the month when I turned eighteen I waxed poetic over the beautiful dozen yellow roses (my favorite) he sent. But in February it was the end. I was dating someone at Denison, I confessed, and wasn't sure about my feelings for *him*. I conveyed this information in a letter. I was afraid if I called Ben, I'd run out of money in the middle of what I had to say. It was a gloomy undertaking harking back, as I wrote, to "so many silly, wonderful things" we'd done together. Sitting next to him at his house eating dinner, shedding tears on his sweater causing the sweater to stain his T-shirt, wrestling with him, lying together on the grass outside school, looking for Christmas presents in the Village, and making love. I couldn't get it out of my mind how wonderful he made me feel. If only I could compare him to someone and be sure. "But I can't," I concluded woefully, "for I have known you for so long and I don't know anyone as I know you." We had to disconnect, I explained. "That's what must happen. I won't ever do what I did as a junior in high school again," I said referring to four auxiliary flirtations back then. "I love you too much. But I don't know what kind of love."

When I told Dick about my dad having been locked up and the former chairman of the Committee on Un-American Activities of the House of Representatives, J. Parnell Thomas, being a fellow inmate, he was blown away. Something opened up, he said. All of a sudden the world got a little bigger and more interesting. He said his political education, which had begun the summer before at The New School, got a "good nudge."

Dick was mostly a jock—a good guy—in high school who swore off sports in college. However, he shared my scorn for Denison being so middle-class WASP. The school had only two black students when I was there, for God's sake. There was Brenda, a writer. Older than I. An exchange student from

Howard, I think. Somebody said she must be a foreign student from Africa because Denison didn't have blacks. Brenda became my friend. And I remember somebody named Harry, who, because he was Jewish, was given honorary status (like a goddamn mascot) rather than full membership to one of the elitist fraternities.

Dick himself was a member of Sigma Chi. He joined because it was supposedly a cool house with the most popular college fraternity song in history, "The Sweetheart of Sigma Chi." In my sophomore year I wore his fraternity pin and got serenaded by the brothers. Dick was surprised I was willing to undergo such a silly tradition, but he concluded the severe part of me (the word his mother used to describe me) was partly a cover-up for a wonderful sentimental me. Severe as in serious, his mother meant. I didn't mind letting it be known that I was appreciated by a member of a trendy outfit. Of course, I wouldn't have been caught dead donning a white cross (the symbol of this commitment) around my family, and ultimately I was instrumental in encouraging old Dick to disengage from the organization, which had a bona fide whites-only policy. He said I helped him wake up to the world.

I went through sorority rush my freshman year. I didn't get into some of the clubs because of my father's politics (I learned later) but I'm sure I didn't get into some all on my own. An odd bunch took me in. By the fall of my second year, however, I was in the midst of the deactivation process. You had to undergo a series of events, almost like a goddamn obstacle course, to get released from sisterhood. The president of the sorority suggested that some of the girls would be hurt by my departure. This rather puzzled me because I thought any active member would feel my attitude would be a burden to the continuing existence of the organization. For I, with my multiplying antagonism, would be apt to spread ill will. It was all a bother, but I was sure that the conferences with chapter advisers, etc. would be more enjoyable than the weekly chapter meetings and the monthly cash giveaway called dues.

While I was stranded in this strange environment my father decided to blast to the world in *The Saturday Evening Post* in an article titled "My Life on the Blacklist" that he'd been a Communist when he took his position before the Committee on Un-American Activities. He admitted this publicly for the first time at the prompting of the magazine's publisher. The committee's assaults on freedom of thought had motivated witnesses who could answer "no" to the Communist question to remain silent, along with those like my old dad, whose factual response would have been "yes." He *had* been, he said, a member of the Communist Party, in whose ranks he had found some of the most thoughtful, witty, and generally stimulating men and women in Hollywood. He went on to say he had also encountered a number of bores and unstable characters, which, for him, seemed to bear out George Bernard Shaw's observation that revolutionary movements tended to attract the best and worst elements in a given society. My father's political activity had already begun to dwindle by the time Mr. Thomas posed the question, but he prolonged his affiliation until the case was finally lost. At that point he could terminate his membership without confusing the act, in his or anyone else's head, with the quite distinct struggle for the right to embrace any belief or act of beliefs to which his mind and conscience directed him.

I loved the *Saturday Evening Post* piece. There were, of course, stupid comments at school, but Dick got the bulk of them from a few fraternity brothers. Some fool asked me if I was a Communist and I naturally replied that I was. *The rest have been good questions*, I wrote to my parents. *I get annoyed though when Dick and Joyce* [my roommate] *offer as an apology for the silly overtones the old "they don't know anything about it."* Because they *should* know about the blacklist, I thought. But as I remember it, Joyce bought up a batch of the issue from a store in Granville to have on hand for curious prospects. And Dick said he remembered a snobbish pride he had being in my company knowing what my family had gone through. He didn't remember anybody giving him a hard time about me. Beatnik maybe, but that sounded good to him.

In any event, after two years at Denison I was history.

The Tunnel

Somewhere in this point in my life I entered a tunnel or whatever you want to call it. A misty bog. A foggy scene. And, dear reader, for those of you who need it spelled out about the why and wherefore of my subtle descent into same—it's only in hindsight that I can shed light on it. For at the time I was clueless and scared. And here (in no particular order) are some of the things I didn't know. (1) Choosing to deal silently with the tormenting ghosts of yesteryear is a perilous resolve. (2) Fears not faced are like termites ceaselessly chomping at the foundation of whatever kind of life you're trying to build (I dodged them whenever possible). (3) There was a big hole I was trying to fill. (4) This is a fleeting world: a star at dawn, a bubble in a stream, a flash of lightning in a summer cloud, an echo, a rainbow, a phantom, and a dream. Everything changes. (I, however, viewed it as a fixed unwelcoming place—I lived for the future, not in the present, in a state of continuing expectation with a terrible sense of isolation, and a feeling I didn't quite belong. I grasped after pleasant things, hoping that by holding them they would somehow last. Drugs and alcohol kept me from facing my life.)

And then, when I was looking for more to say here, I had this dream. . . . So there I was in a cafe indulging in a split of red wine (after years of abstinence); my present manuscript and bag were parked on a chair nearby. And a joint mysteriously appeared. I sat there suspended in time. (I didn't order any food. I didn't need it.) It didn't matter that I was alone. The pain had moved away. I swear I could have stayed in this capsule forever if the cafe hadn't shut down for the night. (I'm reminded that alcohol and drugs, for a while anyway, made me whole. They calmed down my thoughts and feelings—I didn't know I was numbing them.) Next I dropped the contents of my wallet trying to pay. In real life I had just cleaned it. But here I was coming undone. I left, but I left the manuscript behind. And here's the main thing, I didn't know that I would ever tell the truth about the wine (secrets were okay in the capsule).

"I guess I've got to paint this little picture here for you," said my mother one day. "You've got this very needy little girl," said Frances in reference to herself. "With this crazy mother," she continued. "A needy little girl for a number of reasons. First starting with her babyhood neediness—with this whole fantasy of the prince papa and the Jewish mama and my royal lineage— and Russian and Turkish and French and Greek and all mixed up." (Besides Russian and English, my mother's father, Leon, spoke a little French. In Constantinople he picked up Turkish and some Greek. And my mother spoke some of the above.) "And living in Brownsville, East New York," she said. "All that shit, you see, which helped provide for this peculiar, strange person who was probably an alcoholic at birth but didn't know it because my father was probably alcoholic . . . whose neediness was so great I might as well have been Marilyn Monroe. Love me love me love me somebody love me."

Well, I didn't say anything at the time that my mother said this because, for one thing, I got kind of hung up on the picture of her and Marilyn as one. But if she could really be here right now, I'd say, Mom, I wish we'd come together on this neediness thing.

MY FATHER HAD TOLD ME that a splendid exit was a vital part of any performance, but I remember sitting on the steps to my Denison dorm bewildered. Something didn't seem right. Besides Dick, a boy named Jim had declared his interest and I couldn't do anything about it. For one thing I had a paper way overdue. And there was Michael in New York. His family resided in our apartment building on West End Avenue and both of us recognized something had occurred between us during a brief encounter over a school break. Something to think about. I mean, I immediately heard from him when I returned to school. His letters were poetic. He even surprised me with a visit to Ohio. I walked out of the life science building after an anatomy and physiology lab period and he was sitting on the front steps of the building. Dick, somewhere in the vicinity at the time of Michael's arrival, proceeded to smash a hole in his room while listening to Wagner.

I transferred to New York University. I was briefly successful in my academic activities there, which for the most part I found wearisome. I read some good stuff. And at the curious age of nineteen I found that I had to function as a king in a Nativity play in dance-drama workshop. But I got excused from making an appearance in Literary Heritage. I spoke to the professor on the matter one afternoon after he'd delivered a detrimental lecture on *A Portrait of the Artist as a Young Man*. I had listened to him speak of Stephen Dedalus with tears drifting down my face as he butchered the lad. My talk with the professor afterward coincided with the returning of an A paper on the Norwegian playwright Henrik Ibsen. I was thanked for my essay and told that attendance wouldn't be required as long as I did the work. I didn't do the work. I received an F and I drifted away.

Meanwhile I saw Michael on weekends—sometimes at Princeton, where he was doing graduate work—and he wrote lyrical letters in between. I was still in love with Dick, I told a friend, "but my relation with Michael seems to approach fullness." I studied dance with Anna Sokolow. And before the culmination of the school year, I relocated to the Columbia University School of General Studies.

John called again. I first heard about him one night late during the summer after my freshman year, when I was indulging in lethargic conversation with my parents. Previously he had been simply the son of a remarkable ear specialist. He'd gone through Harvard College, a Columbia University College of Physicians and Surgeons internship, and was soon to become a pediatrician. But my parents had spent the evening with close friends, and the talk at one point had fixed itself upon me and my certain attributes and upon John and his similar qualities. I was told that he might call. Then I thought of him in fanciful terms. He did phone about a week later. His voice was moderate, gentle, and I resolved that he must be small. His conversation was unruffled. His adjectives, unique. He said, "I got your happy phone number from Irene Diamond." I saw him once or twice before the previously mentioned cold-shoulder episode and my retreat into the Diamonds' pool. He was English-looking and shy. Then a year and a half later he reappeared.

His father was also blacklisted. Because of his parents' strong support of Henry Wallace in the 1948 election and their evolving friendship, his father's medical practice significantly dwindled despite a superb reputation as an ear specialist. And it didn't help that some kind of organizing committee gathered at their country home following the Peekskill concert featuring Paul Robeson (August 27, 1949) that never took place. Robeson was a close family friend. The proceeds were to go to the Harlem chapter of the Civil Rights Congress. For a number of years Robeson had given concerts for the group. The *Peekskill Evening Star* had run a front-page story on his upcoming appearance with a three-column headline: ROBESON CONCERT HERE AIDS "SUBVERSIVE" UNIT—IS SPONSORED BY "PEOPLE'S ARTISTS" CALLED RED FRONT IN CALIFORNIA. The editorial on the inside claimed, "The time for tolerant silence that signifies approval is running out," and it printed a letter from an American Legion officer headlined SAYS ROBESON AND HIS FOLLOWERS ARE UNWELCOME.

Paul telephoned from Grand Central before boarding the train the day of the concert to say he had heard there was trouble. Some kind of organizing against him. And instead of taking a taxi from the Peekskill station to the concert grounds he asked Helen, John's mother, to meet him. John's father was laid up with a broken leg. So Helen set out with fourteen-year-old John, who insisted upon going along. "Nobody's going to hurt my Paul," John proclaimed.

Paul arrived without incident, and then a two-car caravan escorted him to the performance site. But as they approached closer and closer they could hear shouting and noise and some screaming. An anti-Robeson mob had taken over. Concertgoers were being attacked. The stage was smashed, the chairs torched. A jeering crowd on the sidelines yelled "Dirty Commie" and "Dirty kike." Police were visible on the sidelines. Some were smiling. And no one was making a move to interfere with the mob. Helen saw a burning cross on the hill and instructed John to take cover on the floor of their station wagon. She then ran to the car behind her, where Robeson was. "Get Paul the hell out of here!" she yelled. "Get him the hell out of here. Get him to New York."

The next day fifteen hundred people showed up at their home to begin planning the rebuttal concert. Already inundated with hate calls, Helen asked for protection from the state police. They promised to be there, but nobody came. John strapped on a .22 he had around for target practice and he and a friend booby-trapped the driveway with wire fencing. Then they personally patrolled the place. "There was plenty of FBI undercover baloney after Peekskill Number One," says John, "and well into Peekskill Number Two." There was also loads of hate mail and threats of physical harm.

There were no more concerts for Paul after that. No theater auditorium could rent to him because the place might be burned down under "mysterious circumstances." Carnegie Hall wouldn't rent to any group that would include him. You couldn't put a sign in a store advertising his records. You couldn't play Paul Robeson records on the radio and keep your job. The point was to isolate him.

"The attempt of the enemy was to cut off the progressive people from the great masses of the Americans," said Paul. "In my own case it was to cut me off from the Negro people from whom I'm born. Imagine," he said, "somewhere somebody says I, born a Negro—that because of my beliefs, my fight for peace, my fight for friendship between nations, my fight for the complete liberation of my people—that somewhere I'm not an American. That I should be cut off from the very people from whom I was born."

It was partly through John's feelings for Paul Robeson that his sensitivity was revealed to me. He was crazy about Paul. John was eight years older, introducing me—at nineteen and a half—to an adult world. He took me to restaurants where I'd never been. We drank before-dinner drinks and wine with dinner. I liked Bloody Marys with no ice and Johnny Walker Black. I remember feeling wonderful. (As my dad said, alcohol just made it easier to forget things.) I ate frog legs and Brie cheese and crème caramel and *moules marinières*. We got drunk and I stayed thin.

John picked me up in his Mercedes and I stayed overnight at his apartment, a racially integrated cooperative on Fifth Avenue—and he gave me clean towels. I don't remember if we slept together that night. It seemed terribly grown-up and when I came home from another man's house, my parents told me Michael had called. I announced I didn't have any secrets, including from Michael. My father said some secrets were good.

I had trouble sleeping. John gave me sleeping pills. I felt taken care of and I slept. I was going to Columbia and taking literature courses and painting on huge canvases. I also took modern and jazz dance classes.

I saw more of John. He was a doctor and I thought he knew how I felt. He gave me Tuinal, Seconal, and Dexamyl. We got married in New Milford in the study with the family gathered around. (Granny wasn't there. She died when I was in high school. Thanks to her I had funds for college. She left Joe and me an inheritance as the surviving children of David.) John gave me the most beautiful ring. We picked it out together. Jade and gold. We celebrated that night at my parents' home in the city with a party we called (on the invitation) a shivaree. (My father's idea.) I thought I hurt Michael badly. When I had a miscarriage that first year I hoped we were even.

I cried a lot with John and I got angry. I hated it if it rained and if I gained weight. I would get high on pills and make late-night phone calls when John was at the hospital. He got me presents and left me notes in the early morning before taking off and he kept me supplied. John says (as he remembers it) that was the primary way (with sleeping pills) or, at times, the only way that I could get to sleep.

I went to school and danced, and after the miscarriage became preoccupied with having a child. I was convinced I couldn't. After major surgery I did get pregnant. I continued going to school and I danced for nine months and I left Columbia very pregnant. I was still taking pills and I ate lots of hard candy and I dieted. I didn't really enjoy anything. I did want my baby. I drank bourbon and ate Petit Beurre cookies. *Little butters*, I called them, and waited for my child to be born. My son made me happy.

John gave me lessons in how to hold him. He was very patient with me. For the longest time I would wake up in the morning and I was happy knowing my son was in the next room. But I never felt I was doing enough.

Carlo, Ellis, Kate, and John

I had a daughter. Another wonderful light fell upon a foggy scene. She was two weeks late. I had become convinced she would never be born. I went to movies in Times Square by myself and I read *Story of O*, a French erotic novel by Pauline Réage.

I saw my first therapist after the miscarriage. He suggested I get a kitten. John was allergic. We kept the cat anyhow. I saw my second therapist sometime after my daughter's birth. I don't know when. I nursed her late with my cat on my lap and bourbon in my hand. I remember watching Woody Allen subbing for Johnny Carson. I remember telling my little girl it was going to be all right. But John had put his hand on my breast and I didn't feel anything. And this was a big deal for me. I went to see some analyst. I told him about the hand on the breast and not feeling and he told me that some women never felt anything on their breasts. I was lucky, he was saying. He wasn't addressing me. We discussed putting me in a hospital. I liked the attention. I'm sure I thought I was being overly dramatic. We settled on pills and therapy with another therapist. I started analysis. I never said anything in analysis and neither did the doctor.

In the spring of 1969, when I was still married to John, I met Tommy. He was a senior at Harvard. We did a movie for public TV. (I had started acting a couple of years earlier.) After the film we talked on the phone and wrote each other letters even when we were both in New York. I got a post office box.

In the fall John and I separated. I hurt John terribly.

Tommy and I didn't live together right off. He'd spend the night and leave before the kids got up in the morning. We married in August 1970.

April 1971 my father won the Academy Award for writing the movie *M*A*S*H*. In 1968 he'd read the galleys of a comic novel about a medical unit during the Korean War. The novel was

Kate, Tommy, and Ellis

MASH and he felt it was excellent source material for a movie. He went back through the gates of Twentieth Century-Fox, the studio that had fired him, and pitched the idea. Fox bought the rights and it became known as one of the great war comedies of all time. The screenplay brought my father his second Academy Award. Tommy and I watched in New York on TV at the Hunters' apartment and jumped up and down as the actress Eva Marie Saint handed him the statue in LA. "At long last," said Ring with a smile, "a pattern has been established in my life. At the end of every twenty-eight years I get one of these," he said, holding Oscar. "So I will see you all again in 1999."

Shortly thereafter Tommy and I were driving the previously mentioned motorcycle north on Riverside Drive. A car cut in front of us and I catapulted over him and over the car and I went flying in the air and I landed. I had a compound fracture of the right femur and they operated and put me in traction and I stayed in the hospital for seven weeks. When they told me I was going to have to stay I told them I couldn't. "You don't understand, I have two children," I said.

Tommy would bring the children and he would also come alone. Sometimes twice a day. To make it better I went back on sleeping pills. My father's friend Ian Hunter would bring me THC and I would snort it, and Tommy and I smoked grass and he would then light up a cigar to cover the smell. He'd push something against the door and get into bed next to me and we made love.

Ian would come with an artist's model and she posed naked in the window and we drew—until they laid on us the no-naked-model-in-the-hospital-room rule. I went home in a body cast and I was a piece of sculpture. I took Percodan. So did Tommy.

I had two leg casts. My leg didn't heal properly. I switched doctors. I had more surgery.

The night before going to the hospital, the dryer door was open and our Siamese cat Curtis walked in to sit on the warm clothes. I didn't see him when I shut the door. And you know the rest. I screamed. And I remember Tommy taking the kids on his lap and saying, "Babies, I have something to tell you." Tommy and I had gone to Brooklyn to purchase the two kittens for the children. We kept them hidden in Tommy's dressing room (he was in a play on Broadway called *Four on a Garden*) and they spent the night under our bed. They had been a huge Christmas success.

The night before flying thirty feet in the air off the motorcycle we had taken LSD and ridden stoned through Central Park and seen *Lawrence of Arabia*. I remember thinking I was glad we hadn't been drinking.

I don't remember my drinking. I remember Tommy's.

I was lured out to Freeport Hospital on Long Island by an alcohol counselor once a week to learn about alcoholism. I went to some Al-Anon meetings.

We talked about going to California. There was an agent there who knew what to do with Tommy's career. His drinking scared me. He stopped. I remember him telling his grandfather, Archie Lee, whom he loved, that he couldn't drink. I was encouraged.

We sublet our apartment. I got a driver's license and we all moved to Los Angeles.

I kept Tommy company not drinking.

September 1975 we moved into a cantilevered house in Laurel Canyon. The kids went to the Wonderland School.

We borrowed some beds and a couch and got acquainted with Los Angeles.

Tommy looked for work.

We bought a blue '67 Camaro.

Tommy found a 1960 red Ford pickup truck, which he and the kids called Wonder Truck. I sometimes drove Wonder to auditions and to take the children to school. I liked driving my pickup listening to country-western music.

We got a yellow cat at Ralph's whom we named Rose, for the Yellow Rose of Texas.

Two Scenes from a Marriage

I

We colored Easter eggs.

Tommy walked around the kitchen playing his guitar. My daughter, Ellis, put another decal on her egg. "That's a remarkable egg," I said. She said she was experimenting and that she had used toothpicks and thread. I asked Tommy if he'd seen the egg.

"Yeah, she's makin' good eggs this year," he said.

"I'm going to make one for you," Ellis told Tom. "I am going to make it with your name on it."

"She's real good with eggs this year," Tommy said again. "You didn't lay those yourself, did ya?" Tommy put down his guitar. "Anybody want to give this chili the taste test?" he asked. He was making chili.

"I will, not now, but a little later," said Ellis.

I was waiting for an empty pot. I wanted tea.

"Damn! That's good chili, you all. I want you to know it." Tommy knocked on the table three times. "Katie, have some chili," he whispered.

(Eventually we smoked dope. I remember sometimes wishing Tommy would drink. That was something I understood. I had learned something at Freeport about drinking behavior. I was told he was a dry drunk.)

II

We were having dinner. I had cooked chicken stuffed with wild rice, and made a salad. Jerry Jeff Walker was playing on our cassette player. My son Carlo was eleven and my daughter Ellis was ten.

"When I came home this afternoon I saw a big black dog with a lot of courage or dumb. Either one. He was eating an onion roll he'd pulled from the garbage, which he'd tore a hole in," says Tom. This is the first thing he's said cheerfully all evening. He looks around to make sure everyone's paying attention. "I was standing up by the eucalyptus tree by the garage. I picked up a couple of rocks and threw them at him."

"Did you hit him?" I asked. "I hope not," I said.

"I hope not, too," said Ellis.

"I don't know," said Tom. "He went limping off as fast as he could go. If we lived in the country I'd take a shotgun to a dog who got in the garbage. We'd be hauling off a lot of dogs."

"All right," I said. I'd had it.

Tommy picked up his dinner and went into the living room where he ate his dinner alone reading *TV Guide*.

Carlo said to leave him alone.

Tommy did a film called *Jackson County Jail* and some television shows. He played Howard Hughes. He did the movie *The Betsy*.

I couldn't get it out of my head that time was running out for me and babies. I didn't even know if this was true. Tommy talked about accepting a four-picture deal offered him by Universal Studios to have money for a house, for a baby.

"What baby?" I had said that I couldn't have a baby until I had worked more. Not until I was further along.

How much further along he wanted to know.

"I'll know," I said. "This makes me feel lonely," I said.

"Can you imagine how lonely it makes me feel to be told I can't have a child?" he said.

Tommy held me and said I was safe from all fear. He said to let everyone know he gobbled up formless fears with his breakfast. I couldn't take the time then to have a baby. I'd always thought we'd have a big fat Indian baby. Tommy is part Indian.

My husband was becoming famous. As a child I had thought I was going to be famous.

We bought an eight-room house with a pool and a Jacuzzi in Los Feliz in the De Mille estate area that had been built by Cecil B. De Mille for his daughter Katherine and Anthony Quinn.

Tommy was in New York doing *The Eyes of Laura Mars*. I was in California doing a film for public television. I remember sitting in my kitchen and this man (from an acting class) I barely knew was asking me if my husband loved me. Yes, I said. We were drinking. We made love on my living room floor. My kids were sleeping. I remember it was getting close to morning and my daughter came looking for me. She found me downstairs standing there with this man she'd never seen before.

That same night Tommy slept with someone else.

I hired a babysitter for the kids while I worked. She was taking Thorazine and I went looking for it in her bag; I took pills from her not quite knowing what they did.

I came to New York for Christmas and I saw that Tommy had gone back to drinking and I got scared. We spent a hellish week in his hotel getting ready for Christmas. Christmas was hell in the country with my parents, and Grandma Marie, and my children, and my cousin, her husband, and their children. Tommy was drinking in the kitchen. He'd stolen sleeping pills from my father. My cousin asked me if Tom was trying to get into a fight.

John came and picked up the children and took them with him for the rest of the vacation, and Tom and I headed back to town. He was weaving in and out on the Merritt Parkway and I talked him into letting me drive. He told me what a nice guy he was for letting me. He said he wanted to separate. I said let's talk about it in the morning.

The next morning he brought it up and I packed some stuff and went downtown, running into Tom's agent on the way.

I went to my friend Julie Garfield's (John Garfield's daughter) and sat around drinking with her and Rip Torn. Tommy called up and said, "Baby, come back," and I said I couldn't or something. I didn't mean forever.

The Gift

As my grandfather said, in order to get from one perilous situation to the next, in one of my favorite stories, "the lease said the soonest mended." Well, I made it out of the tunnel, dear reader. I pulled through the fog and the bog. How I emerged is another story. But I don't drink or take drugs or smoke dope anymore. I haven't for some time.

And speaking of good news, the story about the guy peddling magazines at the foot of the bed has a happy ending as far as I'm concerned. Back then, the night after he infiltrated my room, my defending of my beliefs may have gone unrecognized. But my father—the trailblazer in this department—revealed to me much later that it showed him a kind of extreme sensitivity that in the end he felt he had to respect. He never dragged me out of the closet or anything. But the unabridged rendition of how he felt about the whole business trickled down to me over the years as a result of the periodic inquiries on my part. I wanted to get to the bottom of things.

Dad, I wrote in an e-mail on my last attempt. [Dad] . . . *some time ago I reminded you . . . in Santa Monica you spanked me for using the word nigger. . . .* "Fortunately I don't remember this,"

Maude, Frances, and Ring

you said, "but ... it had a good effect [you thought]. ... *In your teens you were more sensitive to this issue than ... your parents."*

[Well] *what issue?* [Dad.] *What issue? I wish I ... asked you then. I didn't, so I'm asking ... now.* [And] *... say more about that word sensitivity ... my extreme sensitivity?* [Please say more.] This was the gist of a dispatch about ten sentences long. Signed "With love from your daughter."

Pretty extreme, remarked my dad in reference to the fact that I hid rather than collaborate with the law lingering in the living room. ... [Y]*ou apparently felt,* he wrote, *... merely affirming their suspicion made you an accomplice. ... I wouldn't have done it but I loved you for it. And still do,* replied my dad in an e-mail titled "meanings."

Well, I'm glad I asked. How the hell else would I have known that my father treasured the closet affair. How would I have understood that love had anything to do with it. And in the nick of time one could say. Because that was in the middle of the winter of 2000 and my father died in the fall. On Halloween. Not that he gave a damn about Halloween. The caregiver Doxie Forrest said she didn't know it would be that night. She's from St. Catherine, Jamaica, West Indies. Before I got there that evening she told Ring I had a surprise for him. Something to brighten him up. Doxie said he turned his eyes toward me as if he wanted to say something when I went to get my glasses and the notes my brother Jim had given me about *The Fishermen of Beaudrais*. An agreement had just been reached to produce the screenplay that my dad wrote with Dalton Trumbo in the early forties. Based on a story by Ira Wolfert, it concerned the French Resistance in World War II.

My father didn't say anything when he heard the news.

My mother, on the other hand, was ecstatic. She bounced up and down on her bed. My father was occupying a hospital rendition smack up against the one they used to share. Due to a memory problem that revealed itself after a head injury sustained in a car crash two years before, my mother wasn't fully grasping the situation. Until the collision, as my dad said, she was the much healthier specimen of the two. But after, her short-term memory slipped away. We were told it would return, but pretty soon it became clear that her recovery would remain incomplete. She has Alzheimer's. My mother had three acting jobs, however, lined up at the time of the wreck. One was *Earthly Possessions* with Susan Sarandon for HBO. But despite her partial view, that night, she seemed to detect some of the basics. And being in the middle of some good news and bad, she was unabashedly pouncing on the good. "That's the best news ever!" she shouted.

My father didn't say anything but as I told him about the deal we held hands. He couldn't hear worth a damn so you had to talk into something called a PockeTalker II through a tiny plug-mounted microphone hooked up to huge earphones perched on top of his head. Jim had replaced the mini earphones that came with his personal, versatile listening system for a mammoth set.

I remember when the hearing equipment began getting complex. We were in the huge playground at Ninety-first and Riverside Drive and the place was swarming with kids. My mother asked me how it was going, referring to an earlier version of this chronicle. She had wanted to know where it would begin. She said I could start in a meadow or on a mountain where something catches my eye that transports me to the past. My mother was seventy-five then, and had gotten a face tuck and gone to Hollywood the previous winter for pilot season.

Then my father turned up. He'd just had his ears checked by a specialist and reported he was so deaf in his right ear he was probably going to abandon the hearing aid in that ear because it was no longer doing any good. In a couple of weeks, he told us with a grin, he would begin experimenting with a device behind his right ear that would transmit sound to the left. "It won't be binaural," he said. My mother said that was okay. "We'll just have to love him—like we have to love Maude." Maude is my youngest daughter (three and a half at the time) who flapped her arms up and down and squeezed her nose when she got excited. My mother then asked my father to take out his right hearing aid. She got up close and said, "I can't stand it," which my father couldn't hear. So she said to me, "We can get away with murder." My parents had just returned to New York from Sundance, Utah, where my father worked intensely (for five days) coaching screen-writers at Robert Redford's institute. They came to the park to see Maude and me before taking off for their country home in Weston, Connecticut. (In the early eighties they sold the house in New Milford and bought one in Weston.) It was a hot day in June.

The sprinkler was on. Maude was in the sandbox. Then she joined us and we all sat down on a bench, where Maude consumed a peanut butter and jelly sandwich. My parents told her she should eat chicken sometimes—something besides peanut butter and jelly. And Maude said, "Get a grip on reality," which had to be repeated for my father who hadn't caught every word.

A couple of nights before my dad had squeezed my hand for dear life but the hand-holding this night was quite steady. Quite even. Quite steady really. Normal hand-holding you could call it except there had never really been any hand-holding before my father got sick. But this night, as I was saying, it was an even exchange.

The hospice nurse said hearing was the last to go. He could still hear even though he was traveling, said Doxie. And I hoped to hell this was the case even if the person couldn't hear worth a damn to begin with. Words had taken a backseat in the last couple of days, but I had another thing to say. There was something else I needed to pack in. One last thing to push through the little mike. I wanted to thank Ring for being my dad. I thanked him for taking my brother Joe and me on after David was killed.

Then Doxie and I changed his shirt while he pushed his left arm in the sleeve of the gray T-shirt to help us. My father was in some pain when we moved him, and that was about the time the horrible noise began. A heavy rattle and the rattling was sounding louder and louder. I remember thinking this must be the death rattle I read about in books. Something was rattling like in Tolstoy's *The Death of Ivan Ilyich*. I rubbed my father's chest to eradicate the din. His emaciated body twitched. Then the rattling and wheezing gradually diminished.

We were told no more liquid by the hospice nurse on call.

Put a pillow behind his back, the woman said. We were just about to place the pillow when Denise arrived. Doxie's replacement. So Doxie sat Ring up and asked Denise to place the pillow. While she was raising him, Doxie talked to herself. "I don't like the way how he look." She repeated it but not to me. Neither one of us had ever seen anyone die before. Only Denise. We noticed my dad's features changing. I said something about blood on his shirt. "It was the water that catch his shirt and give it a dark look in the night." It wasn't blood, Doxie told me. I saw the water coming out of his mouth. The color of his skin changing. Doxie bent over to look into Ring's mouth and the tongue was way up in his throat like it was going back. His face was getting white. She saw the tongue in his mouth getting dark like a bluish look.

"He's dying," she said. "He's dying." She screamed it. "Oh, my God, he's dying!"

"Don't say that," said my mom.

But I was glad she did. I took it as a cue to put my arms around my dad so I could hold him on through this final passage. I took my mom's hand.

We were getting to the "gapping" part, as Doxie called it. "That's how the breath leave the body," she said. Everything was going swimmingly really. My father was moving on. The direction was clear. When, what do you know, old Denise began shouting out of a clear blue sky, "Call a priest! Call a priest!" As I say, she had been through it. She had seen old relatives die and that's what they did. She wanted to pray over my dad. Her family gets on the goddamn floor.

"Stop it!" I cried out. "Just stop it," as I crossed my arms in defense of my father's atheism. Everybody knew he was a non-believer, for God's sake. He subscribed to the *Skeptical Inquirer*, for example. And in the hospital when a priest came into view,

"There's the collar," he remarked, ducking under the covers, feigning sleep. Denise asked if I wanted her to leave. No, I said. I didn't want her to leave. But I hoped she'd change the tune. She forgot where she was, she later explained.

The breath was leaving the body slowly now. We lowered my dad down in the bed. Doxie gave him a little more than a spoon of water.

"Why did you give him the water?" I asked.

"Back in our country that's all you can give him to go home is a spoon of water. Old tradition." He was "gapping" slowly, very peaceful though, no struggling.

"I love you, my dad."

My mom was standing over the bed talking to him, touching his face, touching his nose. "You're fine. You're going to get through this," she told him. "You're going to be fine."

I left the room after removing my dad's black Swatch watch. I took it with me.

"He died at home," remarked Denise. "He could have died in the hospital. It was very peaceful. It was sweet."

Doxie said she prayed for him, asking the Lord to have mercy on his soul. "May his soul rest in peace."

I CAN'T HELP DRAGGING the plundering girl back in here. I was contemplating the relevancy of the cat disaster stories or, more to the point, my need to share them with everyone when the little black wretch entered a dream. She was waiting to steal when I nabbed her under the covers. Well, as you may remember, I ultimately responded with sympathy, posting my episodes of theft for the world to see. I then led her to the chest of drawers where pre-Columbian treasures lay. And she chose from among them one of the ancient pottery shards. A blacklist relic. Sometimes people need a little something to lure them from under the covers or out of a closet. I let her help herself to a token before taking off and now I was making an exit with my dad's Swatch watch in hand.